Rocky Mountain National Park Hiking Trails
— including Indian Peaks

By Kent and Donna Dannen

D0797025

The East Woods Press

Fast & McMillan Publishers, Charlotte

Copyright 1978 by Fast & McMillan Publishers, Inc.
First Printing.

All rights reserved. No part of this book may be reproduced without
permission from the publisher, except by a reviewer who may quote
brief passages in a review; nor may any part of this book be reproduced, stored in a retrieval system or transmitted in any form or by
any means, electronic, mechanical, photocopying, recording or
other, without written permission from the publisher.

Library of Congress Cataloging in Publication Data
Dannen, Kent, 1946-
    Rocky Mountain National Park Hiking Trails.
    Bibliography: p.
    Includes index.
    1. Hiking — Colorado — Rocky Mountain National Park — Guide-
books. 2. Rocky Mountain National Park — Guide-books. I. Dannen,
    Donna, 1949-   joint author. II. Title.
GV199.42.C62R623   917.88′69′043   77-25701
ISBN 0-914788-06-X

Cover photograph of Kent Dannen by Donna Dannen.
Drawings by Donna Dannen.
Maps reproduced with permission from U.S. Forest Service, Region 2,
Denver Colorado.

Typography by Raven Type.
Printed in the United States of America by The Delmar Company.

East Woods Press Books
Fast & McMillan, Publishers
6000 Kingstree Drive
Charlotte, N.C. 28210

To our parents, who showed us ancient paths:

Martha and Don Harward   Mary Ellen and Dwight Dannen

Ask for the ancient paths
where the good way is; and walk in it
and find rest for your souls.

Jeremiah 6:16

About the Authors

Donna and Kent Dannen starting out from the northeast end of the Mummy Pass Trail. **photo by Dwight L. Dannen**

Kent and Donna Dannen have guided hikers over the trails of Rocky Mountain National Park and Indian Peaks for a combined total of more than twenty years. Both began their professional guiding activities as hikemasters and naturalists for the YMCA of the Rockies and have led hundreds of hikes covering thousands of miles. Kent now works as a writer/photographer, teaches a nature photography course for the National Wildlife Federation and is a contributing editor of *Backpacker* Magazine. Donna is a ranger-naturalist with the National Park Service and a free-lance nature artist. The Dannens live in Estes Park, Colorado.

Acknowledgments

The authors wish to thank fellow hikers in the National Park Service and U.S. Forest Service who checked the manuscript of this guidebook, refreshed our memories, supplied information on recent and future trail alterations, made many helpful suggestions and caught mistakes. The value of this aid cannot be overstated. The staff of Rocky Mountain National Park paid us a special compliment by vehemently debating among themselves their criticisms of our text (the war of the marginal notes). These proofreaders will see much of their own effort in this book as they read it from cover to cover — with sharp red pencils ready.

We have done some underlining of our own in the text to make descriptions of various destinations easier to find. We did not follow a logical system in our underlining, but made our decisions about what to emphasize by intuition based on many years of answering hikers' questions. What to underline was, in the words of George Armstrong Custer, a command decision.

Cover Photo

Kent Dannen checks his map above Forest Canyon in Rocky Mountain National Park. Longs Peak, the park's tallest, is in the background. Photograph taken by Donna Dannen.

List of Maps

Contents

TRAIL DESCRIPTIONS

Preface

On Rocky Mountain National Park trails it sometimes seems as if the whole world has heeded Jesus' command to "rise, take up your bed and walk." A conservative estimate indicates that 600,000 people hike the park trails each year while additional thousands hike the trails in the national forests that nearly surround the park.

Obviously, there is a quality to these mountains that multitudes of people want to experience. Just as obviously, that quality eventually will be stomped out by lug soles if we are careless in our use of this spectacular stretch of the Rockies.

In writing this guidebook we have two goals, neither of which is to encourage more people to hit the trail — an activity needing no encouragement. First, we want the book to help both novices and experienced hikers to enjoy the backcountry more fully. Second, and even more important, the guide is intended to help everyone use the Rocky Mountain wilderness in a disciplined way so it will not be loved to death.

Understanding the ecology of Rocky Mountain National Park greatly increases the enjoyment of its trails. Accordingly, the guide contains three very detailed descriptions of parts of three different trails, called nature walks. These walks, none more than three miles long, represent the workings of various life zones. By reading the three descriptions, hikers will begin to understand how natural history functions along other trails situated in the same zones.

All the trail descriptions are relatively detailed. In fact, knowledgeable fellow hikers in the National Park Service and U.S. Forest Service who kindly reviewed the manuscript suggested that it might be too complete. They feel that knowing exactly what to expect takes some of the adventure out of backcountry experiences. Their criticism certainly is valid. Nevertheless, we believe that knowledge usually is preferable to ignorance. Although the information furnished here will eliminate some (but only some) of the physical adventure that accompanies error and uncertainty, it will also, through increased understanding, open additional paths of spiritual and mental adventure.

Frankly, though, this book can't cover everything, because backcountry management is complicated. The National Park Service tries to protect the landscape and the visitor from each other and, at the same time, to make re-creation (as well as recreation) possible for visitors. To meet the constantly changing demands of such a difficult task, the Park Service almost constantly changes the details of its backcountry management. Designated campsites are here one summer and elsewhere the next. Stretches of trail are altered in various ways to better preserve the land. Guessing the exact site of outhouses gives modern hikers a kind of adventure Daniel Boone never imagined.

We mention almost no trail signs in the guide. Signs often are present along the trails to help hikers find their way. But predicting exactly where signs will be and what they will say next week makes long-range forecasting of mountain weather seem sure and simple by comparison.

Another criticism of the original manuscript was that it contained information about trails that are harmful to the land — old trails running to destinations now served by newer paths built with land protection in mind. After considering each of the old trails carefully, we decided we agreed with the criticism, so we eliminated their descriptions from the book.

This trail guide is meant to be used during the five months of the year that are appropriate for hiking in the Colorado Rockies — June through October. We prefer post-Labor Day hiking because of the comfortable temperatures, yellow aspens and smaller crowds. But each month offers its own unique and worthwhile joys.

Note on the Maps

The maps for *Rocky Mountain National Park Hiking Trails* were adapted from Resource Base Maps prepared by the U.S. Forest Service, Region 2, Denver, Colorado. All but two of the maps were reduced to a scale of one inch to the mile. (The Wild Basin map and the map of North Inlet and Tonahutu Creek trails and Onahu Creek-Green Mountain Circle have a slightly smaller scale.) The contour interval is 40 feet. For ease in estimating distance, all maps are criss-crossed by lines marking off square miles. Although the Resource Base Maps were the most accurate and up-to-date maps available for this area, we made many corrections based on our hiking experience.

If you desire maps with a larger scale, we recommend ordering 7.5 minute, 1:24,000-scale quadrangle maps from the U.S. Geological Survey, Denver, Colorado 80255, or from the USGS at National Center, Reston, Virginia 22092. Although not completely accurate, especially with regard to man-made features, quads are very good. Their current cost, which can be expected to go up, is $1.25. The names of the relevant quads for Rocky Mountain National Park and Indian Peaks are (in descending order of usefulness) McHenrys Peak, Longs Peak, Trail Ridge, Fall River Pass, Allens Park (yes, we know this spelling differs from our text; who are you going to believe — the USGS or the U.S. Postal Service?), Isolation Peak, Estes Park, Grand Lake, Mount Richthofen, Bowen Mountain, Ward, Monarch Lake, Glen Haven, Pingree Park, Comanche Peak, Chambers Lake, Clark Peak, Trail Mountain, Granby, Strawberry Lake, Gold Hill, Raymond, Panorama Peak, Crystal Mountain, East Portal and Nederland. Circumambulating these maps when they are laid out together is a pretty long hike in itself.

Trailhead Locator

MUMMY RANGE

1. Pingree Park (9030')
2. Corral Creek Trailhead (10,000')
3. North Fork Trailhead (7960')
4. McGraw Ranch (7840')
5. Gem Lake Trailhead
   on Devils Gulch Road (7740')
6. Twin Owls Trailhead (7920')
7. Lawn Lake Trailhead (8540')
8. Chapin Creek Trailhead (10,640')

MORAINE PARK

9. Cub Lake Trailhead (8080')
10. Fern Lake Trailhead (8155')

BEAR LAKE ROAD

11. Hallowell Park (8400')
12. Bierstadt Lake, Boulder Brook-Storm
    Pass Trailheads (8850')
13. Glacier Gorge Junction (9240')

BEAR LAKE TRAILHEAD

14. Bear Lake (9475')

LONGS PEAK AND NEARBY GOALS

15. Longs Peak Ranger Station (9400')

EAST EDGE SUMMITS

16. Twin Sisters Trailhead (9090')
17. Storm Pass Trailhead (9110')
18. Lily Mountain Trailhead (8780')
19. Marys Lake (8046')

WILD BASIN

20. Copeland Lake (8312')
21. Finch Lake Trailhead (8470')
    and Wild Basin Ranger Station (8500')

INDIAN PEAKS, EAST OF THE DIVIDE

22. St. Vrain Mountain Trailhead (8800')
23. Camp Dick [Middle St. Vrain] (8638')
24. Beaver Reservoir (9161')
25. Mitchell Creek Trailhead (10,480')
26. Long Lake Trailhead (10,480')
27. Rainbow Lakes Campground (9960')
28. Buckingham Campground (10,121')

INDIAN PEAKS, WEST OF THE DIVIDE

29. Roaring Fork Trailhead (8281')
30. Monarch Lake (8346')
31. Junco Pond (10,040')

TRAIL RIDGE ROAD

32. Gore Range Overlook (12,020')
33. Ute Trail Crossing
    of Trail Ridge Road (11,440')
34. Beaver Meadows (8440')
35. Deer Ridge Junction (8930')
36. Milner Pass (10,750')
37. Timber Lake Trailhead (9000')
38. Holzwarth Homestead (8884')
39. Baker Gulch Trailhead (8864')
40. Onahu Creek Trailhead (8765')
41. Green Mountain Trailhead (8794')

PHANTOM VALLEY TRAILHEAD

42. Phantom Valley Trailhead (9060')
43. Lake Agnes Trailhead (10,300')

GRAND LAKE AREA

44. Tonahutu Creek and
    North Inlet Trailheads (8545')
45. East Inlet Trailhead (8391')
46. East Shore Trailhead (8390')
47. Green Ridge Campground (8400')

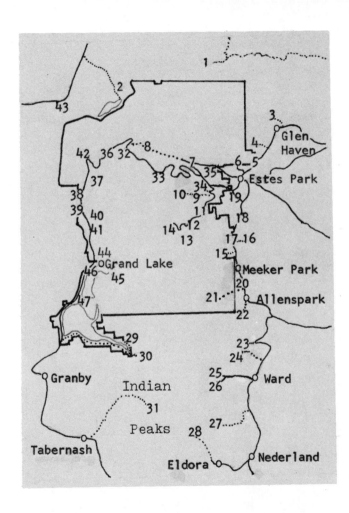

Clark's nutcracker on subalpine fir

What to Wear and Carry

"The Nonessential Backpacker" is a section in *Backpacker* Magazine featuring gadgets, clothing, food and miscellaneous exotic stuff for hikers to carry into the wilderness. Our favorite item from this feature is a Colorado product — a down-filled necktie. No longer is there any excuse for sloppy hikers!

A certain amount of silliness is unavoidable as advancing technology in materials and equipment design makes hiking and backpacking ever easier. As potential customers for hiking products increase, the incentive for manufacturers to supply both quality and crud to satisfy needs and desires increases proportionately. Any detailed list today of what is needed in the Rocky Mountain National Park backcountry would be obsolete tomorrow.

Nevertheless, although equipment and clothing (terms with indistinct distinctions) constantly change, there are some stable factors, for the human body and the mountain environment do not change much.

The park's mountain environment is made up of two important categories: terrain above tree line and below tree line. That below tree line is the more moderate. Venturing very far above the trees, in the alpine zone, necessitates more preparation for varying conditions.

As for the human body, it experiences two important states: comfortable and uncomfortable. The state of discomfort can be subdivided almost infinitely, with "sissy" at one end of the scale and "casualty" at the other. Most of us are willing to risk some discomfort during our backcountry experience to achieve a certain amount of relief from too much weight while hiking. The trick is in determining the degree of risk.

For instance, starting out for Dream Lake on a warm, sunny August morning without carrying sweater or raingear is perfectly reasonable. The chances of a dangerous ambush by the elements are negligible. But starting out for Longs Peak on the same morning without the burden of extra protection for your body is foolhardy and could cause you significant harm. Between these two extremes range a number of less simple situations requiring decisions about what to wear and carry.

Below tree line it is possible, though unlikely, for the temperature to vary as much as 50 degrees F. during a single day. The chance of being caught in an afternoon shower is fairly high, but wind usually is not bothersome.

Wind, wetness and temperature all figure in discussions about hypothermia. Hypothermia is a newly popular word describing what used to be called exposure. The new terminology developed along with a better understanding of the weather conditions and physical stresses that cause this dangerous phenomenon. Essentially, the victim's internal heating mechanisms break down because of repeated draining away of body heat by combinations of low air temperatures, wetness and wind. Hypothermia can occur in temperatures as high as 50 degrees and in locations below tree line. But it probably won't occur below tree line unless a nearly naked, fasting hiker, traveling alone off-trail and unknown to anyone, suffers an incapacitating injury.

Below tree line the risk of serious injury from exposure to inclement elements is not very significant. On the other hand, who wants to be even miserably uncomfortable? If you plan to be more than a mile from the trailhead, a cotton shirt, long pants and rainwear are the minimum items necessary to avoid significant risk of discomfort. Additionally, sunscreen lotion, food, water, a sweater and a pack to carry it all in are advisable. And some hikers do manage to survive with less than 15 pounds of camera equipment.

The alpine zone has greater extremes. The temperature varies much more than below tree line. Unfortunately, the sun probably will pour down in the morning when you are climbing and generating plenty of your own heat. In the afternoon, when you are descending and generating much less heat, clouds often will shade you while the wind picks up to a stiff gale.

Therefore, while hiking above the tree line you need to be able to add or shed layers of clothing. You should have some way of covering the full length of arms and legs. Raingear helps to cut the wind. A sweater is the minimum extra clothing you should carry just for warmth, and a hat, gloves and jacket may be very welcome. You will need more water than when below tree line because deeper breathing and high winds suck moisture from the body.

Protection from the sun is vital in the shadeless environment of the alpine zone. People differ, of course, in their sensitivity to the burning of ultraviolet light. But tolerance experienced elsewhere is irrelevant at high elevations where thin air screens out far less UV radiation than at lower elevations. On snow the exposure to UV is much greater than on earth or rock, because the snow reflects back much of the burning radiation, greatly increasing the dosage you receive. In the Rockies a large percentage of the attempts to achieve suntan end up as sunburns. Colorado has the country's highest rate of skin cancer, because thin air gives so little protection from radiation.

Do everything practical to keep the sun off your skin. Long sleeves and pants are obvious. When they are too warm, apply sunscreen lotion with abandon. Turn your collar up to cover the back of your neck. Wear a hat with a brim. Sunglasses are essential.

As frequently as people underprotect their skin while hiking in the mountains, they overprotect their feet. Plain old over-the-ankle work shoes with cork composition or rubber soles or even mere tennis shoes are adequate for most trail hiking. For off-trail hiking (as to mountain summits) or for backpacking — times when it is more important to keep feet dry — heavier (but not very heavy) hiking boots made of full-grain leather are helpful. The all-too-familiar neoprene lug sole is the best sole for traveling over rock, although a pattern with shallower and closer-set lugs than currently popular would work just as well and cause less wear and tear on the landscape. Unfortunately, a large percentage of hikers and backpackers wear heavy, reinforced boots that are far more burdensome and expensive than needed. Most of them are bought as much for show as for moving their owners from one place to another. People who wear huge "waffle stompers" for hikes that require less footwear present a ludicrous picture.

On the subject of excesses, many hikers carry more food than they need, but because they like to eat. If you are enthusiastic about food, eating in the unequaled beauty of the wilderness certainly will enhance your gustatory delights. On the other hand, that same beauty can compensate for a good deal of deficiency in the food line.

High calorie food that is bad for your health at home, such as hard candy or chocolate, may be just what you need for dragging your body up a steep slope. Most dried fruits and the multiple variations on the familiar "gorp" are good. A list at the back of this guide includes books devoted to eating in the wilderness. It is in the culinary arena that some of the most enthusiastic backcountry creativity is expressed.

Yet, if the truth be known, food is the least necessary item in the pack for all day-hikes and for most backpacking trips. You should have some food, but you do not need much. Anybody can manage to skip a meal or two. From the standpoint of total joy derived from a wilderness experience, an extra roll of film or pair of gloves can be a good deal more important than an extra sandwich.

Furthermore, there is an undeniable relationship between amount of food consumed and amount of defecation, and human defecation has become a serious pollution problem — not to mention aesthetic — in Rocky Mountain National Park. Small garden trowels for the burying of human wastes are not carried and used with nearly enough frequency.

For this reason, it is much more important to carry water than to carry food. DO NOT DRINK FROM STREAMS IN ROCKY

MOUNTAIN NATIONAL PARK. Although you might get away with it for a while, making a habit of drinking unboiled or untreated water eventually will cause illness — usually of a dysentery nature and always at the worst possible time.

Just as preventing illness is preferable to curing it, preventing accidents is preferable to first aid. Still, one member of your hiking party should carry a first-aid kit. Band-Aids®, in particular, are useful and have magic healing powers far beyond any rational explanation. First-aid knowledge usually is more important than first-aid supplies, and it is infinitely more lightweight. Our book list contains good references for wilderness first aid; they should be learned from rather than carried along. The extra weight would be no fun, and if you have to take time to look up a first-aid technique, you probably would be too late in executing it.

On the other hand, the book you are reading is well worth its weight in the energy you save by not getting lost. A map is the absolute minimum reference needed by hikers not intimately familiar with the terrain they hope to cover. You probably can get along without a compass if you can orient yourself in relation to prominent mountains, especially Longs Peak. But if rare low clouds obscure the peaks, a compass may help you to get out of the wilds at a time when you do not care to waste hours in being lost.

Finally, there is no need for such equipment as an ax, saw, sheath knife or cavalry sabre. The only necessary cutting tool is a pocketknife. Some multibladed pocketknives have a lot of useless extra stuff attached (a corkscrew?!), but screwdrivers, scissors, file, awl, magnifying glass or tweezers can be very handy for makeshift equipment or body repair.

Backpacking, of course, requires much more equipment than hiking — frame pack, sleeping bag, tent, stove, mattress, ropes, telescope, wetsuit, inflatable raft, hot air balloon, helicopter, whistle, four Sherpas, this trail guide and a partridge in a pear tree. Further information on what backpackers need can be found in the excellent books on this subject listed at the back of our book. If they fail to mention a down-filled necktie, please remember that it is very hard for even the best of us to stay current.

Pika (cony)

Lightning: One Strike and You're Out!

The weather was deceptively clear, even balmy, as we began to walk up Old Fall River Road after a successful climb of Ypsilon Mountain. This unpaved road, which climbs to 11,800 feet at Fall River Pass, had not been reopened to summer auto traffic. It had been necessary for us and our hiking companions to hike down the old road to Chapin Pass from the Alpine Visitor Center on Trail Ridge Road before ascending Ypsilon.

Climbing back to our cars, we were less than a half-mile from safety when the sky quickly blackened and thunder echoed ominously. It was a difficult situation. We were much closer to the Alpine Visitor Center than to the tree line. Yet, the higher we climbed the greater our danger of attracting lightning. Since all alternatives were bad, we decided to try to reach the visitor center, from the east, before the storm reached it, from the west. Of course, we lost the race.

Rain and hail pelted us in sheets. We tried counting five-second intervals between lightning and thunder to estimate the number of miles to where the bolts were striking; our count yielded only four seconds for the thunder to travel to us from the strikes. We hoped we could get inside an old cabin nearby that had sheltered road workers many years before, but it was locked.

Under its eaves, we at least found protection from rain and hail. Now that we no longer generated heat by frantically hurrying uphill, we began to chill. There were dry, warm jackets in our packs. Leaving hiking companions strung out along the cabin wall, we ran around a corner of the building; the recess of a door on the other side would give us a bit more shelter for putting on the jackets.

We barely had turned the corner when the universe erupted and was transformed to one all-encompassing boom. Its volume knocked us to the ground. Back on our feet, we returned to our friends and found them thoroughly shaken. Lightning, they babbled, had struck right where we had been standing seconds before! Sparks had flown off and hit the individuals standing on either side.

No one was seriously hurt, but all of us were seriously terrified. Lightning does strike twice in the same place — frequently, in fact — and it was thundering all around. We scattered quickly for the lowest depressions we could find, trying to stay away from each other and from water courses and rivulets that could conduct currents along the ground to us from lightning strikes.

Actually, our friends were wrong. Had lightning struck exactly where we had been standing, the hikers on either side would have been badly injured or killed. Lightning did hit nearby, though, and the strike's voltage had diffused through the ground along lines of least resistance, dissipating in strength as it traveled.

One line of this "step voltage" had radiated to a piece of an old shovel lying on the ground under the eaves. Had we not moved, it would have radiated to us, instead, and caused injury or death. Most people who are hit by lightning are victims of step voltage rather than of direct strikes. But the time between strike and conduction of step voltage is a very small fraction of a second, far less than human senses can perceive. It certainly seemed as though lightning had smashed directly into the midst of the group.

Rain pelted down on our hollows of scant safety, and we wished we had sleeping pads or climbing ropes to squat on for insulation from the ground and from more exposure to step voltage. Such equipment, unfortunately, is unnecessary for reaching the summit of Ypsilon Mountain. We could only stay as low as possible with as little of our bodies as possible touching the ground.

At last the storm passed over. Its fury actually had lasted a scant few minutes, but it seemed much longer. Looking west, we could see another storm following close on the heels of the first.

Lightning was striking the Never Summer Range and heading our way fast.

We ran for the shelter of the visitor center at Fall River Pass. Now, running a half-mile at full speed, laden with heavy boots and packs, up a 45-degree slope in oxygen-short air at 11,500 feet poses definite problems. On the other hand, lashes of lightning and extreme fear are marvelous incentives to effort. As we ran we heard sirens wailing across the tundra and hoped that rescuers were coming for us.

We were on our own, though, and were nearly dead from exhaustion when we stumbled, gasping, into the safety of the visitor center. The second storm hit as the door swung closed behind us.

Nearly dead does not count. We learned then where the sirens were going: to a parking lot on Trail Ridge Road where a woman had been struck directly by lightning and killed. Standing on the equivalent of a mountaintop, she probably had died from an "upward stroke" of lightning. This type begins in the ground and sparks up to clouds. The huge amount of electricity exposes the conducting object (in this case, a human body) to a temperature as high as 50,000 degrees F. Death is almost inevitable.

The victim might have been struck by a "down stroke," with about the same result. Yet strikes that originate in clouds usually dissipate in the surrounding air so that the actual strike consists of only a few thousand volts. Seventy percent of the victims of down strokes survive.

The amount of shock a person receives from voltage running along the ground depends on the nearness of the strike and on the conductivity of the ground surface. The chances of survival depend largely on the reaction of people nearby. The victim may look very dead because heartbeat and breathing usually are stopped at once by the electrical shock. Nevertheless, closed heart massage and artificial respiration should be commenced immediately. The heart frequently will start up by itself; the lungs will not. Although lack of oxygen for long periods can cause brain damage, victims have recovered completely after having no oxygen for as long as 22 minutes. There are additional injuries from lightning that may need first aid: burns, cuts, shock, internal bleeding, broken bones from falling. Some of them may kill if not tended.

It is easy to understand why many mountaineers are fatalistic about lightning. Their attitude is unfortunate, for it fosters carelessness, and there are some ways to avoid being hit. Obviously, you should not be the highest object around when a storm threatens. If at all possible, get below tree line. You will be very safe in a forest. This is quite different from huddling under a lone tree, which would make you an excellent candidate for receiving strong step voltage. If you can see an old lightning scar twisting around the trunk of a nearby tree, you are too close to the tree.

If caught unavoidably above tree line by a storm, you should stay away from edges of cliffs and from high boulders; also from rock debris and vegetation at the bottom of cliffs, for both conduct step voltage. Cracks and shallow niches in the mountainside also should be avoided.

The best procedure is to crouch among flat-topped boulders. Since such ideal places are scarce on the tundra, a depression may have to do. But depressions containing water are annoyingly uncomfortable and are dangerous because of step voltage.

There are a few local hints for minimizing the danger from lightning in Rocky Mountain National Park. First, because storms tend to gather in the afternoon, you should begin hikes to peaks early enough to reach the summit and leave it by about 1 p.m. Having to end a hike by climbing to a trailhead above tree line, such as Gore Range Overlook or Fall River Pass, is less than ideal.

Second, certain places apparently are preferred lightning targets and might be avoided during storms. On the list are Deer Mountain, Specimen Mountain and Mills Moraine. Trail Ridge seems like a favorite target, but that may be because it swarms with so many potential victims. Longs Peak, of course, is the highest point anywhere around — except for climbers who are standing on top of it.

All in all, lightning is nasty stuff. It is the only summer danger in

Rocky Mountain National Park that a fit, properly equipped and experienced mountaineer cannot overcome. Nevertheless, fear of lightning can inspire evasive action which will reduce the chance of being hit to very acceptable odds. Only the foolish lack such fear.

Douglas-fir branch and cone

Hikers as Caretakers

Rocky Mountain National Park is a better place now than it was when we first hiked its trails in the 1950s. The improvement has occurred despite a huge increase in visitation of all kinds and an explosion of backcountry use. The statistics are awesome. For example, there was a 700 percent increase in backpacking between 1965 and 1975. We are reluctant to quote statistics, though, because they constantly are outdated by greater increases.

Today there is considerable evidence that mushrooming crowds have reversed the trend toward improvement and that the park is headed toward wilderness degradation. But the reversal is not inevitable just from the point of numbers. Better educated, more enlightened, more loving use of the land can preserve the park for future generations.

Although most of the park's improvement should be credited to the National Park Service, the time has passed when we should count on rangers to look after our wilderness interests. Every day we hear more calls in more areas for government to do this and that and to relieve individuals of personal responsibility. Because we hikers and backpackers value the freedom we feel in the wilds, we must accept the responsibility for taking care of the land over which we walk in Rocky Mountain National Park.

As caretakers, each of us must act as though the salvation of the park's wilderness depends on us alone rather than on regulations for preserving the backcountry. Our wilderness will be preserved, in fact, only if we exceed the minimum requirements of regulations. For instance, the National Park Service requires that all backpackers obtain a free permit allowing backcountry camping at certain sites on particular dates. Campfires are permitted only at sites equipped with steel fire rings. The regulations specify that only dead and down wood should be burned.

In reality, there is no room left in this park's backcountry for campfires of any kind, anywhere. Even the dead and down wood has a place in the ecosystem; each link in the chain of life is important to the whole. Research in other mountain wilderness areas has revealed that some insects that pollinate wildflowers nest in dead and down wood. When thousands of campfires consume all the dead and down wood — and insect nesting sites — within a wide radius of many campsites, they eliminate the insects and the plants as well, without a single blossom being stepped on.

The backpacking stove with liquid fuel is the hiker's only acceptable source of fire in the wilderness of Rocky Mountain National Park. Stoves are much more convenient and clean than campfires, so virtue has its reward.

We must not only pack out all we pack in but pack out all the litter left behind by other hikers. Park regulations prohibit hacking on trees, ditching tents, removing rocks from their natural sites and blackening rocks in fire rings, because these practices permanently inflict human presence on heavily used areas. But we should take greater care; at campsites we should wear moccasins or some other soft footwear to minimize the effect of concentrated walking.

When there is no outhouse, Park Service regulations call for human waste to be buried in the zone of decay six inches underground and at least 100 feet from all watercourses. We should do more. When we must answer the call of nature, we should remove the ground cover intact with our trowel before digging a hole, and replace it later, as cannily as a fur trapper used to hide his cache of pelts. Really good caretakers even cultivate backcountry constipation.

The hiker's role as caretaker of Rocky Mountain National Park extends further: we must abandon our normal reluctance to intrude on other people's activities. When we observe other hikers acting contrary to good wilderness ethics, we must take it upon ourselves to educate the offenders in the friendliest way possible about proper backcountry behavior. For instance, we can explain how hikers must travel on trails and not short-cut across switchbacks because making shortcuts destroys vegetation and causes erosion, which will wash away the trails. And we can insist that wash water for dishes, bodies and everything else be carried away from watercourses and campsites for dumping.

We need to educate ourselves extensively about the ecology of Rocky Mountain National Park wilderness so that we will not damage it out of ignorance. We must stress to fellow hikers the delicacy of all life on this austere land. We can point out how slowly plants grow in the mountains, especially in the alpine zone. By word and example we must urge the utmost care in subjecting mountain plants to the absolute minimum of stress, for their already stressful lives can stand little more. Where trails already exist, we will stay on them. Where there are no trails, we will avoid fellow hikers' footsteps to disperse and minimize the impact of our passing.

Many of us have pets we would enjoy taking into the wilderness. But when dogs, cats, canaries or goldfish enter the backcountry, they unavoidably increase impact on the wilds in various ways. So many human beings want to use Rocky Mountain National Park wilderness that pets cannot be allowed. A sympathetic explanation of this necessity to hikers with pets is far better than the typical rage and muttering and certainly will have more of an effect on their future behavior.

The role of caretaker demands that each hiker and backpacker make these sacrifices and more so wilderness may live long after we are gone, just as it lived long before any people saw it. We must sacrifice out of love for the wilderness; it benefits us in so many ways, and it is beautiful and needs our protection. As we urge others to practice good wilderness ethics, we must feel kindly toward them, for they are potential allies and fellow caretakers of Rocky Mountain National Park.

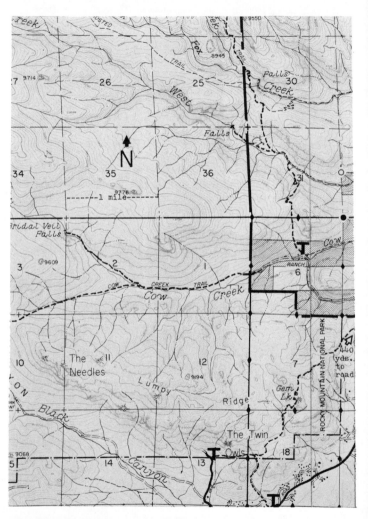

Gem Lake and Trail from McGraw Ranch

Mummy Range

The Mummy Range is the most diverse and complex hiking area in Rocky Mountain National Park. From trailheads scattered all around its base, a network of trails crisscrosses the mountains, giving hikers and backpackers wonderful choices of routes and destinations.

Gem Lakes Trail

"How could two miles be so long? When do we reach the darned lake, anyway?"

Such reactions are frequent among the many hikers who are lured onto the Gem Lake Trail because it seems fast and easy — the lake is only a two-mile walk from the two trailheads closest to Estes Park Village. The trail, however, winds through open, south-facing ponderosa pine woods at a lower altitude than most park paths; thus, midday heat in summer can sap hikers' energy significantly.

Many folks are disappointed by the Gem Lake hike. But their disappointment arises from their inability to see and understand the fascinating natural events occurring at trailside. With a quart of water per person, three hours to spend, and a knowledge of what to look for, they would find the Gem Lake Trail unique and enjoyable. It is best hiked early or late in the day, not only for physical comfort but for grand vistas of dramatic light falling on the Front Range.

To reach the two Gem Lake trailheads, drive north on MacGregor Lane (which becomes Devils Gulch Avenue and then Road) from the city park in the middle of downtown Estes Park.

After about a mile, the road bends east at the entrance to MacGregor Ranch. One trailhead for Gem Lake is reached by driving through the ranch. You may have to open a gate; if so, be sure to close it behind you. Stay on the paved road (.8 mile long), which dead-ends at a parking lot below Twin Owls, a large rock formation perched on Lumpy Ridge.

To reach the second trailhead, continue on Devils Gulch Road past the MacGregor Ranch entrance. After the road bends north again, you arrive at a parking lot on the left side of the road 1.8 miles from the middle of town.

The first .8 mile of trail from the parking lot at the second trailhead passes through private land. Much of the access corridor is fenced on both sides as it crosses level open meadows. At the trail's second right-angle turn, look up at Lumpy Ridge. The highest "lump" to the left is Twin Owls, a favorite formation for technical rock climbers. From other viewpoints it really does look like two owls.

The next formation to watch for comes into sight as you approach a small creek bed bordered by moisture-loving white-barked aspens. Before you reach the trees, look to your left to note on the ridgeline a trio of rock figures called Hen and Chickens. If you have the gift for seeing images in rock formations, you will find no better place to exercise it than on the trail ahead.

Soon the way grows steeper, and a pull on your water bottle may seem appropriate. There is no point in being Spartan about it; you should be carrying enough water to take a drink whenever you want one. After a couple of switchbacks, you arrive at last at the park boundary where the trail from Twin Owls joins this one.

The trail from Twin Owls is a bit shorter than the one from Devils Gulch Road. Furthermore, its trailhead is 180 feet higher, and its path climbs more gradually. It is the somewhat easier way to Gem Lake, and all within national park boundaries. If the Twin Owls parking lot is full, however, you may want to begin at the other trailhead. Please do not park your car so as to block the driveway of the house at Twin Owls.

NATURE WALK TO GEM LAKE (MONTANE ZONE)

The Twin Owls parking lot is a good place to visualize the broad outlines of the geology of Lumpy Ridge. Forty million years ago (give or take a day or two) the ridgetop was part of an ancient plain. It was raised to its present position a mere five to seven million years ago, by which time the plain had been deeply penetrated by weathering, the process that breaks up rocks and decays them into soil. This decay had occurred along a network of fractures in the granite underlying the plain. As the sides of granite blocks outlined by fractures disintegrated, their unweathered cores remained as solid rock surrounded by weathered debris. The debris later eroded away, especially as the ridge was raised.

The cores are the "lumps" of today and also the huge boulders that eventually tumbled down the slopes of Lumpy Ridge. The boulders could be mistaken easily for rocks deposited by melting glaciers, but glaciers never extended to this spot.

The rounded appearance of the rocks comes from the way in which they weather. Masses of granite in areas of slight rainfall split off plates or shells in successive layers like those of an onion. The process, called exfoliation, begins when water invades tiny cracks in the granite and dries more slowly than on the surface. Some minerals in the granite are slowly dissolved by the water and form claylike material. The clay expands and wedges off plates parallel to the surface.

The action, of course, takes a very long time. We casually drop millions of years here and there throughout Lumpy Ridge geology. Human life is too short and human experience too limited to enable most imaginations to encompass so long a period of time. Such mind-numbing ages remind us of part of Psalm 39, which says, "Lord, let me know how fleeting my life is! Surely man stands as a mere breath! Surely man goes about as a shadow!"

The trail begins amid quaking aspens and large chokecherry bushes. This is the most common wild cherry (*Prunus virginiana*); varieties of it grow throughout most of the United States. It is a marvelous shrub, with long white flower clusters of almost overpowering sweetness in spring. The blossoms evolve to masses of dark purple or black cherries, much favored by birds and jelly-makers. In fall the leaves of the bush turn orange-red.

In the drier areas along the trail two kinds of juniper grow. Common (or creeping, or dwarf) juniper is a low shrub with short, sharp needles. Rocky Mountain juniper (often called cedar) is a small, many-branched tree with flat, scalelike foliage. The female plant of both kinds bear blue cones with a waxy covering which makes them resemble berries. Juniper "berries" are used to flavor gin. They are not tasty, and after an experimental nibble, few hikers venture to try more.

Wild rose is another common and edible-if-you-are-desperate shrub on the first part of the Gem Lake Trail. After its fragrant pink flowers have faded they are transformed to rose hips, well known as a source of vitamin C. These red fruits taste no better than bland, mealy apples; they also have annoying hairy seeds. So unless an advanced case of scurvy is causing your teeth to fall out, it would be best to leave the rose hips to grow prettily and to be eaten by the wildlife that favors them.

Growing among the rocks and in draws on the hillside is Rocky Mountain maple. Although the leaf's shape is familiar to most hikers, this many-stemmed shrubby representative of a noble and valuable family seems like a stunted poor cousin. Well, it is the only maple we have, and we like it! It puts up with excessive dryness and poor soil which the big, showy maples never could tolerate. In size and shape it reflects the general harsh austerity of the West, yet in fall its leaves turn a showy red and yellow like the magnificent sugar maple of the East.

Ponderosa pine is the dominant tree in the montane zone of vegetation through which the trail passes. It has moderately long needles growing in bundles of two or three. The bark of young ponderosas is dark gray, and that of mature trees is thick, deeply grooved and rusty red. These picturesque mature pines, which may be as old as 500 years, stand apart from each other, giving a ponderosa woods an open, parklike appearance.

Perhaps the most interesting inhabitants of ponderosa forests are the tassel-eared (abert) squirrels. They are the most magnificent squirrels in North America and need no description beyond that of the children who call them "squabbits,' for squirrels with rabbitlike ears. Aberts come in two distinct color phases, black and gray-and-white, and there are some dark brown individuals.

Less spectacular but more pugnacious are the red squirrels, which are more gray than red. Chipmunks (striped back and face) and golden-mantled ground squirrels (larger, with striped back and plain face) also abound. In grassy areas near the base of the trail, unstriped Richardson's ground squirrels are common. Locally they are called gophers. Yellow-bellied marmots, western cousins of the woodchuck, often are seen sunning themselves on rocks about a quarter-mile up the trail from Twin Owls.

Common birds to watch for as you hike toward Gem include tiny pygmy nuthatches, mountain chickadees, yellow-rumped warblers, gray-headed juncos and raucous Clark's nutcrackers. Two thrushes seen more frequently along the lower part of the trail than in other areas of the park include Townsend's solitaire and the rust-and-blue western bluebird, which is not to be confused with the very common blue-and-gray mountain bluebird.

In the moister areas among the ponderosas, Douglas-fir grow in groups or singly. Their cones, with three-pointed bracts protruding from under the scales, are quite distinctive. In the Pacific Northwest, the Douglas-fir grows to a huge size and is extremely important for lumber. In our semiarid climate, however, a specimen a yard in diameter qualifies as an old giant.

After a double switchback below Twin Owls and a stretch of trail running just inside the clearly marked park boundary, watch for an interesting antelope bitterbrush growing closely over a trailside rock on the left. Bitterbrush does not look unusual; it has many branches, small leaves and small yellow blossoms in May and June. Yes, it tastes very bitter. But it is an important brouse plant for mule deer. (During the last century market hunters wiped out the antelope of the plant's name in the Estes Park area.) The warm period of each spring day is longer near the rock's surface because the surface reflects and absorbs heat. In response to the advanced season of this inch-thick microclimate, the branches of the plant growing nearest the rock are the first to leaf out and bloom.

By now, a pause to take a swig from your water bottle probably is welcome. The view over the pastures of MacGregor Ranch, established in 1874, is dominated by Longs Peak, the tallest peak in sight. At 14,255 feet it is the highest point in Rocky Mountain National Park. Mount Meeker, to the left of Longs, is the park's second-tallest peak — 13,911 feet. To the right of Longs stretch other 12,000 and 13,000-foot summits of the Front Range.

Nearer at hand, the hillside is dotted with many dead ponderosa pines killed by mountain pine beetles. Now and then you will see lightning-killed trees, too. Beetle trees are good hunting grounds for hungry woodpeckers such as common flickers, whose red wings and white rumps flash in flight. All the dead trees provide holes essential for nests of swallows, bluebirds, wrens, chickadees, nuthatches and many more cavity-dwelling birds.

Farther up the trail, in especially dry and sunny areas, prickly-pear cactus begins to appear. The blooms in June are a showy yellow and red. The big, nasty-looking spines at all times of year are a dramatic warning to keep away. But they are not dangerous, for you can see them. The real threat comes from the minute spines growing close to the surface of the fleshy stem.

In a national park, the prickly pear, like everything else, is of course left unmolested. Elsewhere, where it is more abundant, it is gathered and eaten, and then the small spines come into play. The big spines are easy to break or burn off, but the little ones seem immune to any type of removal. Most folks cannot even see them without a hand lens; under magnification the rows of barbs on each spine stand out like fishhooks. The barbs can work their way into the flesh of careless hands and cause pain for days.

The small spines were found by an archeologist in 90 percent of the feces collected from ancient ruins at Mesa Verde National Park.

Not content with the romance of examining centuries-old feces, the archeologist tried eating fresh prickly pear with its tiny spines intact. Oddly, martyrdom for science was not the result. The only negative sensation was a prickling of the tongue. Please refrain from this kind of experiment, though — especially in national parks!

A safer, if not better-tasting, addition to the Indian diet was squaw currant; abundant squaw currant grows along the trail as it climbs the ridge. This bush has the typical rounded, lobed leaf of a currant, and trumpet-shaped pink flowers which ripen to red berries. The berries are used by some jelly makers, but they need much spicing up to make the product more than insipid. They are, however, an important food for birds and small mammals.

As the trail bends to the left, it climbs across a gulch between Lumpy Ridge and a minor ridge extending south from the main slope. Although you may not be able to feel a change, you are entering a cooler, wetter climate. Plants are more sensitive to climate than are people, and here Douglas-fir is the dominant tree rather than ponderosa pine, which is adapted to drier slopes.

More water trickles into this gulch than is available to plants on the surrounding hillsides. The sides of the gulch are shaded during much of the day, and in winter the north-facing side receives hardly any sun because it shines from the south. Then each snowflake that is protected from the sun's direct melting rays serves as a tiny reservoir of water to nourish thirsty plants. Additionally the shade slows evaporation at all times of year.

The trees change again as the trail climbs over the minor ridge. The ridgetop is exposed to high winds, especially in winter. Here grows limber pine (*Pinus flexilis*), whose tough, flexible branches bend easily before the wind but rarely break. This tree normally is associated with tree line, several thousand feet higher in the mountains. Its needles are shorter than the ponderosa's and grow five to a bundle, giving each branch a scrub-brush appearance.

After crossing the ridgetop, the trail from Twin Owls descends slightly to join the approach from Devils Gulch Road. Past the junction, the combined trail climbs steeply along the edge of an aspen grove in an often-dry creek bed where there is a heavy growth of bracken ferns. Soon excellent views beckon to the south and west, necessitating short detours from the trail. Looking south, you will see the bumpy summit of Twin Sisters across the valley east of Longs Peak. Lake Estes and associated civilization are obvious in the valley immediately below you.

Essentially similar views continue until the trail turns into a shady canyon with a small stream. The canyon is refreshingly cool, and out-of-place Engelmann spruce has found a foothold similar to its usual home higher in the subalpine zone. An occasional subalpine fir also grows here. Aspen, water birch, chiming bells, shooting star and other moisture-loving plants, along with mosquitoes, inhabit this oasis.

After crossing the stream, the trail is closed in by canyon walls. Exit is via two series of short switchbacks, at the top of which appears *Paul Bunyans Boot*, a rock formation which constitutes a must photo. Chemical weathering even has put a hole in the boot's sole.

Natural sculpture and balanced rocks are common on Lumpy Ridge, as are potholes in the granite. On cliffs above Gem Lake, itself a big pothole, these formations of chemical and mechanical weathering seem too fantastic to be natural — more like a Disneyland invention.

The hollowing out of rock basins begins when falling rain picks up a little carbon dioxide from the air to form extremely mild carbonic acid. The acid tends to break down certain granitic minerals into various clays. Some of the rock surfaces are structurally weaker and more susceptible to this chemical weathering than are the surrounding surfaces. Further weak acids formed by accumulations of decaying vegetation can accelerate pothole formation, as can wind and frost-wedging, expansion of ice that enlarges cracks in rocks. Weathering sometimes creates holes all the way through rock.

Below Gem Lake there are three series of short, steep switchbacks built to make the trail easier for horses, not for humans.

The trail emerges from trees to run along steep-walled rock slabs, which collect the sun's warmth and radiate it back on hikers. You get steadily hotter. Then you face one more long dusty switchback and reach the lake — at last.

"Ugh, that's it?" is the typical reaction. Folks expecting a typical alpine lake always are disappointed. Gem covers only .2 acre with a maximum depth of five feet and an average depth of one. It is stagnant, fed by rain and snowmelt, with no visible outlet. Various interesting but unglamorous creepy-crawlies call it home.

Yet Gem is a joy, for there is no other body of water like it in the park. White-throated swifts, uncommon elsewhere, dip and soar over the lake. Picturesque limber pines and Douglas-fir decorate the sandy shore. Stroll 200 feet to the opposite end of the lake where pine branches will frame a photo of Gem with spectacular peaks in the background. Details of the patterns made by orange lichens on the rock cliffs provide additional good picture subjects. The examples of exfoliation and chemical weathering are unexcelled.

The acoustics of this natural amphitheater are such that your heartbeat seems to echo. This phenomenon can be a disadvantage if a large group (say two) of noisy children is present. The hike to Gem Lake is excellent for kids, but remember that you would not let them scream and yell in church.

There are comfort stations around the corner of the cliff at the north end of the lake. Between them and the lake lies the easiest route of ascent to the top of the cliffs, about 200 feet above. It is worth the climb for the different photographic perspective of the lake (for which a wide-angle lens is helpful) fantastic potholes and views of the surrounding peaks.

The trail continues past the comfort stations and descends for a mile and a half to end on the road to McGraw Ranch (also called Indian Head Ranch). Interesting rocks are less abundant on this (north) side of Lumpy Ridge. Douglas-fir are abundant, though, closing in the upper part of the trail and restricting views to a few glimpses of the Mummy Range. The lower part of the trail crosses more open country, passes through a gate in a fence at the park boundary and then traverses other land to reach the McGraw Ranch Road. Public access here is a point of contention. You should check current access with the National Park Service before hiking down this side of Lumpy Ridge from Gem.

We recommend against beginning hikes to Gem from the McGraw Ranch Road because there is no good parking area at this spot. An accommodating friend who can drive there to pick up hikers who have traversed Lumpy Ridge via Gem is the best arrangement. The driver can reach the McGraw Ranch Road by continuing along the paved Devils Gulch Road to a point 3.9 miles from Estes Park. There the paved road bears right, and the unpaved McGraw Ranch Road continues straight ahead. The end of the trail is located at the top of a hill 1.1 miles from Devils Gulch Road. It is *not* obvious unless hikers are waiting at the rendezvous point. A utility pole on the right side of the road bears the metal numbers "2140."

Most hikers probably will prefer to return from Gem via the same route they ascended. It all looks different going down.

North Fork of the Big Thompson Trail System

Everyone is destination oriented. This trail guide of necessity reflects hikers' obsession with getting to a particular place. But on the North Fork trail system there is much to be said for no-particular-destination hiking. Most destinations are far from the trailhead. The national park itself is 4.4 miles from the starting point in Roosevelt National Forest.

The land around the North Fork of the Big Thompson River has been less used for day hiking than other sections of the park, Bear Lake or Glacier Gorge, for instance, because of the long distances to specific destinations. But backpacking has greatly extended the range of wilderness walkers, and travel along the North Fork is increasing.

It was the North Fork's remoteness that attracted one of the most colorful characters in Estes Park history in the 1870s. The Earl of Dunraven, an Englishman, had attempted to gain control of the Estes Park region to preserve its beauty and wildlife from despoliation by the three or four summer tourists who drifted in weekly. By fraudulent means, Dunraven gained title to enough land to turn Estes Park and the entire Big Thompson drainage to the north, west and south (including the North Fork) into his own private hunting reserve.

When Americans paid no attention to his titles, land or otherwise, Dunraven saw that his plan would fail. He reversed his goals and opened a posh hotel to capitalize on the growing fame of Estes Park as a summer paradise. Meanwhile, he escaped the frustrations of civilization by building a hunting lodge for himself along the North Fork.

Dunraven's name lives on in a glade, trail, mountain and lake in the North Fork drainage. His memory adds romance to an area which would be very pleasant and interesting even without a colorful history. The day hiker on the way to nowhere in particular will have an enjoyable trip along the North Fork.

To reach the trailhead, drive north from Estes Park on the Devils Gulch Road to the little town of Glen Haven. At a sign about two miles past Glen Haven, turn left on an unpaved road. Somewhere along this road is the lost site of Dunraven's hunting lodge. Perhaps someday excavation for construction of a new summer home will turn up the whisky cache that the earl buried one fall and was unable to find the following spring.

A few miles down the unpaved road on the left-hand side is the North Fork Trailhead, a U.S. Forest Service parking lot. On the other side of the parking lot the _Dunraven Trail_ begins by heading up a small ridge in what seems to be the exact opposite of the proper direction. But the path soon drops steeply down a forested slope to parallel the North Fork. To the left, the trail extends down through a deep, narrow canyon to Glen Haven — an easy pleasant walk of less than two miles. To the right, the trail extends much farther than two miles — not all easy, but mostly pleasant.

Passage to the right does start out easily, through the shade of

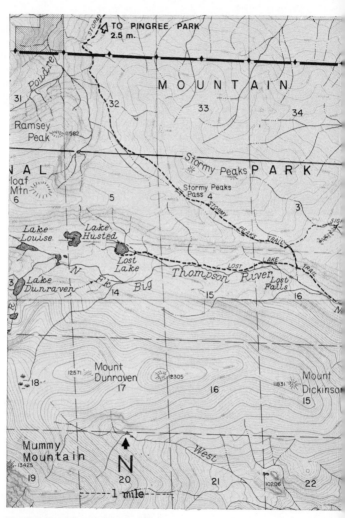

North Fork of the Big Thompson

thick blue spruce and Douglas-fir. In late August and early September, you may have trouble walking quickly past raspberry bushes laden with delicious fruit. As this beautiful canyon widens, the trail passes from national forest property to private land. While you are on private property, be especially conscientious about staying on the trail.

Before long you find yourself walking on a jeep road, which narrows again to trail dimensions until breaking out of the trees at *Deserted Village,* three miles from the trailhead. Wagons carried hunters to this turn of the century resort, which still has one cabin in more or less upright condition. A dysentery epidemic in 1909 had a poor effect on business, and the place was abandoned once and for all by 1914. The earl's hunting parties called this site Dunraven Meadows; a 1907 map labeled it Dunraven Park.

Lest you duplicate the unpleasant intestinal symptoms of wilderness visitors in 1909, *do not drink the water* straight from the North Fork. Treat it chemically and/or boil it first.

Ponderosa pines close in on the trail as the meadow narrows toward its upper end. Some of them have grown around strands of barbed wire that used to be attached to fence off someone's land interest. Dunraven probably did not bother to erect fences along the North Fork; people ignored his other fences anyway, running cattle over much of the land he claimed. His dream of preserving the wilderness and its wildlife for himself was a $200,000 flop. After one last hunt up the North Fork in 1880, he left the region for good. Preservation along a more typical American pattern was accomplished in 1915 with the establishment of Rocky Mountain National Park.

Almost a mile inside the park border, the North Boundary Trail begins on the left. Despite its name, it follows the eastern boundary south to West Creek and out of the park. This trail is described below, but for now you may wish to note that it passes the North Fork Ranger Station less than 200 yards from its junction with the Dunraven Trail.

Past the junction, the trail along the North Fork is called the

Lost Lake Trail. It proceeds along the bottom of the valley on a fairly mild grade for about 1.5 miles. It then climbs steeply away from the river. At a spot 2.3 miles from the North Fork Ranger Station, the trail forks. The Stormy Peaks Trail (see below) is the right-hand fork. The Lost Lake Trail continues left over a relatively young terminal moraine, missing Lost Falls but passing through Lost Meadows. It parallels the creek to reach Lost Lake.

Lost Lake itself was lost once to the national park. After Dunraven gave up his dream, the need for preservation became evident. A dam was built on the North Fork, enlarging Lost Lake into a reservoir. In the early 1970s, the National Park Service acquired the reservoir and began allowing the dam to disintegrate. Gradually Lost Lake is returning to its original level.

The trail fades away beyond Lost Lake, but easy routes exist to points farther on. Two lovely, unnamed alpine lakes sit on the other side of a ridge southwest of Lost Lake. There you are close to the base of Rowe Peak, and the rocky cliffs of the mountains rise dramatically from the tundra.

The North Fork descends into the upper lake via a small noisy waterfall tumbling out of an interesting gorge that extends down from *Lake Dunraven*. Rather than climbing the gorge to Lake Dunraven, you may prefer to use it for your descent, since a much easier route to the earl's lake begins at the outlet of the lower of the two unnamed lakes. After crossing the outlet, worm your way through the least dense section of Krummholz, traverse the bottom of a talus slope and then head straight up the ridge which hides Lake Dunraven.

To climb *Mount Dunraven*, continue on up the ridge. After it becomes somewhat less steep, descend slightly to cross an unnamed drainage to reach and ascend the main bulk of Dunraven. Dunraven is the first summit on a spur extending east from the Mummy Range. The second is unnamed and in the way if you wish to continue along the spur to *Mount Dickinson*, at the end.

From the Mount Dunraven spur you can climb to a saddle on the main section of the Mummy Range between *Hagues Peak* and

Mummy Mountain. Although the approach from this side is less steep, these peaks usually are climbed from Lawn Lake because that approach is shorter (see below, Trails North of Horseshoe Park). From Mummy you can descend to the Lawn Lake Trail via a south slope and a trail from the sometimes dry *Potts Puddle*. If *Lawn Lake* itself is your goal, descend the steep tundra slopes from the Mummy-Hagues saddle, following cairns to reach the trail between Lawn and Crystal lakes.

You can climb from Hagues to *Rowe Peak* and *Rowe Mountain* by dropping a few hundred feet to below the tarn at the base of Rowe Glacier. From there climb steeply north to Rowe Peak. Losing and regaining altitude is easier than fighting the ragged spires on the knife ridge extending above the glacier between Hagues and Rowe.

There is a circle route back to Lost Lake via *Icefield Pass*, north of Rowe Mountain. Two more alpine lakes, *Lake Louise* and *Lake Husted*, add further joy to an easy meander across the tundra above Lost Lake.

Back at the North Fork Ranger Station, the *North Boundary Trail* heads south through fairly thick forest, crossing two streams as it winds steeply up a ridge. Then it descends to Fox Creek, then up again and down again to West Creek, then up again and down again to Indian Head Ranch (also called McGraw Ranch), six miles from the North Fork.

As you can imagine, all this up and down becomes tiresome and dulls the mind to interesting details at trailside. Yet, because spectacular views are infrequent, sharp attention to detail is essential to make the North Boundary hike worth the effort. This trail is not the park's best for hiking. Horse riders have it pretty much to themselves. But for hikers with both the endurance and perception of John Muir, there are some nice spots. It definitely should be hiked from north to south, so you will be climbing on the relatively cool, somewhat less steep northern slopes and descending the more open and warm southern slopes. Some details:

Fox Creek Falls is pleasant though not spectacular. On the map, it is reached by a trail extending from private land at the Trail's End

Cheley Camp, west of Glen Haven. It can be reached also from above by following Fox Creek down from where the North Boundary Trail crosses it, just outside the national park boundary.

Above Fox Creek, the North Boundary Trail passes what used to be the _Husted Trail_. The Husted now evaporates in a "research natural area" kept so unaltered that all horses and camping are prohibited. Hikers who lack a scientific motive probably will want to continue past the Husted Trail.

Another trail junction comes up soon, this one with the _Fox Creek Trail_, on the left. Unless you have some personal reason for following Fox Creek to the east, there is little point in paying much attention to this trail, which soon descends a very steep slope through switchbacks. It is used almost exclusively for horse trips.

Past the Fox Creek Trail junction, the North Boundary Trail descends to West Creek. As you reach the valley floor, but before you reach the creek, a spur trail cuts back sharply to the right, extending one-half mile upstream to _West Creek Falls_. You have more than a mile of steep walking ahead to Indian Head Ranch, and the hiker's natural urge is to get on with it. Nevertheless, you may find it worthwhile to expend a little more effort in the pleasant side trip to the double-tiered falls, where the creek rushes through a rocky amphitheater.

West Creek Falls is so lovely that it undoubtedly would be a popular hiking destination if access were easier. The best route is via the south end of the North Boundary Trail, which is none too good. Begin by asking permission to park your car at Indian Head Ranch. Permission usually is given along with advice about how to reach your hiking goal. The ranch is located at the end of McGraw Ranch Road (2.3 miles, unpaved), which leaves Devils Gulch Road 3.9 miles from downtown Estes Park.

The North Boundary Trail leaves the ranch with a sharp right turn after you pass the first gate beyond the ranch buildings. There is no sign to mark the point. Head straight uphill on a meadow to the spot where the trail climbs to the lowest point on the ridge. It is very steep, much eroded and often sunny and hot.

From the ridgetop the trail switchbacks steeply down through Rocky Mountain maple and Douglas-fir to West Creek, 1.4 miles from the ranch. Cross the creek and turn left (west) at the trail intersection; the trail follows a gentle grade along the stream to West Creek Falls. The trail to the right follows the valley floor, eventually recrossing West Creek and circling back over the ridge to Indian Head Ranch.

The southern end of the *Stormy Peaks Trail* branches away from the Lost Lake Trail 7.6 miles from the North Fork Trailhead parking lot, immediately after a very steep section. Past the junction, the Stormy Peaks Trail is even steeper for almost a mile. The grade becomes less grinding near tree line where you get a fine view of Rowe Peak and Rowe Mountain above Lost Meadows. (You may want a wide-angle lens for photos at this point.) Stormy Peaks Pass is another mile up a less-steep section of trail. The effort required to make a short climb from the pass to the top of Stormy Peaks is amply rewarded by an excellent view.

From Stormy Peaks Pass you can skirt some rocky bumps for an easy walk west over the tundra to *Sugarloaf Mountain*. As you climb Sugarloaf, walk to the edge of the North Fork Valley for a spectacular view of the lakes below and the main peaks of the Mummy Range. From Sugarloaf you can descend via *Skull Point* and *Icefield Pass* to Lost Lake.

The Stormy Peaks Trail continues north below Stormy Peaks Pass. The path is faint in a few spots but easy and pleasant to follow downhill to the park boundary and out of the park through subalpine woods. The northern end of the trail is located at an entrance gate to the Pingree Park Campus of Colorado State University, about 7.5 miles from the Lost Lake Trail. The Stormy Peaks Trail affords good views of Pingree Park; its "campus" is more like a camp.

Stormy Peaks Pass is 9.7 miles from the North Fork Trailhead and just over half that distance from Pingree Park Trailhead. If your goal is the Stormy Peaks area, it is obviously easier to hike from the northern end of the trail.

To drive to Pingree Park from Fort Collins, leave U.S. Highway 287 north of the city and drive 27.5 miles north and west on State Highway 14. At that point, two miles past Fort Collins Mountain Park, turn left and drive 14 miles south to Pingree.

From Estes Park or Loveland, follow U.S. Highway 34 to the Masonville Road, about three miles east of the Big Thompson Canyon. Drive on through Masonville to the spot where the road ends in a T-junction. Turn left (west) and drive northwest along Buckhorn Creek. You will run out of paved road after a few miles, but keep on until you reach a fork in the road more than ten miles from Masonville. The right-hand fork goes to Stove Prairie; take the left-hand (lower) fork west to Pennock Pass and down to another T-junction, about 25 miles from Masonville. Turn left and drive approximately five miles on a two-lane gravel road to Pingree Park. Take the left fork about 500 feet before reaching the entrance gate. A sign marks the trailhead on the left side of the road.

Some maps show a *Signal Mountain Trail* heading from the Stormy Peaks Trail to the park's eastern boundary. This "trail" is hard to find and has disintegrated to the point where trying to follow it amounts to cross-country navigation. It can be traced in some sections (watch for old blazes on trees) but you will lose the path now and then and have to wander about, searching. When it disappears at last in an expanse of boulders accented with magnificent old limber pines, head for the ridgetop and try to retrieve the trail there. It never was located where maps indicate, on the side of the ridge, and it disappears completely above tree line on South Signal Mountain. Head straight up to the summit or circle on its left (northern) flank to climb the slightly taller Signal Mountain just outside the park boundary.

The U.S. Forest Service trail from Signal Mountain down to the North Fork is well maintained. It is steep in some stretches and very steep in the rest. As it descends Bulwark Ridge, most of the trail passes through open limber or lodgepole pine forests which normally are sunny and hot. The trail is used mainly by horses; hikers ascending it face a difficult grind. Signal Mountain Trail ends at the unpaved road west of Glen Haven at a gate marking the boundary between Roosevelt National Forest and private property. The road at this point is closed to public vehicles, but the North Fork Trailhead parking lot is located a few hundred yards to the east.

Mummy Pass Trail

Mummy Pass Trail runs from the Long Draw Reservoir Road to the national park's northwestern boundary to a spot above Pingree Park beyond the northern boundary. Both ends of the trail are in Roosevelt National Forest. It passes through what once was the remotest part of the park. The improvement of the road to Long Draw Reservoir to accommodate ordinary passenger cars has made the park's northwestern corner more accessible, but it still is relatively uncrowded and the best place to spot deer and elk. During hunting season it is heavily patrolled by rangers to frustrate the criminal intent of poachers.

To reach the Pingree Park end of the trail, drive to the Tom Bennett Campground turnoff on the north side of the gravel road about a half-mile before reaching the gate to Colorado State University property (see above, North Fork of the Big Thompson Trail System). Turn right past the campground, over the South Fork of the Cache La Poudre River and up around a curve to a fork in the road. If you have a normal passenger car, park it and start walking up the left fork toward Cirque Meadows and Emmaline Lake. If you have a high clearance pickup truck or jeep, you should be able to drive the road for another 2.5 miles to the beginning of Mummy Pass Trail.

The road fords Fall Creek, and about a quarter-mile later the trail heads left (south) from the road. After switchbacking through subalpine forest for a couple of miles, it winds out of the trees and into the national park. Above tree line, the trail steepens somewhat until you reach the broad, nearly level top of a bench leading to Mummy Pass. On the way, you must descend into a lush little valley holding two ponds and a multitude of flowers.

After hiking on out of the valley, you can turn right (northwest) off the trail and climb steeply over tundra to _Fall Mountain_. The opposite (northern) side of the peak is glaciated dramatically, as is the entire ridge leading northwest to _Comanche Peak_. On the way to Comanche, skirt the big rocks at the heads of the cirques that indent this ridge but walk to the edge now and then for the view.

From the top of Comanche, it is a long way north to any higher mountain. It also is a long way down to Emmaline Lake, Cirque Lake and other smaller tarns at the head of Fall Creek. These lakes can be seen from intermediate peninsulas that project from the Fall-Comanche ridge. But the best view is from Comanche's summit.

A circle route back to Pingree leads east down the north ridge above the Comanche cirque. Below this ridge you will hit a trail from Emmaline Lake that leads to the jeep road. Follow the road down to your parked vehicle.

Mummy Pass sits on a broad tundra plateau between the Hague Creek drainage and the South Fork of the Poudre drainage, 2.2 miles from the northern boundary. As the trail winds across tundra and through subalpine forest, you see the Mummy Range from a unique if not particularly spectacular angle. More scenic from the plateau is the Never Summer Range to the southwest, with dramatic Mount ·Richthofen and Nokhu Crags dominating the skyline. Just past the crossing of Mummy Pass Creek, 1.8 miles from Mummy Pass, you arrive at a junction where the Mirror Lake Trail runs to the right (north).

Since more hikers approach _Mirror Lake_ from the western end of the Mummy Pass Trail, we will jump in seven-league boots to the Corral Creek Trailhead. To reach this trailhead, drive along State Highway 14, which runs between Fort Collins and Walden. About four miles north of Cameron Pass or two miles south of Chambers Lake, turn southeast onto the two-lane gravel Long Draw Road (U.S. Forest Service Route 156), which travels through Box Canyon and Corral Park, eventually ending at the western end of Long Draw Reservoir.

Drive about eight miles on this road to the Corral Creek Trailhead, which is on the left (east). The U.S. Forest Service plans to

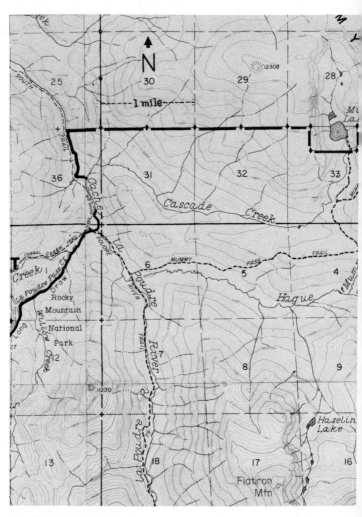

Mummy Pass Trail System

build a parking lot there as a substitute for roadside parking; we hope the plan has been carried out by the time you read this. There is a campground, Long Draw, about a quarter-mile south of the trailhead.

The Mummy Pass Trail begins as an old jeep road following Corral Creek but soon becomes a path. After less than a mile, you reach a T-junction. Turn right (southeast) and cross the outlet from Long Draw Reservoir. Almost at once the Cache La Poudre River appears; you cross it on a substantial bridge into the national park. Another .6 mile of easy walking brings you to a junction with the Poudre River Trail. The Poudre River Trail (see "Trail Ridge Road," Trails from Milner Pass) branches right (south); the Mummy Pass trail continues east.

The Mummy Pass Trail meanders north of Hague Creek along a gentle open valley until a left bend takes you steeply up through thick woods. The grade moderates at the ridgetop, rising gradually to the junction on the left with the Mirror Lake Trail, 4.5 miles from the Corral Creek Trailhead.

The climb to Mirror Lake is an easy walk through subalpine forest until you reach a meadow where Cascade Creek flows still and wide, .7 mile from the Mummy Pass Trail.

There, branching sharply right from the main trail, a path heads straight upslope through the forest. Above tree line the route is steeper yet. Following cairns up the mountain, you eventually cross out of the park into Roosevelt National Forest. The trail levels west of _Comanche peak_. There is nothing to be gained from striking out for the top of Comanche until the path flattens; premature departure probably will put you on an annoying false summit. Beyond Comanche Peak, the trail descends across tundra slopes to another junction; a sharp right turn there leads down after about four miles to Comanche Reservoir. This artificial lake is situated at the end of the road branching off the Pingree Park Road to Tom Bennett Campground (see above).

It may seem odd that some maps call the trail to Comanche Peak the Mirror Lake Trail when, from the point of view of most hikers, it cuts away from Mirror Lake. The trail was named, though, when most visitors to the lake approached it from the north.

The final mile of the trail to Mirror Lake passes through forest and flowered marshy meadows before reaching its destination. The lake, a classic tarn, was scoured by a glacier in the rock of a long cirque. This is tree line, so the lake at its outlet end is bordered by both erect subalpine fir and the shrubby Krummholz version of the same tree. The far shore is rocky and barren, rising straight up to cliffs and snowbanks. The peaks that tower over the lake are no less dramatic for being unnamed. The lake itself has been short-changed with a very common name for an uncommonly beautiful place.

Trails North of Horseshoe Park

The most popular Mummy Range trails are those above Horse-shoe Park, starting at the Lawn Lake Trailhead. This trailhead is a parking lot on the right (north) side of Fall River Road a short distance from the spot where the road branches off U.S. Highway 34.

The beginning of all the trails switchbacks steeply up a ponder-osa-covered lateral moraine. Hikers cutting up or down across these switchbacks have caused severe erosion. The National Park Service is trying to restore vegetation and repair some of the damage to the land. Please do not frustrate these efforts by short-cutting.

Above the switchbacks, the grade becomes less steep, heads into lodgepole pines and aspens above Roaring River, then divides 1.3 miles from the trailhead. The right branch follows Roaring River north to Lawn Lake (see below).

The left branch goes to _Ypsilon Lake_. It crosses Roaring River among aspens and climbs a moraine through lodgepole pines. Once on top of the moraine, the trail levels a bit, still among lodgepoles. Some hikers find this section of trail boring despite occasional close views of the snow-filled gullies that form a huge Y on the face of Ypsilon Mountain.

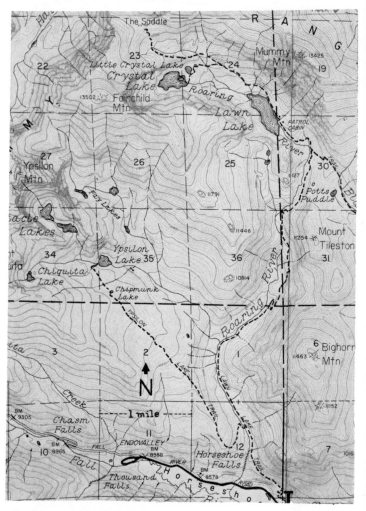

Trails North of Horseshoe Park

When the trail descends to _Chipmunk Lake_, pause to take a photo of Fairchild Mountain reflected in this tiny pond (assuming a calm day). Then leave the trail and walk through the woods to the pond's swampy eastern shore. If the air is still, you will get numerous mosquito bites and a superb reflection shot of Ypsilon Mountain. A wide-angle lens is essential.

The trail ends on the west side of Ypsilon Lake amid large glacial erratics and subalpine forest. A waterfall tumbles down a steep slope nearby before the stream flows into the lake. It is a pleasant spot but lacks the majesty of _Spectacle Lakes_, a hard, steep half-mile farther on. These lakes, which look like giant eyeglasses from the top of Ypsilon Mountain, sit on a ledge 800 feet higher than Ypsilon Lake. Above them rise dramatic Y-couloirs on the classic glacial cirque which is the east face of Ypsilon Mountain. A photographer caught here without a wide-angle lens faces certain frustration.

Reaching spectacular Spectacle Lakes is something of a trial. The best of two routes is up the stream that flows into Ypsilon Lake. This route is steep above the waterfall and blocked by rock outcrops and glacial erratics. You will have to crisscross the creek to circumvent the obstacles.

In an often-flowery meadow, the terrain levels out, and the stream branches. The lay of the land probably will cause you to arrive between the two forks. You can follow the left fork to _Chiquita Lake_, about a mile from Ypsilon Lake. The right fork leads to Spectacle Lakes. Below the lakes, the stream tumbles through a waterfall from the shelf on which the lakes sit. Getting up onto this shelf involves a rock climb which many trail-accustomed hikers find disturbing.

An alternative route that avoids the rock work begins by ascending a gully above the treeless northern edge of Ypsilon Lake. You can see the starting point from the trail at the western shoreline. The gully leads up to a ridgeline, where you turn left and climb above the trees. From this area, angle left again around to the west side of the ridge and descend to the lower Spectacle Lake.

This alternative route involves a greater total expenditure of energy than does the first. It also leads you to an inconveniently cliffy spot on the lower lake, from which it is difficult to reach the best vantage point, at the outlet. On the other hand, this is the route for hikers who absolutely will *not* climb the slabs below Spectacle Lakes!

To reach *Fay Lakes*, three small bodies of water in the valley between Mount Ypsilon and Fairchild Mountain, follow the southern shore of Ypsilon Lake to its outlet. Cross over and make your way northeast through the forest, climbing steadily until you reach the stream from Fay Lakes, less than half a mile from Ypsilon Lake. Follow it upstream to the lakes, which are strung out at half-mile intervals.

Fishing is prohibited in Fay Lakes to protect the very rare greenback cutthroat trout. The greenback once was a widespread native in this area until alien fish were introduced to improve angling. It was not realized that the more aggressive aliens would compete with the greenback and drive the species to the verge of extinction. The greenback now is recovering through careful management by wildlife biologists and eventually will be common once again.

From the turnoff for Ypsilon Lake, 1.3 miles from the Lawn Lake Trailhead, *Lawn Lake Trail* follows an easy grade along Roaring River. After the trail veers east from the river, a set of two long switchbacks marks the beginning of gradually increasing steepness. Above these switchbacks, head uphill from the trail if you wish to climb *Bighorn Mountain* and/or *Mount Tileston.* The ascent is steep without benefit of trail and runs through fallen timber. Picturesque limber pines compose the tree line on Bighorn and Tileston. Mountain sheep concentrate on Bighorn, but you are just as, and perhaps more, likely to see them from U.S. Highway 34 in Horseshoe Park.

Continuing up Lawn Lake Trail through more switchbacks brings you to a small basin and good views of the cliffs on Mummy Mountain, to the north. A trail junction on the right, 5.6 miles from

Bull elk

the trailhead, marks the beginning of the Black Canyon Trail (see below). Although Lawn Lake is .6 mile farther on, some maps refer to the trail between this spot and the lake as the Black Canyon Trail. This appellation arose in the early part of the century, when the trails were mainly horseback routes and the usual destinations were somewhat different from today's. In this book, "Black Canyon Trail" refers only to the path between Lawn Lake Trail and Cow Creek.

Past the Black Canyon Trail junction, Lawn Lake Trail curves left through subalpine forest to emerge in a grassy, often flowery, meadow below Lawn Lake. In 1911 a dam was built to enlarge the lake. Now agricultural demand for water often causes its level to be lowered, greatly diminishing its beauty. If you catch it while full, however, Lawn Lake is very attractive, with _Hagues Peak_ and _Fairchild Mountain_ towering in the distance.

Hagues and Fairchild can be climbed by following the trail to the northern end of the lake and then on up a much steeper grade than that below the dam. Four hundred feet above and a half-mile beyond Lawn Lake, the trail divides. The left branch heads uphill past an unnamed pond and _Little Crystal Lake_ to _Crystal Lake_. Crystal sits in a magnificent cirque on the side of Fairchild and probably is the deepest lake in the park.

If a mountain summit is your goal, you probably should not take the time to visit these lakes, wonderful as they are. You will get good views of them from the right-hand branch of the trail as it ascends to _The Saddle_ between Hagues and Fairchild. Well below The Saddle, Fairchild climbers should leave the trail as it angles to the right (north) in a relatively level alpine meadow. Bearing left, ascend the steep ridge that extends southwest to Fairchild's summit, a simple but strenuous boulder-hopping climb at this elevation.

If you wish to climb Hagues Peak or _Mummy Mountain_, head east from the main trail before reaching the Crystal Lake junction. (A sign may still be in place pointing the way to Rowe Glacier on the northern side of Hagues.) Bearing right (east), follow rock cairns up a very steep slope to the saddle between Hagues and Mummy. The first part of this climb is the worst; try to step gently on the tundra.

Tassel-eared (Abert) squirrel on ponderosa pine

From the saddle, it is a relatively easy hike to either Hagues or Mummy. (See description of these peaks in North Fork section, above.)

The easiest route up Mummy and Hagues probably is not from Lawn Lake but from the *Black Canyon Trail*. East of its junction with the Lawn Lake Trail, where the Black Canyon Trail levels, strike off to the left (northeast) through struggling pines over large rocks to tree line. Pick out the least steep route to the top of Mummy; the summit is 2200 feet higher than the Black Canyon Trail, an elevation gained in approximately one mile. A false summit 500 or so feet below the top could fool and disappoint you.

Back on the Black Canyon Trail itself, the path soon begins to descend. There are many ponds amid the large boulders. One of the largest ponds is *Potts Puddle*, which can shrink to nearly nothing in a dry summer. As it crosses Black Canyon Creek several times, the trail becomes gradually dimmer ("unimproved" is the local euphemism) but never disappears entirely. Eventually, it begins to become clearer, crosses a saddle between Dark Mountain and Lumpy Ridge and descends to Cow Creek. There it meets the trail to Bridal Veil Falls slightly more than one mile from Indian Head (McGraw) Ranch.

Bridal Veil Falls normally is reached from Indian Head Ranch. The ranch is located at the end (2.3 miles) of (unpaved) McGraw Ranch Road bearing left from the Devils Gulch Road at a point 3.9 miles from downtown Estes Park. Ask permission at the ranch, which is private property, to park your car. Permission usually is given along with instructions about how to drive to the trailhead. (It probably is unnecessary to stress that all road gates that you open should be closed behind you.)

The trail to Bridal Veil Falls is an easy three miles through open montane zone vegetation. It can be hot at midday in midsummer. There are many lovely beaver ponds, though, along the trail as it follows Cow Creek. And Bridal Veil Falls ranks among the prettiest in the park.

Chapin Pass Routes

Chapin Pass is the back door to Mount Chapin, Mount Chiquita and Ypsilon Mountain. Although the rugged, glacially carved east faces of these popular peaks are very visible and beautiful from the valleys around Estes Park, the unglaciated, less-precipitous western slopes rising above Chapin Pass offer the easiest routes to the top. Beyond Ypsilon you can continue to Desolation Peaks, Flatiron Mountain or Fairchild Mountain. Chapin Pass is the highest point on the Chapin Creek Trail.

The easiest way to Chapin Pass is to drive to a small parking area by the side of the unpaved Old Fall River Road about 6.5 miles from its beginning at the western end of Horseshoe Park. (This uphill road is one-way; after the hike you will have to continue on to Trail Ridge Road at Fall River Pass.) From the parking area, follow the road for a few yards to the spot where the Chapin Creek Trail starts on the right (northern) side. Then follow the trail a short distance straight uphill to Chapin Pass.

If the Old Fall River Road is not yet open for the season and if you are determined to hike through Chapin Pass, you must drive over Trail Ridge Road to Fall River Pass and begin there. Walk down the Old Fall River Road nearly to tree line. There you should angle off to the left and follow the ridgeline downhill to Chapin Pass, thus avoiding having to ascend to the pass from farther down the road.

Beginning at Fall River Pass adds almost three miles to the hike. It means that the final part of your trip, when you are tired, will be an ascent above tree line to reach your car. Furthermore, lightning-filled clouds may roll some excitement your way, forcing a retreat below tree line prior to climbing again toward Fall River Pass. (See "Lightning: One Strike and You're Out.")

To climb _Mount Chapin_, _Mount Chiquita_ and _Ypsilon Mountain_, head east from Chapin Pass on a faint ("unimproved") path that branches off the main trail. The branch trail soon climbs out of the trees, cuts around the southern flank of a hill on the ridge and disappears amid rocks and tundra. Do not fret if you miss the trail;

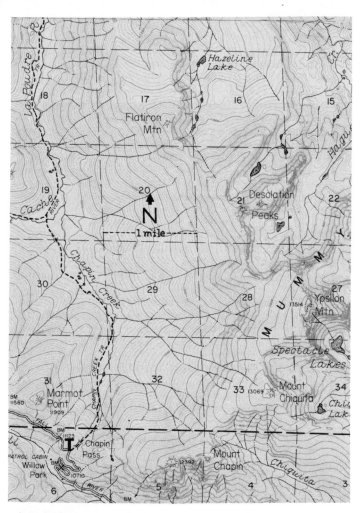

Chapin Pass Routes

once above tree line, it is a simple, steep trudge up the ridge to Chapin, the rounded summit farthest to the right.

Ascending this ridge to Chapin seems like a steeper and harder climb than either Chiquita or Ypsilon. Many hikers bypass Chapin and head directly for these two higher peaks via the saddle between Chapin and Chiquita. By so doing, they miss seeing good views down onto rock spires that rise from Chapin's rugged southern side. As you approach the top, bypass Chapin's western summit and head for the taller eastern one.

From Chapin descend about 400 feet to the Chapin-Chiquita saddle, then ascend 1000 feet to the top of Chiquita. You walk about a mile from summit to summit. The grade is not terribly steep; only the 13,000-foot elevation may pose minor problems. Chiquita is the easiest "thirteener" to climb in Rocky Mountain National Park.

If you are pressed for time or have a more distant goal, you can skip Chiquita and head straight for Ypsilon, a mile farther on. From the top of the snow-filled gullies that form a Y on the east face of Ypsilon, there is a spectacular view straight down to Spectacle Lakes, more than 2000 feet below. Since you are likely to see this view in the morning, the sun probably will be glaring off the water. A polarizing filter over the lens will eliminate the glare from photos.

Beyond Ypsilon the going gets tougher. _Desolation Peaks_ are located two rugged miles of ridge-clambering and cirque-skirting north of Ypsilon. It is a similar mile-and-a-half beyond Desolation to _Flatiron Mountain_.

Fairchild Mountain, northeast of Ypsilon, usually is climbed from Lawn Lake (see above, Trails North of Horseshoe Park). But Fairchild can be reached also from Ypsilon, a route which necessitates losing and regaining 1000 feet of elevation over a couple of very steep and rough miles. If you plan to go to so much trouble, you might as well descend Fairchild via Lawn Lake and arrange for transportation at the trailhead in Horseshoe Park.

Back at Chapin Pass, the _Chapin Creek Trail_ descends very quickly to the marshy drainage of Chapin Creek. You probably will reach the valley floor in less than 20 minutes; we will refrain from guessing how long it will take to climb back out. This three-mile trail is followed mainly by backpackers on their way to somewhere else via the Poudre River Trail (see "Trail Ridge Road," Trails from Milner Pass). Your chances of seeing elk along Chapin Creek or the Poudre are excellent.

Moraine Park

Their easy accessibility and great beauty have made the trails west of Moraine Park very popular since before the national park was established. The two main trailheads, for Fern Lake and Cub Lake, are situated within a mile of each other on an unpaved road west of Moraine Park Campground. The proximity of the trailheads and a connecting link between their trails make a circle hike reasonably simple.

To reach the trailheads, turn onto the Bear Lake Road two-tenths mile west of the Beaver Meadows Entrance to the park, or 2.7 miles south of the junction of U.S. Highways 34 and 36 on Deer Ridge. Follow the Bear Lake Road for 1.2 miles over a ridge to Moraine Park. A few yards past Moraine Park Visitor Center, a paved road branches right toward Moraine Park Campground.

Follow this road for a half-mile and turn left on the still-paved road to the trailheads. (If you reach Moraine Park Campground, you have missed the turn.) After 1.2 miles the pavement ends. The parking area for Cub Lake Trailhead is 1 mile ahead on the right; there is another on the left after a few yards more. The Fern Lake Trailhead and its parking lot are located a mile up the valley, at the end of the road.

Fern Lake Trail System

From Fern Lake Trailhead the path meanders for 1.5 miles along the Big Thompson River to The Pool. Because this stretch of trail is relatively flat and easy to walk, many hikers hurry along it. Of

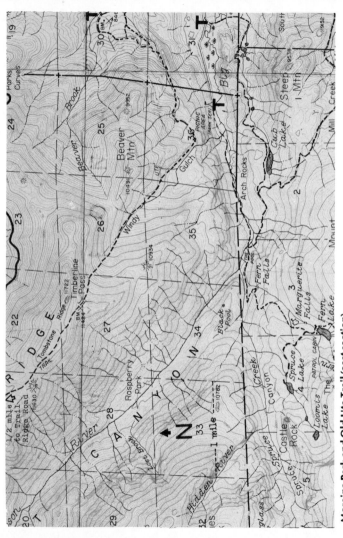

Moraine Park and Old Ute Trail (east section)

course, they get hot and sweaty in the process and blame the trail for being too warm and dull. Such hikers should travel at a more comfortable pace and take time to see the many interesting features which make the trip to The Pool such a joy for an alert and observant hiker.

A little more than a mile from the trailhead, Fern Lake Trail winds beneath _Arch Rocks_. It is tempting to think that these giant monoliths were put there by a retreating glacier, but they more likely fell from the cliffs after the glaciers melted. The best place from which to photograph the entire configuration of Arch Rocks is along, or in, the river a few hundred feet to the west. Afternoon sunshine, if available, is the best.

The trail crosses the Big Thompson River on a substantial log bridge at _The Pool_ where water swirling between steep stone walls has formed a pool in the rock. Past the bridge, the path divides. The left-hand branch passes along the valley floor through a meadow that is in the process of reverting to pine. As you begin to climb along a northern slope, thick forest closes in. Less than one-half mile from The Pool, a lovely brook flowing down Mount Wuh intersects the trail through a patch of Rocky Mountain maple. Farther on there are views of Stones Peak, to the west, but you will get better photographic composition of the mountain from Cub Lake. The trail levels out, and a path to Mill Creek Basin branches off to the right about a mile from The Pool. It is easier to walk this 1.5 mile path from the other direction (see "Bear Lake Road," Hallowell Park Trails). The trail to Cub Lake leads straight ahead and reaches the lake after .3 mile (see below).

The Fern Lake Trail runs straight ahead from the Cub Lake trail junction. Circling around open south-facing slopes, the trail to Fern Lake soon climbs along the side of a gully and enters deep subalpine woods. After crossing Fern Creek, you ascend a rather noisy ridge between the roarings of Spruce and Fern creeks.

Continuing on the somewhat steep slope parallel to Spruce Creek, watch for brownie ladyslipper orchids (*Cypripedium fasciculatum*) at trailside. Presently the path switchbacks along a fairly level grade.

As you curve up the hillside, the roar of _Fern Falls_ announces its presence before you see it.

After climbing 480 feet in the mile from The Pool, you probably will be ready to cool off in the spray from the falls. Because Fern Falls is surrounded by dense woods of Engelmann spruce and subalpine fir, the best light for photography hits the falls in midday, when most hikers arrive.

Past the falls, the trail climbs rather steeply again, away from the creek, and the immediate rise in temperature and reduction of noise are always surprising.

A switchback brings you more or less parallel to Fern Creek, but you cannot see it until just after the junction with the Spruce Lake Trail (see below). Crossing Fern Creek at the outlet of Fern Lake, you walk onto the open shoreline for a fine view of Notchtop Mountain and the Little Matterhorn, which rise beyond subalpine forest on the other side of the lake.

For the best photographic effect, back up a bit to include lodgepoles or spruce as a frame for your picture. If you think the near shoreline looks slightly overtrampled, find a position where bushes in the foreground will block it out. A few yards farther along the shore you can take similarly composed photos of Stones Peak and an unnamed neighboring summit to the right.

Leaving Fern Lake, the path crosses a boulder field and climbs through classic subalpine forest. Shade and moisture-loving flowers such as various species of pyrola are common along the mile of trail between Fern and Odessa lakes (see "Bear Lake trailhead," Odessa Lake Trail).

Spruce Lake Trail begins back in the open forest amid moss-covered rocks just before you reach Fern Lake. The .8 mile path climbs at an easy grade, then drops through glacier-deposited boulders to cross an outlet creek and enter the marshy meadows that surround Spruce Lake. Convenient sitting rocks are somewhat difficult to appropriate at the lake; the best ones are partly submerged. Stones Peak rises massively beyond the lake. Even more spectacular are the chimneylike spires of Castle Rock, which loom directly overhead.

To reach _Loomis Lake_, recross the creek and circle to the southwestern shore of Spruce. Then follow its inlet stream uphill through the forest, scrambling over logs and boulders to a rocky, marshy pond about a quarter-mile from Spruce Lake. A final climb over a ledge brings you into the amphitheater containing Loomis Lake. Dramatic, craggy cliffs rise on three sides of this emerald tarn.

Spruce Lake is the best starting point, also, for climbing _Stones Peak_. Head north from the lake over the thickly forested low ridge below Castle Rock. On the other side of the ridge you'll find Spruce Canyon, which contains Spruce Creek. Follow the drainage upstream to tree line and a huge cirque between Sprague Mountain and Stones Peak. Pick the least steep route past _Hourglass Lake_ and on up to a glacial shelf. Via the very steep slope to the right of an unnamed pool on this shelf, climb to the low point on the ridge that connects Sprague and Stones. Then turn right and climb the ridge to Stone's summit.

The top offers the best possible view of Sprague Glacier and the tarn into which it descends. South of you lies impressive Rainbow Lake. To the west, you look down on the crags of Hayden Spire rising from Lonesome Lake. (For an alternative route up Stones, see "Bear Lake Trailhead," Flattop Mountain Trail System.)

Cub Lake Trail

The Cub Lake Trail is known for its variety of wildflowers. It is an excellent trail, also, for successful bird-watching. The variety of both flowers and birds is created by many different types of habitats through which the trail passes in 2.3 miles. For driving instructions to the trailhead, see the beginning of this chapter. If both parking areas are full, please do not park on the side of the road. Additional parking is available only .3 mile farther on.

From the trailhead, you cross a footbridge which spans old swampy beaver workings. In the wet meadowland beyond, the trail is lined with willows and thinleaf alder. Watch for various species of warblers, particularly yellow, Macgillivray's and yellow-rumped

(Audubon's). Just past the third bridge (this one crosses the Big Thompson River), watch for pink shootingstars growing at streamside, especially from late June through mid-July.

The trail continues amid water-loving shrubs that obviously have been broused in winter by elk. Before long you arrive at a mixed grove of ponderosa pine and Douglas-fir. There are large, glacially scoured rocks to the right (west), and white-barked aspens to the east (left). This is a good area in which to watch for warbling vireos and western tanagers.

An aspen grove a bit farther on, amid signs of beaver activity, is home to several species of hole-nesting birds — mountain chickadees, swallows (tree, and violet-green), house wrens and various woodpeckers. Just past a second aspen grove, a short uphill section of trail climbs over bare, rounded glacially scoured bedrock. Large boulders, glacial erratics, perch isolated on the bedrock where the glacier left them 13,000 years ago. Views to the east show a long even-topped ridge of unsorted rock dumped by the glacier along its edge. That is the classic lateral moraine for which Moraine Park was named.

Yellow-bellied marmots frequently are seen among the glacial erratics at trailside. These larger cousins of the eastern woodchuck are especially appealing in early summer, when the young animals scamper about after emerging from their mothers' hibernation dens.

Pause at a large round erratic sitting right in the middle of the trail. If you feel beneath the rock, you will perceive at once the difference between the glacially polished surface protected by the erratic and the rough bedrock elsewhere, exposed to weathering for thousands of years.

From bedrock the trail descends to more wet meadow and reaches the junction of the Cub Lake Trail and a horse trail which follows the lateral moraine. When hiking here in spring or fall, look for elk tracks in the wet soil.

Bear right at the trail junction and follow the edge of the meadow in a westerly direction. The path is nearly level, with ponderosa-covered hillsides on the right and a series of old beaver ponds on the left. Although beaver sightings are unlikely, you may see a muskrat cutting a V in the water.

The scarce and spectacular wood lily grows by the ponds in late June or early July. Picking any wildflowers in national parks is, of course, both illegal and wrong. But picking one of these rare blossoms would be an especially grievous offense.

Past the old beaver ponds, the trail begins a series of switchbacks uphill through aspens. Rather steep in places, it soon levels a short way before you reach the lake.

Cub Lake is very shallow. It is excellent habitat for beautiful yellow pond lilies, and for less beautiful leaches. From the eastern end, you can shoot a good photo of Stones Peak with the lily-covered water in the foreground. A short telephoto lens would be helpful in composing the picture.

The path runs west along the north shore of the lake. At the western end, it passes through a small area of lodgepole pines which burned in a forest fire in 1972. Then the trail arrives at a junction with trails from The Pool (see above) and Mill Creek Basin (see "Bear Lake Road," Hallowell Park Trails).

Mule deer doe and fawn

Bear Lake Road

Bear Lake Road provides access to one of the most popular areas in the park. Various problems have come about as a result of this popularity. The most obvious, if not the most serious, is awful automobile congestion — the epitome of what a national park experience should not be.

The National Park Service is striving heroically to deal with traffic congestion, but it is a complex problem because of the lay of the land and the distances involved. While this book was being written, plans were being laid to establish a mass transit system, which appeared to be the only way to save visitors from the soul-destroying battle against traffic jams on Bear Lake Road. To learn how mass transit should work in this unique situation, the Park Service planned to run an experimental system for a few summers.

A bus route was to begin at a parking lot on an old gravel pit across Bear Lake Road from Glacier Basin Campground, 4.8 miles from the beginning of the road near the park's Beaver Meadows Entrance. Freed from their cars, visitors to Bear Lake and other points along the road were to catch a free bus ride and save both fuel and incredible wear and tear on their nerves. At first, intervals between buses and hours of service were to be determined experimentally. For more up-to-date details about the system, you should check with the National Park Service.

Perhaps more than everyone else, hikers should benefit from a mass transit system. We hikers and backpackers tend to be more upset by traffic problems than other park visitors. Part of the reason we walk into the backcountry is to escape infernal automobiles. It is

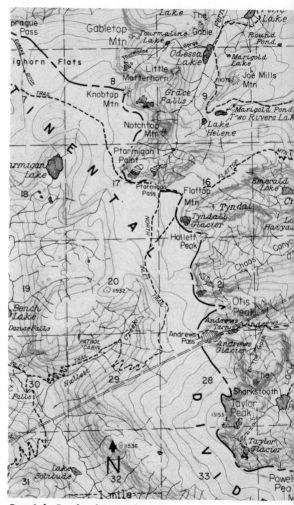

Bear Lake Road and Bear Lake Area

menacing to have them snapping and growling and roaring and lunging after us right at the trailhead. Buses should do much to ease our jangled nerves.

More important, there will be increased flexibility. With a mass transit system in operation, we can start hiking at one trailhead and end up at another. Buses should make possible the very desirable one-way hikes which previously posed logistical problems too great to bother solving. As a result, hikers will be distributed more evenly instead of being concentrated at two or three trailheads.

The bus system probably will not lessen the crowds on the trails because many more people are going to realize the joys of hiking. But more even distribution should help to keep the backcountry population from resembling the crowds we are trying to escape.

Hallowell Park Trails

The Hallowell Park Trailhead is reached by a short unpaved road that leaves Bear Lake Road 3.5 miles from Beaver Meadows. Turn right (west) and drive a few hundred yards to a parking area. From there a broad, clear trail runs up Mill Creek Valley for 1.6 miles to _Mill Creek Basin_.

The most notable features of this easy, pleasant walk probably are the stands of aspens and recent beaver workings along Mill Creek. The area was used for timber cutting and sawing in the 1880s, and the aspens and lodgepole pines may be a result of that clearing operation.. These are the trees that begin to grow in places cleared by fire or lumbering.

Additionally, Mill Creek Basin is an excellent place to look for hawks. The broad, bushy flats of Hallowell Park provide the birds with good rodent hunting. The aspens and cliffs along Mill Creek offer well-watered nesting sites. Hence, this relatively small area gives hawks the essentials needed by all wildlife — food, water and shelter.

From Mill Creek Basin a trail leads left (south) up the side of Bierstadt Moraine to _Bierstadt Lake_, a mile away. Most hikers reach

Bierstadt Lake from Bierstadt Lake Trailhead or Bear Lake because those trails are shorter and more scenic (see below; see "Bear Lake Trailhead," Flattop Mountain Trail System).

A right (north) turn in Mill Creek Basin takes you over the ridge between well-named *Steep Mountain* and *Mount Wuh*. The trail is a 1.5 mile link with the trails west of Moraine Park, especially the ones to Cub Lake. It is more easily walked from south to north than north to south. But it is not hiked much because there are easier and more interesting ways to Cub Lake (see "Moraine Park," Cub Lake Trail).

Boulder Brook and Storm Pass Trails

The trailhead for the Boulder Brook and Storm Pass trails is situated on Bear Lake Road 6.4 miles from Beaver Meadows, on the left (south) side immediately before the Bierstadt Lake Trailhead. The junctions of trails a short way south of the road are so complex that they defy verbal description. One trail dodges swamps for 1.5 miles to Sprague Lake and Glacier Basin Campground. Another intersects it after approximately paralleling Glacier Creek and the road the entire distance from Bear Lake. The Storm Pass Trail leaves the Glacier Creek Trail a half-mile from the road. The Boulder Brook Trail cuts across this tangled web, heading due south and straight up Boulder Brook. Numerous short spur trails complete the confusion by connecting the trails in various ways. To sort all this out, refer to the map and pray that signs are in place.

These trails tend to be used mainly by horse riders. But the Boulder Brook and Storm Pass trails, at least, attract some hikers as well.

The *Boulder Brook Trail* is fairly easy to follow. Just stay on the path that always seems to head uphill. Past the junctions, the trail stays close to Boulder Brook, a small stream bordered by aspens. Eventually, you arrive at an area which is still very open because of the forest fire of 1900. Amid many rocks, scraggly trees struggle for life where fire burned even the organic humus of the old forest floor.

Boulder Brook and its trail meet the North Longs Peak Trail (see below) 2.5 miles from the road. The Boulder Brook Trail perhaps is best reserved for fall hiking, when the aspens have turned yellow, but it serves as a useful link between Longs Peak and Bear Lake Road throughout the hiking season.

The _Storm Pass Trail_ strikes uphill from the Glacier Creek Trail one-half mile from Bear Lake Road. Following an easy grade through thick woods, the trail winds to the top of a ridge and drops down a bit to marshland at the head of Wind River, 2.5 miles from the starting point. Beaver activity is obvious here where aspen and willow dominate.

An unimproved trail leads 2.2 miles down the northwestern side of Wind River to a road just above the East Portal of Adams Tunnel, a key link in the Big Thompson Irrigation Project. (The road is closed to public vehicles, however, at the east end of the East Portal lake.) Beyond Wind River, the Storm Pass Trail winds uphill through heavy forest for 1.7 miles to Storm Pass, southwest of Estes Cone (see "East Edge Summits," Storm Pass Trail to Estes Cone).

Bierstadt Lake Trail

Bierstadt Lake Trailhead is located on Bear Lake Road 6.4 miles from Beaver Meadows. The starting point and parking area are on the right (north) side of the road immediately past the Boulder Brook-Storm Pass Trailhead.

The 1.4 mile trail to Bierstadt Lake switchbacks up the south side of Bierstadt Moraine. A forest fire in 1900 cleared the area, which was reforested by quaking aspen. In summer this climb, a sunny one, can be rather hot. In fall, however, when days are cool and the aspens are yellow, the trail is a magical delight. Its views of the Front Range framed by aspens are hard to beat at any time of year.

On top of the moraine, lodgepole pines take over from quaking aspens. The grade levels, and the trail has been built up over marshy areas in a few places. Essentially, it skirts bogs on the southern shore of Bierstadt Lake and leads you by an indirect but easy route to the western side.

Soon you arrive at the junction with the trail from Bear Lake. Bear right, and also at the two junctions that soon follow, to reach the Bierstadt lakeshore, a flat half-mile from the first junction. The view of Longs Peak from the lake probably will be the one you choose to photograph. Arriving early in the morning will give you the best light, possibly a still lake surface for reflections, and certainly the most comfortable hiking.

The ideal route to Bierstadt begins at Bear Lake. The trail is only .2 mile longer from there and is much easier to walk. You then can walk down the Bierstadt Lake Trail to Bear Lake Road to meet a national park shuttle bus or other prearranged transportation.

Glacier Gorge Trail System

The second most heavily used trail system in Rocky Mountain National Park is based at Glacier Gorge Junction on the Bear Lake Road. Lately the little parking lot there inside a switchback has been full before mid-morning. We hope a shuttle bus will do much to alleviate the congestion. The case for car pooling and/or taking the bus cannot be made too strongly. It often has been necessary for a driver to drop his fellow hikers at Glacier Gorge Junction and continue on .7 mile farther to the much larger, and often full, parking lot at Bear Lake.

A four-tenths mile path near the beginning of the Dream Lake Trail (see "Bear Lake Trailhead," Dream Lake Trail System) connects Bear Lake and Glacier Gorge Junction. We had not set foot on this connecting path until a few years ago when the parking problem exploded; we have used it often since. Looking on the bright side, the awesome traffic tangle forced us to discover this well-flowered, pleasant little stroll; you might want to walk it just for fun.

The first part of the trail system leads upstream on Glacier Creek to _Alberta Falls,_ .6 mile from Glacier Gorge Junction. The falls are pretty and, except for Chasm Falls beside Old Fall River Road, the most accessible falls in the national park. With extensive beaver workings, a narrow gorge to peer into, a classic white-water stream

81

Broad-tailed hummingbird and Colorado blue columbine

to photograph and abundant golden-mantled ground squirrels, only limited parking prevents the crowds of people on the trail to Alberta Falls from rivaling the teeming throngs at Bear Lake.

On the other hand, the mountain vistas from this section of trail, although good compared with most places, are only fair compared with many other spots in Rocky Mountain National Park. A forest fire in 1900 cleared the area of shade, and the forest has been slow to grow back on such dry land where even the humus soil was destroyed by fire. The trail can get very warm.

A normal length lens will do quite well for photographing Alberta Falls. The slopes of Half Mountain in the background add little to the picture; you may want to lower your sights and include more of Glacier Creek flowing below the falls. Use aspen trunks and branches as a frame in the photo.

Unfortunately, you will find that many aspen trunks have been scarred by hikers' carvings. The soft, white bark seems to invite this kind of vandalism, and because Alberta Falls is an easy destination, the carvers concentrate there. It behooves all of us to put a stop to any further desecration. If you see someone of any age engaged in this activity, do not stone him and dump his body in a river. Rather, use your friendliest persuasion to educate him in proper backcountry behavior and good stewardship. Nearly everyone will respond positively, if somewhat embarrassedly, to such an approach. A common stuttering response will be to ask whether you live in Colorado, as if that makes any difference in a national park.

Past Alberta Falls, the trail winds uphill on a gradual grade through more rocky land slowly recovering from the forest fire. The cliffs of Glacier Knobs appear to the right of the path, then you reach the junction of the North Longs Peak Trail (see below). A short way past the junction, the Glacier Gorge Trail levels and even descends a bit above Glacier Creek at the base of the southern side of Glacier Knobs. You may see pikas or marmots in the rock fields alongside the trail.

Presently, the trail descends into a bowl where there is a pleasant grove of subalpine woods spared by the 1900 fire. In this bowl 1.9

miles from the trailhead, Loch Vale and Glacier Gorge come together, and there is a major parting of the ways. The trail to the right is a mile-long spur to the trail to _Lake Haiyaha_ (see "Bear Lake Trailhead," Dream Lake Trail System). The trail to the left leads into Glacier Gorge (see below). The trail in the middle leads uphill into Loch Vale.

"Loch Vale Trail" has a romantic euphony which must appeal to people, for this path tends to be used more than the Glacier Gorge Trail. Few hikers who opt for Loch Vale are disappointed. At first the path climbs gradually on an open slope above Icy Brook. Less than one-half mile past the junction, you can get a good view of the brook cutting through a narrow gorge, with Taylor Peak just visible over the trees at the top of the gorge.

Switchbacks take you up the mountainside to the level of The Loch, one of the most photographed lakes in the park. With rugged peaks in the background, Taylor Glacier and other snowfields accenting the cliffs and a rocky shoreline made picturesque by limber pines, The Loch presents a limitless number of scenic opportunities. Capturing fully the beauty of this spot is an impossible photographic challenge, but it is fun to try.

The broad cliff that dominates the western end of The Loch is the Cathedral Wall, a popular playground for technical rock climbers. To the right of it you can see Andrews Glacier peering over a forested ridge of Otis Peak.

To hike to _Andrews Tarn_, at the base of the glacier, follow a trail around the right (northern) side of The Loch. Beyond The Loch, the path parallels Icy Brook through subalpine forests to a trail junction .9 mile from The Loch's eastern end. The trail going left from the junction leads to Timberline Falls, Lake of Glass and Sky Pond. The trail going right leads to Andrews Tarn. The trail is heavily used, but Andrews Glacier is not impressive — an unphotogenic field of white above an undistinguished milky blue tarn. As glaciers in this vicinity go, Tyndall Glacier is more spectacular and easier to reach, via the Flattop Trail (see "Bear lake Trailhead," Flattop Mountain Trail System).

There are, however, plenty of other attractions on the way to Andrews Glacier. Andrews Creek presents many scenic spots while flowing through the subalpine woods below the glacier. The valley walls are decked with magnificent rock spires, the most obvious being _The Sharkstooth_, to the south. It was sculpted by a predecessor of Andrews Glacier.

Another notable feature is a large rock mass that dominates the center of the valley beyond tree line. It consists of glacial rubble dumped there by melting ice. The trail winds up the right-hand side of the mass to a shelf on which sits Andrews Tarn. Interesting chunks of ice may be floating in the lake, and the tundra flowers growing around the tarn are lovely.

The Andrews Glacier path is a logical route for ascending Taylor and Powell peaks and a deservedly popular route for descending from Flattop Mountain, Hallett Peak and Otis Peak (see "Bear Lake Trailhead," Flattop Mountain Trail System). But if your hiking time is limited and your goals are less ambitious than Taylor Peak, you would do well to choose the left-hand turn at the junction beyond The Loch and head for _Timberline Falls_ and _Lake of Glass_. (The U.S. Board of Geographic Names perversely calls this tarn "Glass Lake"; everyone else calls it the more euphonious "Lake of Glass.")

From The Loch you may have seen the three-tiered cascade of well-named Timberline Falls, hanging from ledges below and to the left of Taylor Glacier, and perhaps glimpsed the falls through trees near the trail junction. Then it is out of sight as you follow a fairly distinct trail through the forest to the falls. The path avoids marshes, skirts large boulders and probably snowbanks and arrives at the edge of the catch basin at the foot of the falls.

At any time Timberline Falls must rank among the finest in the park. In early summer, when the flow of Icy Brook has sculpted winter's deep snowdrifts around it, the cascade is unexcelled in beauty. The trick is to predict when the sculpture will be just right and to arrive at the spot in the morning, when the light is good for photos.

Climb steeply beside Timberline Falls and then over the edge of the bedrock basin containing Lake of Glass, 4.2 miles from Glacier Gorge Junction. Looking back down the valley gives a nice perspective on The Loch and Loch Vale. Lake of Glass is a spectacular tarn surrounded by rock and tundra. Taylor Peak and Taylor Glacier, together with unnamed 12,000-foot precipices, form a dramatic semicircular wall around the lake.

Lake of Glass rarely lives up to its name, however; stiff breezes usually ripple its surface. Your best bet for catching a photo actually displaying a mirror reflection is to arrive just after sunrise, before convection currents in the air begin to take effect.

Twice as large as Lake of Glass, _Sky Pond_ can be found .4 mile upstream in a similar rock basin. Scoured out by the predecessor of Taylor Glacier, Sky Pond sits below the vertical east face of Taylor Peak. A spectacular view missed by many hikers is gained by making your way around the rocks to the left (south) of the lake's outlet to the southwestern shore. From this point, you can see three dramatic spires much favored by technical rock climbers — The Sharkstooth on the left, the needle of Petit Grepon in the center and The Sabre on the right.

That these pinnacles are not for the novice is indicated by the trouble some hikers have merely getting from Lake of Glass to Sky Pond. The tendency is to climb a series of small shelves to the north of Lake of Glass to avoid a wall of Krummholz. Actually, the wall is too massive to be avoided. Those who try to do so end up fighting their way through it. If you climb one shelf only, however, then walk up the valley toward an ominous-looking mass of close-growing spruce, a gate through the wall opens magically. Once on the path, it is an easy walk to the rock slabs on the other side of the Krummholz.

Between the two lakes, a bog to the left of the path produces masses of marsh-marigolds just after the snow melts. If you caught the sculpture at Timberline Falls, you probably have timed the hike correctly for the flowers, as well. Photos of masses of flowers rarely work, but these flowers have large enough blooms and burst forth from the water in sufficient abundance to make photos successful. Shoot from a low perspective; a wide-angle lens helps.

Back at the major trail intersection located 1.9 miles from Glacier Gorge Junction, the short stretch of the Glacier Gorge Trail to Icy Brook is a good spot to watch for birds. Ruby-crowned kinglets, mountain chickadees and gray jays are easy to find. More secretive is the uncommon orange-crowned warbler. Excellent clumps of Colorado blue columbine bloom near the stream in July.

Past the crossing of Icy Brook, the trail switchbacks through spruce and fir forest to bare bedrock where there are isolated glacial erratics, boulders deposited by the final retreating tongue of ice. The trail disappears, so make a note of where you hit the bedrock. On their return hikers commonly walk all the way to the end of the rock, whereas the trail is located only about two-thirds of the way down. People who have made this error in the past have tended to cut back to the trail, off the rock, and have worn another path which creates erosion. If you goof on the return, which is easy to do, retrace your steps rather than cutting through.

At the top of the bedrock "pavement," picturesque limber pines have grown from remarkably little soil. These fine trees make good frames for pictures of the square, flat-topped tower of Longs Peak, ahead. But later you will find even better composition for Longs Peak photos at _Mills Lake_.

The trail crosses Glacier Creek and passes through a marshy area which displays fine examples of subalpine flowers. The extra water may cause a steep place immediately ahead to be rather slick; be careful and be ready to grab an aspen trunk for support.

Past the marshy area, the path again disappears on bedrock. Watch for cairns to mark the way to Mills Lake, 2.5 miles from the trailhead. Mills is considered by many to be the prettiest lake in the park. We think such praise is too extravagant in the face of Lake Nanita and Chasm and Spectacle lakes. Yet Mills is undeniably grand.

The best light for photography at Mills occurs in early evening; the weather usually cooperates. Frame Longs Peak with limber pines on the left and include glacial erratics on the bedrock shoreline for foreground interest. You might even get a reflection if the water lies still in shoreside pools. If the huge bowl of Glacier Gorge is shadowed by the 13,000-foot peaks to the right, be sure to expose your film for the light on Longs, the Keyboard of the Winds and Pagoda Mountain, not for the much darker slopes below.

The Glacier Gorge Trail follows the eastern shore of Mills for a half-mile to the almost adjacent _Jewel Lake_. Jewel is about as marshy as Mills is rocky. The best picture is from the lake's outlet; a wide-angle lens may help to capture the gracefully bent shapes of marsh grass in the foreground.

The trail continues past Jewel, built up above bogs in some places, paralleling Glacier Creek through wet and flowery woods. The woods eventually open to reveal _Ribbon Falls_ rushing over rock slabs above a lush meadow filled with senecios, tall chiming bells and bistort. A short way past the crest of the falls you arrive at _Black Lake_, 4.7 miles from the trailhead. Make your way for a few yards to the left over boulders along the shore, then traverse through the woods to reach the lakeshore again at one of three inlet streams.

The sheer face of a glacial shelf rises above Black Lake, and the even more sheer east face of McHenrys Peak rises above the shelf. There are appropriate trees on the shore to frame the scene, but getting it all in with a normal length lens is a little tight. A wide-angle lens will be welcome.

A trail of sorts heads steeply up the inlet stream to level out on the shelf. There it degenerates to an occasional cairn and then disappears completely. Rock slabs extend everywhere. The trick is to navigate from one to the other without getting caught in Krummholz. A left turn from the spot where the inlet creek bends right will take you over a crest to the rock basin containing _Blue Lake_, three-quarters mile from Black.

If your destination is _Green Lake_, bend right with the stream. Cross it to the south, which soon becomes its western side. Following the creek, navigate across rock slabs at an easy grade to Green Lake, a mile from Black. A short distance beyond Green is _Italy Lake_,

Elephanthead (little red elephant)

whose unofficial name derived from its maplike shape when viewed from Longs Peak.

To ascend _Pagoda Mountain_, start climbing from the left side of Green Lake, bypassing Italy. The route is obvious — straight uphill over loose rock and slabs to the notch at the end of the Keyboard of the Winds. It also is fraught with all the frustrations of scrambling over loose rock and is very tiresome. From the notch, climb west, scrambling with hands and feet over fairly solid rock to the summit. The top of Pagoda is just as pointed as it looks from below — an interesting place with room for two or three climbers on the very summit. Anybody else has to be draped around the sides.

To reach _Frozen Lake_, the largest of the tarns scoured in the rock above Black Lake, curve west from Green Lake's inlet stream. Hike over slabs below The Spearhead, a sheer and pointed pyramid. Frozen Lake sits on the first shelf immediately to the west of The Spearhead.

Frozen is a well-named tarn that rarely, if ever, is completely free of ice. The glacier that gouged out Frozen Lake cut deeply; the tarn is boxed in and confined by rock walls. Hence, it is best photographed not from the water level but from the rocks above, and with a wide-angle lens to include _Stone Man Pass_ and _McHenrys Peak_.

McHenrys Peak is climbed via Stone Man Pass, whose name came from a man-shaped stone pillar located above the pass to the east. From Frozen Lake circle the base of a ridge below the Stone Man to a narrow gully below the pass. The gully, of course, is full of treacherous, tiresome and trying loose rock. Constant alertness is necessary to keep from kicking rock onto climbers below and to watch for rock falling from above. Early in summer, snow fills the gully, and it is possible to slip into an uncontrolled crashing slide.

Many people reach the gully directly by climbing a shorter and steeper route from Black Lake. From the lake's outlet, they circle right through the timber on the northern shore to climb steeply from the northwestern side of the lake to a shelf below the base of Arrowhead. They then follow this shelf to the base of the gully.

The gully is mercifully short, though not as short as you wish. From the pass, head west, descending slightly over loose rock that is considerably less bothersome than that in the gully. Following cairns, traverse this rock to a ridge and climb diagonally left to a break in the ridgeline.

Before descending into a second gully, located beyond this ridge, turn around and take a photo of Longs Peak from an unusual angle, using the rocks around the break in the ridge for a frame.

This gully is the route to the top, but it can be snow filled and create uncontrolled slides ending in injury on rocks. It is best to climb late in summer or to carry an ice ax and know how to use it.

McHenrys has the reputation of being the hardest nontechnical climbs in the park. That probably is an exaggeration. Several peaks in Wild Basin, for instance, are harder by virtue of longer approaches. McHenrys does require a considerable expenditure of energy, however, and it is worth it. The views from the summit are spectacular in all directions. West to Ptarmigan Mountain above North Inlet is very appealing. And the view straight down to Black Lake rivals that from the top of Longs down to Chasm Lake.

It is very difficult to get a photo of Black Lake from McHenrys that conveys a sense of the true distance down, because all the granite slabs extending from the summit to the lake are the same color and tone. Lack of intervening reference points in the wide-open landscape above the lake adds to the problem. Nevertheless, if a passing cloud throws a shadow on the lake, or better (and luckier) yet, between the lake and the peak, the resulting contrast will break up the sameness and result in a much more gut-grabbing photo. Good luck; it is a long way back to try again.

Thatchtop is an isolated mountain which sits between Loch Vale and Glacier Gorge. Its position makes it a superb viewing platform for spectacular peaks. The same glaciers that created the scenery also whacked off the sides of Thatchtop, however, so it is a fairly steep, if simple, climb from both Glacier Gorge and Loch Vale. And the tundra slopes between the glacier level and the summit are none too flat.

We prefer to climb Thatchtop by a longer but less steep route from the Glacier Gorge Trail. About a mile past the lower end of Jewel Lake, turn right from the trail and cross Glacier Creek on a hopefully handy log below the spot where Shelf Creek flows into Glacier Creek. Staying north of Shelf Creek, climb along a faint trail marked by occasional cairns and blocked first by downed timber, then by rock ledges. All in all , it is an interesting half-mile scramble up to *Shelf Lake*. The hardest part now behind, follow the creek upstream to *Solitude Lake*. Perched on steps between Thatchtop and Arrowhead, these lakes are very beautiful and certainly worthwhile goals themselves.

From Solitude it is a steep trudge straight to the summit of Thatchtop. Descent can be via Loch Vale, following cairns from the summit along the tundra to the top of a famous, steep gully shaped like an S. This gully leads down between cliffs to the Loch Vale Trail.

The S-gully is the most direct and more wearing route of ascent — 3.5 miles as compared to 5.5 miles via Shelf and Solitude lakes. To hike it in the opposite direction, leave the Loch Vale Trail at the first switchback past the major trail intersection located 1.9 miles from Glacier Gorge Junction. Cross Icy Brook and follow a faint track to the base of the gully.

The *North Longs Peak Trail* branches left from the Glacier Gorge Trail east of Glacier Knobs, 1.4 miles from Glacier Gorge Junction. This trail is 2.6 miles longer to Granite Pass than the trail from Longs Peak Ranger Station (see "Longs Peak and Nearby Goals"). In our opinion, an extra 2.6 miles is the last thing you need when climbing Longs Peak. On the other hand, for those who can work out the vehicular logistics of widely separated trailheads, descent by the North Longs Peak Trail is an interesting and worthwhile conclusion to the climb. The trail is well laid out with moderate grades for most of its length. It is in excellent condition and easy to walk.

From the trail junction, the North Longs Peak Trail starts out encouragingly by going downhill. But reason correctly informs you that most trails do not run downhill all the way to the top. Soon you cross a bridge over Glacier Creek at a spot where it is confined narrowly between two steep rock walls. Past the bridge, there is no downhill.

An interesting occurrence that happens now and then on this trail comes about as the result of short-cutting switchbacks. (Short-cutting, of course, is a very bad practice which works significant harm on the landscape by encouraging erosion and trail disintegration.) Hikers inclined to cutting switchbacks come striding down the Glacier Gorge Trail from The Loch or Mills Lake and see the North Longs Peak Trail below them. Such folks generally were not too observant on the way up and have forgotten about the North Longs Peak Trail, if they ever noticed it in the first place. They cut straight down to the trail below them and keep heading downhill — in exactly the wrong direction. Some realize their error when they reach the bridge over Glacier Creek; others do not catch on until they have climbed for a while. Incredible as it seems, an occasional hiker climbs a considerable distance on the trail to Longs Peak and never realizes what has happened. Often he has run ahead of his hiking companions, who miss him only after they arrive at Glacier Gorge Junction.

By then the rangers have to be called to sort out the mess. Sometimes the missing hiker is found on Bear Lake Road, having wandered there via the Boulder Brook Trail. Sometimes he turns up the next day near Longs Peak Ranger Station, having climbed all the way over the flank of Battle Mountain and down the other side. He usually has spent a dangerous night in misery and is in less than great shape when found. After such an experience, he repents of cutting switchbacks — until the next time.

The North Longs Peak Trail is the route followed by climbers headed for _Half Mountain_. Although it is possible to climb straight up to the summit after crossing the bridge across Glacier Creek, a barrier of large boulders discourages using that route. Actually, it is far better to take a less direct route and follow the trail around to the eastern side of the mountain to a point almost three miles from the trailhead. This enables you to gain a good deal of altitude on the trail. Leaving the trail at last, you strike uphill through subalpine forest which very soon gives way to limber pines. Pick the least steep way to the top for a magnificent view of Glacier Gorge. A bonus of the climb up Half Mountain is the abundance of very photogenic limber pines, some still standing as scorched skeletons of trees killed in the 1900 forest fire.

You are doing well if you can find your way down Half Mountain to the trail by exactly the same route you went up. Of course, it would be highly unethical and irresponsible backcountry stewardship to mark your uphill climb on trees and rocks. Besides, there is no assurance that the uphill route will be better than the downhill route.

Back on the North Longs Peak Trail, walking 3.6 miles from Glacier Gorge Junction brings you to a junction with the Boulder Brook Trail. The scraggly forest of limber pines is very open. A series of switchbacks eases you up the mountain by moderate grades to tree line.

Above the trees, the grade steepens, and the tundra seems to stretch on forever. It is only about 1.5 miles to Granite Pass, 6.8 miles from Glacier Gorge Junction, but the "forever" aspect stems from the fact that it is another 1.7 miles of tundra to the Boulder Field (see "Longs Peak and Nearby Goals").

Bear Lake Trailhead

Bear Lake is Rocky Mountain National Park's most popular trailhead. As you walk a few yards from the multi-acre parking lot to the lake, you will see more people at any time of the day or year than at any other spot in the park. A free mass transit system is planned to connect Bear Lake with Glacier Basin Campground, 4.8 miles from the beginning of Bear Lake Road, west of the Beaver Meadows Entrance to the park. We hope the buses will relieve the soul-trying, gas guzzling traffic jams as well as provide many advantages to hikers. Check with the National Park Service for details about the system's operation (see "Bear Lake Road").

Bear Lake teems not only with people but with people-habituated Clark's nutcrackers, gray and Steller's jays, chipmunks, golden-mantled ground squirrels and red squirrels (chickarees). Feeding the animals is against park regulations and can lead to trouble for you or for the next person who happens by and does not pay the peanut toll. The rodents reputedly bite. Additionally, fleas carrying bubonic plague (black death, which once killed 25 percent of Europe's population) have been found on rodents in the park. Human infection by this disease in Colorado is extremely rare, but it never hurts to be wary.

Dream Lake Trail System

A left (south) turn at Bear Lake (there are signs to point the way) starts you on the trail to Nymph, Dream, Haiyaha and Emerald lakes and Pool of Jade. It is one of the most beautiful trails in the park and, for most of the distance, one of the easiest. Of course, it also is the most heavily used.

The first half mile of trail to *Nymph Lake* has been paved because ordinary rock and dirt could not stand the pounding of so many feet. Though unnatural, the asphalt does prevent unacceptable erosion. You can avoid the crowds by starting your hike at 6 A.M.

With an early start, you should arrive at Nymph Lake before the day's breezes begin to ripple the pond's surface. A wide-angle lens will be useful to capture the reflection of Hallett Peak and Flattop Mountain (anything but flat from here) among the still-shadowed lily pads on the surface of Nymph. Take your light reading off the sky, or your meter will be fooled by the foreground shadows and cause you to overexpose the peaks.

As you walk a bit farther around the edge of Nymph, a normal focal length lens will be best to photograph Thatchtop Mountain dramatically framed by burned limber pines. Longs Peak looks good from a bit farther up the hill where it is framed by living lodgepole pines and subalpine fir. The patterns in upturned tree roots around Nymph also make good subjects, but probably are best shot in the afternoon, if clouds are not blocking the sun at that time.

After you leave Nymph Lake, the asphalt runs out, but feet of thousands of hikers have beaten a trail that differs little from pavement. The path between Nymph and Dream lakes is very picturesque, bordered with bright subalpine wildflowers and leading into magnificent views of Longs Peak above Glacier Gorge. About .1 mile downstream from *Dream Lake,* the trail divides. The left-hand branch crosses Tyndall Creek and heads toward Lake Haiyaha (see below). The right-hand fork continues on to Dream, 1.1 miles from Bear Lake.

Dream is the park's most-photographed lake that is inaccessible by car. Photos of the lake with Hallett towering on the left and Flattop on the right should include limber pines in the foreground. A wide-angle lens will help.

Continuing along Dream's right (northern) shore, the trail

follows the valley for .8 mile up to _Emerald lake_. A few places along the way are steep, and occasional "photography" stops usually are welcome. One good place is at a long, banded slab of bedrock smoothed by glaciers and thousands of tramping feet. Tyndall Creek tumbles across the steep rock on the left. The moisture makes possible a belt of green, including some ferns, in large cracks in the slab where soil has accumulated. Walk over the rock for a few yards to the left of the trail to compose a photo of this wild garden with the very rugged spires of Flattop rising in the background.

Forest and trail end at Emerald Lake where casual hikers are left behind by determined rock scramblers. The 1.5 miles on up Tyndall Gorge to _Pool of Jade_ is tough and interesting. Making your way around the south side of Emerald, you face a steep series of shelves. (Do not try to follow Tyndall Creek, which flows from Pool of Jade to Emerald.) As you stumble over and around loose rock of all sizes, you begin to believe that the next level grassy area must hold the pool. You are wrong many times before you are right. Pool of Jade is a good destination for those who want to feel as though they have hiked somewhere remote but do not want to pound many miles of trail in a long approach.

Past the bridge downstream from Dream Lake, the trail to _Lake Haiyaha_ climbs in a series of switchbacks through dense subalpine forest where snow usually covers the trail until July. After the path crosses onto a sunny southern exposure, you get good views of Nymph, Bear and other lakes down the valley. Just ahead, dramatic views of Longs Peak towering above Glacier Gorge are framed by dead limber pines. A normal length lens is satisfactory.

Heading down through limber pines, the trail reaches Lake Haiyaha a mile from Dream. In June a stretch of trail near the lake may be under water, forcing a detour over the big boulders that surround the lake. Haiyaha is said to be an Indian word meaning "big rocks."

At the spot where the trail hits the lake stands a very striking limber pine that we have had trouble photographing adequately. Likewise, photos of the lake with Hallett above are disappointing compared with those from Nymph and Dream. But from the other side of Haiyaha, a short telephoto shot of Longs Peak is good in the afternoon, given a benevolent cloud arrangement.

About a quarter-mile before reaching Haiyaha, the trail branches left to meet the Glacier Gorge Trail System (see "Bear Lake Road," Glacier Gorge Trail System). The mile-long link between the two trail systems is quite charming. Although its views are relatively unspectacular, the path passes through wild gardens of midsummer flowers and rushing water. On this stretch of trail, we are particularly conscientious about picking up litter, scattering remains of illegal campfires, staying on the path and educating the unenlightened about ethical wilderness behavior.

Flattop Mountain Trail System

A right turn at Bear Lake takes hikers a short way along a paved lakeshore path until the unpaved Flattop Mountain Trail departs uphill to the right. (Signs at appropriate places point out both these right-hand turns.) Climbing through quaking aspens, the trail divides after less than a half-mile.

The right-hand branch runs along the top of Bierstadt Moraine through pleasant woods to *Bierstadt Lake*. This route to the lake is easier and cooler, though .2 mile longer, than the path from the Bierstadt Lake Trailhead. If you intend to start at one trailhead and end at another, all sanity dictates starting at Bear Lake (see "Bear Lake Road," Bierstadt Lake Trail).

Before it reaches Bierstadt Lake, the trail divides again; the left-hand path runs down to beaver ponds in *Mill Creek Basin*. A spur trail links the Mill Creek Trail with Bierstadt Lake so that no backtracking is necessary if you wish to descend into the basin directly from the lake. Once in the basin, the trail follows Mill Creek (named for a sawmill that operated there from 1887 to 1880) for a short way before branching yet again. The right-hand fork passes through Hallowell Park to Bear Lake Road. The left-hand fork crosses the creek and winds over the ridge between Mount Wuh and

Steep Mountain. After about 1.5 miles, it arrives at the Cub Lake Trail (see "Moraine Park," Cub Lake Trail).

Back at the first trail junction after leaving Bear Lake, a switchback left turn takes hikers along the more heavily traveled trail to *Flattop Mountain*. On a warm south-facing slope, it climbs somewhat steeply above Bear Lake. It soon levels off, however, passing through Engelmann spruce and subalpine fir which are growing back after the 1900 forest fire.

A little less than a mile from Bear Lake, the trail forks. Continuing on the lower path, to the right, you reach Odessa Gorge (see below). The trail to the left switchbacks uphill through fir and spruce which seem not to cast as much cooling shade as they should. Dream Lake Overlook is a good rest stop just below tree line, with limber pines to frame vistas of Longs Peak rising above Glacier Gorge and of the ever-dramatic Hallett Peak. The view of Dream Lake itself is more interesting than photogenic.

Above tree line you arrive at another overlook, this time of Emerald Lake, 1300 feet below. Ahead are nearly 1.5 miles of moderately steep walking to the top of the mountain. Just up the trail from Emerald Lake Overlook, be sure to notice and reflect upon a sign that warns of the dangers of hiking above tree line in stormy weather. Lightning is the biggest danger, but this sign was inspired by hikers walking over a precipice in a blinding snowstorm, with fatal results.

Be sure to watch closely for two species of interesting alpine wildlife that are common on the tundra. Pikas, round-earred, rabbitlike little creatures, are active though well camouflaged. Their loud sharp squeaks are heard more often than they are seen. Ptarmigan (high altitude grouse) also blend in with their background and materialize suddenly underfoot, only to scamper away.

Shortly before you top out on Flattop, you receive fine views to the south of Hallett Peak's true summit and Tyndall Glacier. Most hikers do not bother trying to find the true summit of appropriately named Flattop. It is a broad uplifted plain which usually serves as a route to more dramatic goals. Among the best goals is *Hallett Peak*, easily reached by crossing the tundra at the head of Tyndall Glacier. Then, as you begin to climb, boulders replace tundra. Pick your own best route over the rocks; the way is short, though steep, and the summit is very nice.

Otis Peak, the next mountain south of Hallett, is climbed in much the same way en route to *Andrews Glacier*. Many hikers later descend via the glacier into Loch Vale for a circle trip back to Bear Lake (see "Bear Lake Road," Glacier Gorge Trail System). Sliding down the glacier is fun, but dangerous crevasses can open up late in the season. Also, icy conditions have led to an out-of-control slide with a sudden, fatal stop on the rocks at the foot of the glacier. It is best to check with the National Park Service about the current state of Andrews Glacier before planning to slide down.

Taylor Peak rises south of Andrews Glacier and is a rough climb if Hallett and Otis are included along the way. But you can skirt those two peaks by staying on the broad tundra slopes west of their summits, more or less level with Flattop's summit. Otherwise, from the head of Andrews Glacier, pick your way over the rocks to the top of Taylor. The ascent is harder than the ascent of Hallett, but the view of Longs Peak and Loch Vale is well worth it. Taylor sometimes is climbed via Loch Vale by ascending Andrews Glacier; this route is two miles shorter than the route via Flattop (see "Bear Lake Road," Glacier Gorge Trail System).

It is fairly simple to follow the ridge from Taylor Peak along the continental divide to *Powell Peak*. But peak-bagging beyond Powell changes from hiking to technical climbing. McHenrys Notch, a 300-foot-deep cut in the divide, is a significant barrier between Powell and McHenrys Peak, which usually is climbed from Glacier Gorge (see "Bear Lake Road," Glacier Gorge Trail System).

On the summit of Flattop, the trail forks at a pair of eight-foot cairns. The North Inlet Trail to the left is the shortest way to Grand Lake, at the park's southwest corner (see below). The *Tonahutu Creek Trail*, to the right, is an older route to the same goal, first walked by Indians. This path follows the continental divide to an overlook above Odessa Gorge, then runs northwest around

Ptarmigan Point and begins to descend the western slope.

   Notchtop, Knobtop and *Gabletop mountains* are climbed by striking northeast from the Tonahutu Creek Trail as it begins to go downhill. Proceed carefully on the tundra, stepping on rocks rather than plants whenever possible. The walking is easy and pleasant; the mountains' gentle west faces contrast dramatically with the cliffs on their heavily glaciated east faces.

   A round trip to Bear Lake can be made by descending from the Tonahutu Creek Trail to Odessa Lake via Tourmaline Gorge, a steep gully on the northern side of the Little Matterhorn knife ridge (see below). Be careful on the rocks above Tourmaline Lake. Below the lake, be clever picking your trackless way through the trees to the trail at Odessa Lake.

   The Tonahutu Creek Trail misses good views of *Ptarmigan Lake* dramatically set at the foot of Snowdrift Peak, but a short downhill detour to the left of the trail below Ptarmigan Point takes you to an overlook at the edge of the cirque containing the lake. Again, tread lightly on the tundra.

   Rather than retracing your steps all the way back up to the spot where you left the trail, walk north, heading gradually uphill to meet the trail as it descends east of an unnamed high point above marshy *Bighorn Flats.* There is a slight chance of spotting bighorn sheep there, but your best bet is on the glaciated cliffs surrounding this uplifted plain. Anywhere you might go looking for sheep would be out of the way, and a long shot.

   In 1902 the *Eureka Ditch* was dug across Bighorn Flats to divert westward-flowing water to Spruce Canyon, on the thirsty eastern slope. In essence it moves the continental divide slightly west. The ditch does not intersect the trail, and there are no significant landmarks to indicate where to leave the trail to find it. You have to watch your map, plot your position on it and aim through the marshes by dead reckoning.

   The ditch looks similar to a natural stream. It probably is not worth the bother to locate unless you have a particular interest in the history of water diversion projects or are headed for *Sprague*

Glacier, Sprague Mountain or *Stones Peak*. To reach the glacier, follow Eureka Ditch to Sprague Pass, at the head of Spruce Canyon. From there hike north up a tundra slope to the top of Sprague Glacier, one of the most remote glaciers in the park.

To climb Stones Peak, walk uphill from the top of Sprague Glacier to Sprague Mountain. A ridge extends northeast from Sprague Mountain to Stones Peak. You must follow it carefully down to the base of Stones, then regain 800 feet of elevation. Retracing your steps to Bear Lake means a round-trip hike of more than 20 tough miles. It all must be done in one day, for there are no campsites along the way.

Afternoon storms and lightning sometimes catch hikers when they have many miles more to go above tree line. At such times it may be advisable to descend into Spruce Canyon, hike through its thick trailless forest to Spruce Lake and exit via the Fern Lake Trail. Better yet, take two days and climb Stones via Spruce Canyon in the first place (see "Moraine park," Fern Lake Trail System).

West of Bighorn Flats, the Tonahutu Creek Trail descends between a few tall cairns through lovely flowered meadows. It then turns sharply right (snow cover may make the way vague in spots, necessitating a bit of casting about) to the head of a very steep beautiful valley. An impressive bit of trail construction leads you easily across a sunny (south-facing) but precipitous valley wall through enchanting subalpine meadows and forests.

The surroundings would be even more enchanting if you were not so tired by this time. Getting a permit to camp in this area is a good idea. Camping will give you time for a side trip to *Haynach Lakes* via a faint trail heading upstream to the right at the spot where the main trail cuts sharply left across a boulder-strewn tributary to Tonahutu Creek. A sign warns that hiking above tree line in stormy weather can be fatal.

The tributary does not extend all the way to Haynach Lakes. There is a short steep climb at the end of it to the bench on which sit the lakes, looking very striking below Nakai Peak. Because the lakes often are approached from the western side of the park, there is another trail extending up to them from farther along the Tonahutu Creek Trail. But when the lakes are approached from Flattop, the route up the drainage is easier, though somewhat marshy.

If you are determined to hike the Tonahutu Creek Trail and return to civilization in only one day, you can grind out the rest of the miles past Granite Falls to Big Meadows. Granite Falls is easy to walk by unawares if you are trail weary. "Tonahutu" is Arapaho for "Big Meadows," and they are big to the point of seeming interminable. The trail is excellent, however, always skirting the bogs and staying just within the forest shade.

At Big Meadows, two trails join Tonahutu at different points — a spur from the Onahu Creek Trail, and the Green Mountain Trail (see "Trail Ridge Road," Onahu Creek - Green Mountain Circle). The easiest route to civilization is 1.8 miles along the Green Mountain Trail to Trail Ridge Road. It is a pleasant, wide subalpine trail and much preferable to the hot 4.4 miles of lodgepole pines along the Tonahutu Creek Trail to Grand Lake (see "Grand Lake," Tonahutu Creek Trail).

The _North Inlet Trail_, which is the left-hand fork at the trail junction on the summit of Flattop, is widely praised for the quality of its scenery, trail construction and campsites. Leaving the junction, it descends between tall cairns over tundra slopes west of Hallett and Otis peaks. Tundra flowers clinging to windy Flattop are spectacular in July and early August. The display becomes even more outstanding as you drop down a series of switchbacks along the steep valley wall at the head of Hallett Creek drainage. Spreading all the way to tree line is one of the most outstanding wildflower displays in the park.

Down in the valley the trail passes a locked patrol cabin, a romantic-looking structure in an alpine setting of glaciated cliffs and snowbanks. Past the cabin, a fairly level stretch through fine subalpine forest is followed by a series of switchbacks affording grand views of cascades along Hallett Creek. Soon after the trail leaves the switchbacks and creek, a cutoff to the left leads uphill to Lakes Nokoni and Nanita (see "Grand Lake," North Inlet Trail).

Below the cutoff, the trail winds its way through the woods and meadows along North Inlet — so named because the creek flows into Grand Lake on the north shore. When the trail branches again, take the left-hand fork, which leads down to Cascade Falls. (The right-hand fork eventually rejoins the left.) The falls is best photographed by climbing to the rocks below.

The trail from Cascade Falls to Grand Lake is easy and frequently used. Maps show a road to Summerland Park, located this side of Grand Lake, but this access to private land in the park is not open to driving by the public. You have to walk 1.2 miles more to reach the trailhead (see "Grand Lake," North Inlet Trail).

Odessa Lake Trail

Among the most popular hikes in the park is the hike to Odessa Lake, from which many people continue to Fern Lake and then to prearranged transportation at Moraine Park (see "Moraine Park," Fern Lake Trail System). From Bear Lake, you travel uphill on the Flattop Trail for .9 mile to the trail junction. The left-hand fork goes to Flattop Mountain (see above). Take the right-hand fork. The path now is easy and level. Thus, after a short, moderately steep climb at Bear Lake, the trail has only a slight up or down grade until it reaches Odessa Gorge, about three miles from Bear. A must side-trip is the very short spur to Lake Helene at the head of the gorge, east of Notchtop Mountain. Retrace your steps to the main trail.

The Odessa Lake Trail now slants down the valley wall with views of Grace Falls hanging on the opposite wall, across the gorge. Crossing snowbanks until mid-July, the path passes below Odessa Lake and eventually arrives at a trail junction. The trail straight ahead goes to Fern Lake (see "Moraine Park," Fern Lake Trail System). The Odessa Trail makes a switchback left turn and crosses Fern Creek. It then heads upstream along a narrow gorge to reach Odessa Lake. The outlet is the best spot for photos; a wide-angle lens may be helpful but is not essential. The most dramatic peaks rising above Odessa Lake are Notchtop Mountain and the Little

Matterhorn. Notchtop can be climbed from Flattop Mountain (see above).

One route up the _Little Matterhorn_ begins from a trail that follows the west shore of Odessa. Leave the trail at the spot where a stream flows into the lake, about a quarter of the lake's length from the outlet. Head upstream, picking whatever route seems easiest through dense forest, into Tourmaline Gorge. Past tree line on the open tundra is _Tourmaline Lake._ Stay south of the lake and climb the steep slope to the top of the Little Matterhorn ridge. As you may have noticed while hiking to Odessa Lake, the Little Matterhorn really is a sharp ridge extending east from the continental divide at Knobtop.

It is possible to climb the ridge, also, from Lake Helene, by traversing the base of Notchtop and Knobtop west of Grace Falls. From the south base of the Little Matterhorn ridge, climb straight up to the ridgetop. This route eliminates the loss in elevation between Lakes Helene and Odessa.

To reach the summit of the Little Matterhorn, follow the top of the ridge eastward, keeping to the north (left) side. There are a couple of places easy to traverse but very exposed to long drops. The final four feet to the tiny summit is extremely exposed, so some folks are content to place their elbows rather than their feet on the very top.

Overall, the hike up the Little Matterhorn is short, thrilling, beautiful and not particularly difficult. But it is also steep and windy, and careless climbers have been killed on the way.

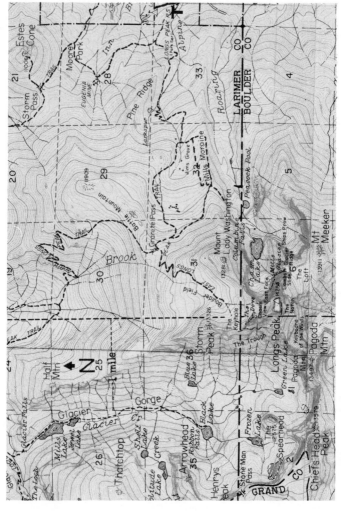

Longs Peak and Nearby Goals and Glacier Gorge

Longs Peak
and Nearby Goals

We huddled cold and fuzzy headed in the utterly dark parking lot at Longs Peak Ranger Station. Pulling ourselves from bed at 1 A.M., we had driven 7.5 miles south of Estes Park on State Highway 7 to a sign indicating a right turn for Longs Peak Campground. After a mile of unpaved road, we drousily had noted a smoother ride as we reached National Park Service pavement. Almost at once we had felt a slight sway as the car turned left into trailhead parking.

Sensing our sleepy reluctance to begin climbing Longs Peak, our leader threw on his pack, jammed his alpine hat on his head and proclaimed to the peaks, "I feel the call of nature." Inspired, we grabbed our assorted equipment and tramped off gallantly single file behind him — right into a nearby comfort station.

So began our first climb of Longs. Many others followed as we, in turn, led various people up the mountain. It is a great peak, the highest in the park (14,255 feet; it shrank a foot in the last U.S. Geological Survey calculations), both photogenic and fun. Longs teaches climbers that *fun* is the best reason to climb — not because the mountains are there, not for an elevated ego trip, not to prove some profound "truth" about the nature of man.

To make the climb more fun, we now sleep late and usually leave at 4 A.M. Nevertheless, we are still groggy as we begin hiking up the steep, dark Longs Peak Trail. Flashlights illumine dimly comprehended ranks of lodgepole pines varied by white aspen trunks near the turnoff to Eugenia Mine (see below). Occasionally, the babble of Alpine Brook disturbs our half-slumber as we somnambulate near the stream. At _Goblins Forest_, 1.2 miles up the trail, twisted limber pines pass vaguely into and out of sight.

We really awaken only when we cross Alpine Brook and LIGHT-NING HAZARD in bright yellow letters jumps out through the flashlight beams in predawn darkness. Less dramatic white letters on the black sign explain what to do should lightning threaten and static electricity cause hair to stand on end.

As we continue uphill to tree line, deformed and stunted trees appear to be battered climbers in the dim light. They struggle constantly toward the heights while storms, jealous of their unshared control, fight to hold the forest back.

Just past tree line, the trail returns almost to Alpine Brook and divides. The left-hand branch climbs along the side of *Mills Moraine* toward Chasm Lake (see below). This path provides opportunities for spectacular photography when alpenglow radiates red, orange and gold in succession from the dramatic East Face of Longs. Mills Moraine, however, is out of the way if you are going to the summit.

The right-hand branch is the main Longs Peak Trail, which recrosses Alpine Brook and enters Jims Grove, a high outpost of picturesque limber pines about three miles from the campground. It heads steeply up the route of an emergency telephone line (now removed) and meets a trail that circles the base of Mount Lady Washington to form a connecting link with the *Chasm Lake Trail*. Ahead are the junction with the North Longs Peak Trail (see "Bear Lake Road," Glacier Gorge Trail System), and Granite Pass. From the pass a series of switchbacks climbs to a giant jumble of rocks called the Boulder Field.

Here the real climb begins as, 1500 feet above, the flat top of Longs catches early morning sun. Dramatic patterns of light and dark spreading across the peaks North Face tempt use of a wide-angle lens. Yet a normal focal length lens produces more striking results.

Formerly, the route to the top was via the North Face. Wire cables used to be bolted to the steepest rock to help climbers ascend straight up from the Boulder Field. The National Park Service removed the cables in 1973 as part of a program to eliminate as many man-made contrivances as possible from the wilderness.

We ascend Longs by a less direct but easier route, through an oval gap in the ridge between Longs and Storm Peak. This gap is called *The Keyhole* and, with two large ledges overhanging it on each side, actually looks like its name.

Clambering over the huge chunks of granite that glaciers and weather have carved from the peak entails gasping for more oxygen than the thin air holds. The Keyhole rather than the summit becomes the immediate goal. On the other side are rest, food and magnificent views to the north into Glacier Gorge.

Just below The Keyhole, near the ridgeline, a stone hut materializes. Built from the same granite as the mountain, the beehive-shaped shelter blends inconspicuously with the ridge. A sobering bronze table is set into the cabin's wall: "Agnes Wolcott Vaille. This shelter commemorates a Colorado mountaineer conquered by winter after scaling the precipice, January 12, 1925, and one who lost his life in an effort to save her, Herbert Sortland."

Agnes Vaille and Walter Kiener had made the first winter ascent of the difficult East Face. Twenty-five hours of climbing so exhausted Ms. Vaille that she was unable to descend to shelter from the storms and subzero temperatures. Kiener had to leave her on the North Face and go for help. By the time he and another rescuer could return, she had died. Meanwhile, Herbert Sortland, another member of the rescue party, could not continue in the adverse weather. He turned back, lost his way, broke a hip and froze to death a short way from the safety of Longs Peak Inn. As for Kiener, frostbite took all but one of his fingertips, all his toes and part of his left foot.

A few dozen others have died on Longs. One accidentally shot himself. Some fell or were hit by falling rocks. One person merely disappeared.

From the tragedy and gloom of the Agnes Vaille shelter, we pass through The Keyhole into the joy and light of Glacier Gorge. Before us, three 13,000-foot peaks west of Longs — Pagoda Mountain, Chiefs Head and McHenrys Peak — form a huge amphitheater at the head of the valley. They sparkle with streams of melting snow which feed many lakes below. Most of the lakes lie in the cold shadow of Longs until midmorning. Some are frozen; others reflect snow and sky.

After a bite of breakfast at The Keyhole, we have to go down to go up. The route, marked by yellow and red bull's-eyes painted on rocks, descends into _The Trough_, a long vertical gully filled with loose stones. Here is is important for climbers to stay close together and catch kicked-loose rocks before they build up dangerous momentum. If one gets away, yelling "Rock!" is the normal warning. Slick snow and ice add further hazards, especially in early summer, when ice axes and ropes are necessary protection in unmelted places.

When we finally leave the seemingly interminable Trough, our reward is traversing a section less arduous and more interesting — the cliffs on the West Face. Here we cross The Narrows, a ledge which looks worse than it really is. In some places it is wide enough to walk two abreast, although the long drop straight down certainly discourages such a practice.

Far below the south end of The Narrows there is a large black rock shaped like and named the Black Hearse. But now is no time for ill omens. We are at the base of the _Homestretch_, a long, steep, smooth slab of granite that ends on the summit of Longs. The thin air at 14,000 feet is supplemented by the nearness of success. We finally arrive!

Once on top, we cluster around the pile of rocks that marks the summit. Wired to this cairn is a heavy plastic tube containing a register in which climbers scrawl their tired signatures.

In good weather we spend a couple of hours on top, resting, eating lunch, photographing marmots and the view, meandering around (the summit covers several acres) and gazing 2000 feet down the East Face into Chasm Lake. As soon as storm clouds appear in the west, prudence demands a descent.

Although it is possible to walk down the very steep Homestretch, many hikers find that the seat of their pants serves as a

Yellow-bellied marmot

convenient brake. This is one of the few places where you can see someone hiking while sitting down. Once we pass The Narrows and are back in The Trough, the view of Glacier Gorge, now brimful with sunshine, is spectacular. The distraction of the view, and fatigue, make falling rocks and slipping even more hazardous than earlier. It always is a relief to reach The Keyhole and the Boulder Field.

The trail is the same one we traveled on the ascent, yet it seems like a new path. At dawn we missed the tiny tundra flowers growing close to the ground. The wind, snow and cold of the mountaintops have failed to deter or distress the little rose crown, moss campion and alpine forget-me-not. Their colors are more brilliant, their blooms more profuse and their beauty greater than that of the big flowers living in relative ease below tree line.

Difficult to see among the flowers and rocks is the little farmer of the tundra — the round-eared, rabbitlike pika. Pikas keep busy harvesting alpine plants to dry in piles for their winter food supply. But they often pause to pipe shrill barks at hikers passing through their hayfields.

We find it difficult to pass by the various tundra flora and fauna without closer examination and picture taking. When lightning-filled clouds begin to roll in, we must push on toward the safety of tree line. We cannot hurry much, however, because feet heavy with fatigue are hard to lift over the rocks that reach up to trip us. Rain usually is popping on ponchos before the day ends.

That sound and the sound of boots thudding monotonously on the trail discourages conversation. Each climber has his own thoughts. Some imagine a big dinner; those who are finishing their first ascent of Longs have more elevated visions. For many, Longs is a high point in their lives. They will remember it always as a great effort and as great fun.

Storm Peak and _Mount Lady Washington_ sit on either side of the Boulder Field as 13,000-foot buttresses of Longs. They tend to be overlooked in the excitement about their 14,000-foot neighbor. Storm and Lady Washington are simple to climb and provide fine vantage points for photographers.

The top of Storm Peak is reached by a right turn and a steep climb from the trail's second Boulder Field crossing of Boulder Brook. Pick the easiest way over the boulders, avoiding snowbanks and the steepest rock. Rest often. The view from the summit gives a unique perspective of the North Face of Longs and of the summits and cirques above Glacier Gorge.

People in a hurry and feeling vigorous can boulder hop up the east slope of Mount Lady Washington from either end of the path connecting the Chasm Lake Trail and the main Longs Peak Trail. An easier, though longer, route heads left from the trail just as it levels above the switchbacks between Granite Pass and the Boulder Field. On this (western) side of Lady Washington, the trail is 1000 feet nearer the summit than on the eastern side. Also, the slope is less steep on the west. Traversing Lady Washington up the western slope and down the eastern one is a favorite route.

From the top of Lady Washington, the view of the East Face of Longs is unsurpassed. For portrait purposes, the East Face makes an excellent background to frame a head-and-upper-torso shot of one or several climbers. The view of Mount Meeker also can be exciting early in the morning when Meeker's rugged slope is accented by the low angle of the rising sun's rays. Do not expect much of a view of Chasm Lake, though. Half the lake is hidden by a rocky bulge on Lady Washington's south slope.

The hike to *Chasm Lake* has infected more than one person with a permanent passion for mountaineering. This trip offers great variety and exciting scenery in return for 4.2 miles of moderate effort. Of course, it is very popular, and the lake often is crowded. It is seen in its best light and greatest isolation by hikers who leave the trailhead at the same time they would leave for Longs.

The Chasm Lake Trail branches off the main trail to Longs Peak at Alpine Brook nearly three miles from Longs Peak Ranger Station. Passing abnormally large cairns, it slants up the side of Mills Moraine to the base of Mount Lady Washington. Unlimber cameras there; the view into Roaring Fork drainage with the East Face of Longs towering above is hard to beat. Peacock Pool stares up like the "eye" in peacock tail feathers, and Columbine Falls hangs as a white accent below the precipice. Climb the rocks a few feet above the trail to include the path and fellow hikers in your picture. A normal focal length lens is perfect.

During much of the summer, the trail crosses a snowbank. Some care is necessary there; a slip could mean an uncontrolled slide far down to rocks, and serious injury. Beyond the snowbank, Colorado blue columbine, the state flower, blooms abundantly among the rocks above Columbine Falls. We probably need not say that picking wildflowers, especially the state flower, is punished by public hanging on the steps of the state capitol and a $50 fine. Coloradans tend to be fussy on this point.

Just above the falls, a lush alpine meadow boasts a flower-lined stream, yellow-bellied marmots which are easily photographed and a picturesque hut. The hut (locked) is a National Park Service storage building for rescue equipment which is used with unpleasant frequency when technical rock climbers get into trouble on the East Face, one of the country's most famous and heavily used rock-climbing areas. Instant popularity among hikers at Chasm Lake rewards foresighted folks who tucked a pair of binoculars for watching climbers into their packs.

The lake itself is a short scramble from the meadow onto the rocky edge of a deep glacier-scoured basin. From behind the stone hut, follow a path up a short gully to a small shelf. Head left from there across a few yards of tundra and rock, then turn right for the last short pull to the lake.

Part of Chasm Lake's beauty may derive from the fact that it hides from hikers approaching from below. Suddenly the lake becomes visible, a large tarn in a setting of unexcelled drama. High crags tower on all sides, but every eye locks on the huge sheer East Face rising straight up for nearly half a mile. It is difficult to realize how far Longs rises above the lake unless climbers on its summit present tiny silhouettes against the sky. Sudden comprehension of the overwhelming massiveness of the scene can induce momentary dizziness in first-time visitors.

Predawn arrival at Chasm Lake can provide an opportunity for magnificent alpenglow photos. Trying to capture the mood and beauty without a wide-angle lens is a certain road to frustration and disappointment. Chasm Lake and the top of Longs can just barely be squeezed into the format of a 35mm camera with a normal lens, but the result is unsatisfactory. With a wide-angle, the East Face and its colorful reflection on the lake's surface, unrippled in the still, early morning air, can appear together in one outstanding photograph.

In Rocky Mountain National Park, _Mount Meeker_ is second in elevation only to Longs. To scale No. 2, you have to try harder. A popular route begins at the stone hut in the meadow below Chasm Lake. From the hut, head south along the stream, climbing for several hundred yards toward the cliffs on Meeker. Avoid the cliffs by veering left (east) and scrambling over loose rocks for about three-eights mile to reach the ridge that leads to Meeker's summit.

A right (southwest) turn up the ridge take climbers eventually to rock slabs on the mountaintop. Meeker has a double summit; the western one is higher. The narrow ridge between east and west summits has been known to make some folks nervous. As elsewhere, care is essential. Essential to all camera carriers is a photographic record of the uniquely blocky aspect of Longs from Meeker.

Be sure to descend Meeker by the same route you ascended. Apparent shortcuts may present themselves, but they probably will take you to the top of an unexpected cliff. (For a description of another route up Meeker, see "Wild Basin," Sandbeach Lake Trail System.)

Eugenia Mine comprises the tumble-down remains of a miner's log cabin, some turn of the century scraps of mining machinery and several piles of mine tailings. The Rocky Mountain National Park area is as poor in exploitable minerals as it is rich in scenery. Local mining efforts fortunately were failures, sparing the scenery the scars of boom and bust.

To reach the mine, leave the main trail up Longs at a right fork a half-mile from Longs Peak Ranger Station. After following fairly level terrain through aspens, the path undulates moderately through various evergreens for almost a mile to Inn Brook and the mine. It forks at the ruins of a once-sturdy cabin which used to house the operator of Eugenia Mine and his family. The left-hand fork leads a few hundred feet uphill to several mine workings. The trail to the right of the cabin passes through pleasant Moore Park and joins the Storm Pass Trail a half-mile from the mine (see "East Edge Summits," Storm Pass Trail to Estes Cone).

East Edge Summits

Conditioning climbs; peaks assigned to desk-bound flatlanders to get them ready for more challenging and higher goals. That is what we used to think about these overlooked mountains south of Estes Park. Now we know better. Peaks on the park's east edge are well worth climbing for their own values. Each mountain is a fine end in itself, even though the tallest barely reaches above tree line. Yes, the high peaks grab the attention of summer visitors to Rocky Mountain National Park, but the lower mountains can be just as rewarding to hikers who have learned how to see:

> *Does not wisdom call,*
> *does not understanding raise her voice?*
> *On the heights beside the way,*
> *in the paths she takes her stand.*
>
> Proverbs 8:1-2

Twins Sisters Trail

To reach the Twin Sisters Trailhead, drive south from Estes Park on State Highway 7. After passing a sign identifying the turn to Marys Lake Power Plant, proceed on Route 7 for another 4.5 miles into the Tahosa Valley. Turn left (east) where a sign indicates the Twin Sisters Trailhead. Drive about .1 mile along an unpaved road to a parking area on the left. A few yards up the road from the parking lot, the trail is clearly marked, running between branches of the road that lead to cabins.

Access to Twin Sisters is through private land; the parking area is situated on private land. Hikers reach Twin Sisters at the suffrance of landowners. Do not make the landowners suffer any more than necessary. Especially, DO NOT BLOCK DRIVEWAYS with your car. Abuse of any privilege will result in the privilege being withdrawn.

You might as well know now, at the bottom: there is no fire lookout on Twin Sisters. There used to be one; we pointed it out to people for two months after the National Park Service removed it in 1977. It had not been used for seven years and had become obsolete as a tool of fire control. Indeed, the official attitude toward fire in the park has changed. In certain places under certain conditions, *lightning-caused* fires are allowed to burn. Such fires are a natural, even beneficial, occurrence and part of the unaltered environment the park was created to preserve.

For instance, the lodgepole pines that line the lower part of the Twin Sisters Trail were able to grow there because fire destroyed a dense forest and created room for the sun-loving lodgepoles. Similarly, a fire in 1929 destroyed a stand of lodgepoles on Twin Sisters, allowing quaking aspens to take their place. This stand of aspens is called the Butterfly Burn. The supposed butterfly shape is rather vague, but butterfly colors appear beautifully on this slope in autumn when the trees turn red and yellow.

Hikers on the Twin Sisters Trail sometimes have cause to regret fires, for a dense woods would make for cooler, more comfortable hiking. The trail heads straight uphill for the first mile through private land. At the park boundary the terrain gets really steep, and the trail snakes through unnumbered switchbacks to the top of a low point on the ridge north of the summit, about 2.5 miles from the trailhead.

At this spot some maps show a feature called Lookout Springs about a quarter-mile east of the trail. Once this spring was a source of drinking water. We doubt its purity and recommend that you skip sampling it and carry your own water.

To help fight the heat of a summer day, you may want to put your water bottle in a freezer the evening before your hike. It will

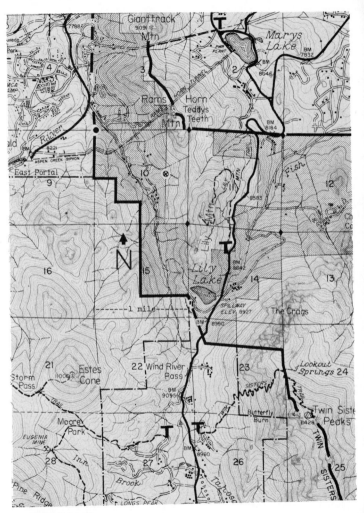

East Edge Summits

Red-tailed hawk

contain a lump of ice when transferred to your pack. Carried next to your back, the ice will absorb heat generated by steep hiking and melt into cold drinking water. Thus the bottle will cool you on the outside as well as the inside.

A better solution is to climb Twin Sisters not on a hot summer day but on a cool summer night. The trail is clear enough to hike by starlight, and a full moon is magic if you can arrange it. A flashlight is worth its weight in confidence.

Starting well before dawn, you should arrive on the ridgetop in time to witness sunrise over the plains, shining with reservoirs. Here a short telephoto lens can be very helpful to photographers; be sure to include the silhouettes of some limber pines in the foreground.

About the time there is enough light to see the trail clearly, the way becomes rockier. It gets steeper, too, and passes through more switchbacks to tree line. In early morning light there is a hard question to be decided: which makes the more dramatic picture — twisted limber pines isolated against the sky, or the remarkable panorama of mountains to the west? The fire lookout was built for watching this wide scene of many mountains. Most hikers end up concentrating on the perfect view of the East Face of Longs Peak, rising directly across the Tahosa Valley.

Some rest and food (call it breakfast if you like) usually seem appropriate on top of Twin Sisters, 3.7 miles from the trailhead. Few hikers are in a hurry to leave; they have literally all day. Yet there is a lot to be experienced on the easy return walk. Pikas squeak their alarms from the invisibility of their near-perfect camouflage among the rocks. Also finding shelter among the rocks is dwarf blue columbine. This rare alpine flower is only a few inches high, an obvious relative of the popular Colorado blue columbine but possessing much stubbier curved spurs. Additional interesting photos of trees present themselves on your way down.

Storm Pass Trail To Estes Cone

Once, while leading a group of hikers to Chasm Lake, we

informed them of a lecture to be given that evening by a man who had climbed Longs Peak more than 50 times. "Fifty times!" exclaimed one panting hiker. "Why, any reasonable man would have stopped at 30!"

Relatively few climbers can claim such a record on the park's tallest peak. Fewer yet may be able to match *our* record on the park's ninety-first tallest peak: one summer we climbed Estes Cone more than a dozen times. Why? Because it's strategically located. Although not very high, it is a good vantage point from which to photograph taller peaks, especially Mount Meeker. Its bare summit has interesting rocks among which hide rare dwarf blue columbine, and photogenic limber pines grow on the slopes just below the summit.

Estes Cone is climbed from Storm Pass. <u>Storm Pass</u> can be reached simply from Longs Peak Campground, 2.6 miles away via Eugenia Mine (see "Longs Peak and Nearby Goals").Or it can be reached simply from Bear Lake Road, more than four miles away on the Boulder Brook and Storm Pass trails (see "Bear Lake Road," Boulder Brook and Storm Pass Trails).

But the shortest, easiest route to Storm Pass is not simple. On State Highway 7, drive .4 mile south of the Twin Sisters road and turn right (west) on an unpaved road. There should be a sign indicating this turnoff for the Storm Pass Trail, but signs are not so eternal as the hills. At any rate, it is the first road south of Longs Peak Inn.

After .2 mile the unpaved road bends 90 degrees to the right and arrives at a three-way fork, .3 mile from Route 7. Continue on the farthest-right fork, which soon veers left at (hopefully) a sign pointing left and reading, "Horse Trail Storm Pass."

About .1 mile past the sign you reach another fork, the left-hand branch of which makes a switchback. Don't take that; drive straight ahead on the right-hand branch. After another .3 mile, you arrive at yet another fork that looks much like the previous one. This time take the sharp left-hand turn and stop in the small parking area on the left side of the road, amid aspens. If there are no empty parking spaces, please do not block the road or someone's driveway.

After all this, following the Storm Pass Trail should be easy. The trail passes through private land for nearly a mile, so it is well marked; landowners like to keep hikers and horseback riders on the trail. Take care not to disturb anything, especially buildings or water supplies.

In June little pink calypso orchids are fairly common among the lodgepole pines on the lower part of the trail. Tuliplike violet-colored pasqueflowers bloom at trailside at higher elevations. In July look for Colorado blue columbine, the state flower, in quaking aspen groves.

Once across the national park border, the trail becomes somewhat less steep, anticipating the levelness of Moore Park, which lies immediately ahead. Bypassing the trail that leads left to Moore Park and Eugenia Mine, follow the right-hand (upper) fork uphill toward Storm Pass. On this sunny south slope, lodgepole pines cast little shade, and it often is warm. If you plan to continue on over Storm Pass, you will feel an obvious drop in temperature when you reach the north slope. Of course, the fact that you will be walking mostly downhill will have something to do with that drop.

If you are headed for the top of Estes Cone, however, pines and warmth predominate all the way. From a classic grove of limber pines in Storm Pass, follow the path that runs uphill to the right. Keep alert to the view on the left through the pines; the first example of Estes Cone's strategic position is a unique perspective of Specimen Mountain, straight down Forest Canyon. The trail at first runs clear and certain, switchbacking excellently up the steep slopes. Then it degenerates to cairns and then not much of anything.

The terrain itself guides you to a spot where a bit of rock climbing is necessary. Please avoid trampling rare dwarf columbine growing among the rocks. The top of this climb is a false summit, but it is easier and more fun to go over the rocks than around them. Next you must descend into a gully and then climb to the cone's summit, on the east side of the mountain.

The panoramas are excellent in all directions from Estes Cone, especially if you started about 5 A.M. Such an early start has the dual advantage of cool temperatures on the way up and the best light for summit photographs. Normal and short telephoto lenses are most useful on this hike, plus close-up equipment for flowers.

Lily Mountain Trail (Roosevelt National Forest)

Lily Mountain is the easiest mountain in this book. Yet it offers a genuine climbing experience. As such, it is an excellent first climb for children whose parents want them to acquire a taste for mountaineering.

To reach the trailhead, drive south of Estes Park on State Highway 7 to a point 2.4 miles south of a sign indicating the turnoff to Marys Lake Power Plant. At present, you park on the shoulder of the highway. There is not much room, which somewhat limits the number of people hiking the trail at one time. Additionally, it is easy to err and drive on uphill past the trailhead. Watch for three major road cuts as the highway climbs the valley wall; the trail begins on the right-hand side (west) just past the third big cut.

The U.S. Forest Service has been considering building a parking area nearby. If it has been established by the time you read this, the trailhead should be easy to find. Such action would allow more people on Lily Mountain simultaneously. Opinions doubtless will vary as to whether that would be a good thing.

The first part of the trail follows a very gentle grade, slightly rising and falling parallel to the road. The slope is partially forested and dotted with interesting rock outcrops. Eventually the way begins to veer left, more steeply uphill and away from the highway. At this point another trail continues straight ahead, dropping downhill. This is but one example of several branching paths that might lure you from the main trail. Ignore the right-hand fork and follow the clearer path to the left. After a series of short switchbacks, yet another false trail leads downhill. Bear left again and climb a few more yards to the ridgetop. Turning left, follow the trail south along the ridgeline toward the summit.

Before you reach the top, the trail becomes less distinct

and then fades away. Here you get to practice the challenge of route finding. Climb a few yards to the right, then cut left directly for the summit. Clambering over the rocks for the last few yards should be easy and fun.

From the top there is a good view of Twin Sisters, to the south over a bump on Lily. Panning to the right from there you'll see Meadow and St. Vrain mountains, the Longs Peak group, the Front Range and, away to the north, the Mummy Range. The extensive red-roofed buildings of the YMCA of the Rockies lie below, in the northwest. In the valley to the northeast, ranchland and residences extend along Fish Creek to Estes Park and Lake Estes. All in all, the summit of Lily Mountain is a pleasant, satisfying sort of place, well worth the effort it takes to get there.

Rams Horn (Teddys Teeth) and Gianttrack from Marys Lake (Roosevelt National Forest)

All parts of the long green ridge running north and south between the Aspen Brook-Wind River drainage and the Fish Creek drainage once were lumped together under the bland and overused appellation of Sheep Mountain. Then more people began to live near and on the ridge, resulting in more imaginative and interesting names for three high points — Lilly, Rams Horn and Gianttrack mountains. From the west, in the vicinity of the YMCA of the Rockies, Rams Horn is called Teddys Teeth because of the three protruding cliffs at the top. They were named after a feature of Theodore Roosevelt's smile as portrayed in political cartoons of his day. Similarly, Gianttrack once gained the name of Holy Hill from the number of clergy who took vacations in summer cabins on its western slope.

Rams Horn draws a goodly number of climbers because it is so dramatic to the thousands of visitors utilizing the YMCA of the Rockies. In recent years, as new houses sprouted on the mountain's western slope, conflicts developed between landowners and hikers. Now it is best to climb both Rams Horn and Gianttrack via a powerline right-of-way leading from Marys Lake, on the eastern side. This is an easier route, anyway; you start 200 feet higher, and the distance to be covered is slightly less.

From U.S. Highway 66, west of Estes Park and just east of the complicated intersection leading into Rocky Mountain National Park, drive south up Marys Lake Road for 1.4 miles to Marys Lake. Park at the western end of this reservoir. Hike west up the four-wheel-drive road beneath power lines that climb to the saddle between Rams Horn (left) and Gianttrack (right). It is a stiff puff-and-pant for the final few hundred yards.

Once on top of the saddle, you can reach Gianttrack by traversing to its southwest slope, which is less steep and where the rock walking is easier. Pick whatever way seems easiest to the top. At the summit there are some interesting limber pines and a cairn.

To reach Teddys Teeth, turn left (south) from the saddle. A path leads through an open area and becomes more distinct with the help of cairns as it passes into woods. Through forested and open stretches with fine views the trail climbs the ridgeline. It becomes quite steep and rocky in one section, beyond which blue paint splashed on rocks marks (or vandalizes, depending on one's point of view) a route to the summit.

From the top of the cliffs, excellent mountain panoramas spread out to the west. Immediately below lies the large complex of roads and buildings which make up the YMCA of the Rockies. Above, you might look for golden eagles or red-tailed hawks, soaring on thermal air currents.

Wild Basin

The views in Wild Basin are not particularly spectacular until you hike in three or four miles. But the creeks are very fine, the woods more so, and the wildflowers usually outstanding. Furthermore, Wild Basin trails are uncrowded compared with Bear Lake Road trails or with Estes Park on the Fourth of July. Trailhead parking is limited, though, and car pooling and/or arriving early are advisable.

To reach the Wild Basin trails, drive south from Estes Park on State Highway 7 for more than 11 miles through the village of Meeker Park to a large sign indicating Wild Basin Ranger Station. Turn right and follow the paved road to Wild Basin Lodge (a few hundred yards). Turn right again on the unpaved road that will extend two miles into Wild Basin to the ranger station.

Soon after leaving the lodge, the road passes over the dam that forms _Copeland Lake_. At the eastern end of the lake is the Sandbeach Lake Trailhead (see below). Copeland Lake is a good place to photograph Copeland Mountain. Early in the morning, the massive, round-topped peak often is reflected by the still waters of the lake, provided the city of Longmont, which owns the lake, has not drawn off the water to use down on the plains.

Past Copeland Lake, much of the road is one car wide and dusty. Whenever you reach a fork, take the left-hand branch; all the left-hand forks go to the ranger station. If you arrive before 9 A.M. you probably will not meet anyone leaving. Driving out will be more difficult later in the day because of increased traffic. Really, the road is perfect — passable in any passenger car without damage to car or occupants — but discouraging to folks who just want a nice

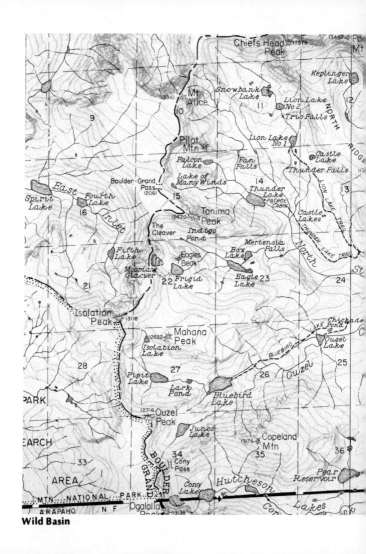

Wild Basin

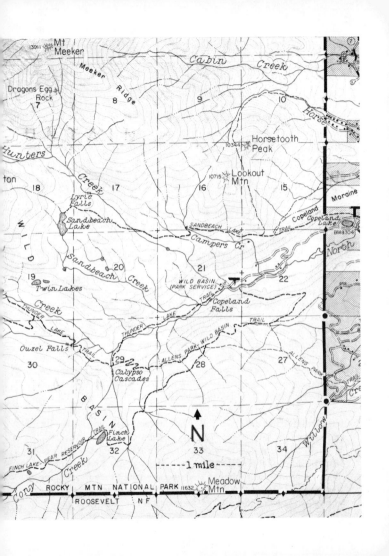

place to take a drive. Park at the end of the road, at the ranger station.

Ouzel Falls Trail System

The Ouzel Falls Trail System begins at a bridge across Hunters Creek, south of the picnic area at the end of the road. A mere .3 mile of easy, pleasant trail brings you to *Copeland Falls*, a somewhat sudden drop in North St. Vrain Creek. It is a pretty spot and well worth a picture (morning light is best) but no more spectacular than several unnamed places along the creek, which the trail follows for the next mile.

A little more than a mile from Copeland Falls, you cross North St. Vrain Creek on a substantial log bridge. Photographers using shutter speeds of 1/125 of a second or faster will stop this spectacular display of rushing water with sparkling droplets hanging in the air. Resting your camera on the bridge railing and shooting at 1/15 of a second will blur the water into cotton-candy smoothness.

Past the bridge, the trail climbs rather steeply for less than a quarter-mile. Where the path bends left, you can walk straight ahead onto a large boulder and look down on the confluence of North St. Vrain Creek on the right and Cony Creek on the left. The trail continues through subalpine forest along Cony Creek to *Calypso Cascades*. Named for the little pink calypso orchids which bloom nearby in July, this outstanding white-water scene is best photographed (oddly enough) at the time when most hikers arrive, toward midday.

There is a trail junction at Calypso Cascades. The trail to the left is a branch of the Finch Lake Trail System (see below). Take the trail to the right for *Ouzel Falls*, crossing Cony Creek via two bridges. You will have a pleasant walk along a fairly level path through woods, oddly quiet now that the creek is behind you. Then, climbing a couple of wide switchbacks, you become able to see through the trees north to Mount Meeker and Longs Peak. Meeker gives the false impression of being the taller of the two peaks because it is closer.

Water ouzel (dipper)

Past the switchbacks, begin to listen for the sound of Ouzel Falls, which ranks among the most spectacular in the park. From the trail's bridge across Ouzel Creek it is possible to see the falls, but the best view is obtained by climbing up the hill just before reaching the bridge. There are worn paths of a sort weaving in and out. None is better than another, all are informal and the very slick rocks can cause a tumble anywhere. The falls can be photographed from many different angles with normal or wide-angle lenses. Morning light, before ten o'clock, is best.

After crossing Ouzel Creek on the bridge, the trail circles below the ridge from which Ouzel Falls falls and reaches a spot where there is another view of Longs and Meeker. At .4 mile from the falls you arrive at another trail junction. The Thunder Lake Trail goes right (see below), and the Bluebird Lake Trail goes left.

The _Bluebird Lake Trail_ climbs steeply south from the junction to the crest of a moraine. Once on top, you will find the grade much more gradual as far as a point 1.3 miles from the junction, where a spur heads left to _Ouzel Lake_. The half-mile spur is often wet but is very lovely, as is the lake itself. Ouzel and Manaha peaks are the most photogenic mountains seen from the lake and are best pictured from the northern shore.

Ouzel Lake is dominated by the imposing bulk of _Copeland Mountain_. To climb Copeland, cross the lake's outlet and fight your way through half-a-mile of heavy subalpine forest to the top of a tree-covered ridge. Bear right there, following the ridge southwest for a half-mile to tree line. From tree line it is a tiresome tundra trudge past innumerable discouraging false summits to the top of this massive mountain. Copeland is the tallest peak on the southern side of Wild Basin, and the view from the top is spectacular.

The Bluebird Lake Trail continues past the Ouzel Lake spur for a half-mile to _Chickadee Pond_. Although you can see the lily-covered pond to the left of the trail, to reach the shore you must strike off through the woods. At the water's edge, follow a marshy track around the northern shore to an ancient beaver dam at the eastern end of the pond, where there often are fine displays of subalpine flowers. You will get soaked knees and elbows photographing them. The Pond lilies plus the strategic location make a photo of Ouzel Peak from Chickadee more interesting than from nearby Ouzel Lake.

Past Chickadee Pond the trail traverses a small boulder field and passes through subalpine forest. The forest is followed by a subalpine meadows where yellow snowlillies bloom in late June. A small waterfall tumbles into this garden all summer. The path runs through rocks and back into trees and ever-increasing flowers to a meadow 5.6 miles from the trailhead. In a marshy area where the trail crosses Ouzel Creek, look for tiny white bog-orchids among the many wildflowers. Often, too, there is an ice cave upstream at the foot of a gully where the creek has carved its way through a deep snowdrift.

After crossing Ouzel Creek, the path steepens dramatically while climbing parallel to the stream, which is out of sight on the opposite side of a narrow ridge. The beaten track frequently disappears on bedrock or under snow, so it may be necessary to search for cairns.

Most hikers are shocked to find a large concrete dam forming a lake at the top of such a lung-popping climb, six miles from the trailhead, but that is the case with Bluebird Lake. The dam is in a state of disrepair, allowing the water to drop many feet below its original maximum level. As of this writing, the city of Longmont holds the water rights to Bluebird Lake. The best view of the lake and of Ouzel Peak rising out of the water is from the southern shore, over and around various rock outcrops.

The trail ends at the lake. To reach higher goals, cross the dam and keep on climbing to the north. After you have gained about 200 feet in elevation above the lake, bear to your left (west) across slabs of rock and tundra. Where the drainage becomes wider and less steep you find _Lark Pond_. West from there it is an easy meander to _Pipet Lake_, about a mile from Bluebird.

Pipet is bleak, despite a rim of bistort and avens. Isolation and Ouzel peaks, stark rock towers, rise on either side. Between them is a barren pass which looks almost as though the glacier that sculpted it melted only yesterday. Few patches of green soften the harsh landscape.

Clambering up to the pass for closer examination, however, reveals that life has taken hold. Patches of tundra are vibrant with the color of alpine flowers, delicate yet rugged. From the top of the pass, a left-hand (south) turn heads along the ridgetop for the summit of _Ouzel Peak_. At first the ridge is narrow and nearly as steep on the west side as on the side you ascended. This is the line of the continental divide. Climb along the west side of the ridge, crossing rocks and tundra below the crest. Eventually, you walk above the area of glacial action onto a broad slope leading to the top of Ouzel. The view is magnificent, of course; you look down into Wild Basin and Paradise Park Research Natural Area.

A walk of an additional mile along the tundra, on the continental divide, takes you to _Ogalalla Peak_. Halfway there you'll bypass Cony Pass, a route of descent to either Junco Lake, south of Bluebird, or Cony Lake in the Finch Lake Trail System (see below).

A right-hand turn from the pass between Ouzel and Isolation peaks leads north along the continental divide to _Isolation Peak_. It is a steep trudge along the narrow ridge past five false summits to the true summit. Since Isolation is higher than nearby Mahana and Ouzel peaks, the view from there is superior. From Isolation the prospect south to Indian Peaks is unobstructed.

A popular route of descent is via the broad saddle between Isolation and Mahana. From the saddle you can descend directly to _Eagle Lake_ or take a side jaunt to _Frigid Lake_. The direct route is to walk north downhill to a broad shelf below the saddle, follow a border of alpine willows to the edge of the shelf and drop down to Eagle Lake. For the side trip to Frigid Lake, circle downhill from the saddle along the base of Isolation and cross snow to the lake. To go from Frigid to Eagle, make your way down to the broad shelf and follow the route described above. You can circle Eagle Lake on the southern (right) shore, descend to Box Lake and exit via the Thunder Lake Trail (see below).

Rather than climbing north and west from Bluebird to Pipet Lake, you can contour south from the dam and ascend the ridge between Bluebird and the outlet stream from Junco Lake. Junco Lake is three-quarters mile from the dam. From Junco it is a rough half-mile uphill to Cony Pass, which is situated south of Junco between a ridge of Copeland Mountain and the continental divide. From Cony Pass you can drop down to Cony Lake and exit via Finch Lake (see below).

Back at the Bluebird-Thunder Lake junction, you can continue straight ahead on the right-hand fork along an easy grade toward *Thunder Lake.* You cross a bridge over North St. Vrain Creek .4 mile from the junction and follow the trail through a tight switchback and up steepening grades. At 1.3 miles from the bridge there is a junction with the Lion Lakes Trail, which goes to the right (see below).

Take the left-hand (lower) fork and continue on through a set of switchbacks and limber pines struggling amid rocks. Then subalpine fir and Engelmann spruce enclose the trail, and the grade becomes less steep. Soon a faint path strikes downhill to the left toward Box and Eagle lakes (see below). Continuing on the level, you cross a large stream, then a smaller one and at last reach the top of a wooded slope above Thunder Lake.

Descend with the trail to a meadow at the eastern end of the lake, 6.8 miles from the Wild Basin Trailhead. The meadow is marshy in spots; stalks of pink blossoms growing there on close inspection turn out to be elephantheads, or little red elephants. A log patrol cabin at Thunder Lake is kept locked, but its long eaves give shelter from afternoon showers. Slosh east through the meadow to get damp feet and a good photo of the cabin, lake and Boulder-Grand Pass with the peaks in the background.

To reach Boulder-Grand Pass, follow a trail around the northern (right) shore of Thunder Lake. Two streams feed the lake from the west. The first one (northernmost) comes from *Falcon Lake*, about three-quarters mile away and more than 580 feet higher than Thunder. The second one flows from *Lake of Many Winds,* a boulder-bordered pond immediately below the pass. Cross both streams. Then, avoiding marshes, climb through woods and rocks to the vicinity of Lake of Many Winds. Circle it on the left and, staying to the right of a prominent snowfield, scramble slowly up loose rock to the pass.

Broad tundra extends downhill from Boulder-Grand Pass toward as fine a string of paternoster lakes as ever a glacier carved (see "Grand Lake," East Inlet Trail). A left turn at the pass presents an uncomplicated ascent over tundra to the top of _Tanima Peak_. Hikers turning right at the pass have a much longer ridgetop journey to the summit of Mount Alice. Most people climb Alice from Lion Lakes and descend via Boulder-Grand Pass.

Leaving the Thunder Lake Trail at 4.8 miles from the Wild Basin Trailhead, the _Lion Lakes Trail_ climbs straight up the hill for about 100 rocky yards. The grade then becomes more reasonable as the trail snakes through large boulders and levels on a crest. After a descent into subalpine forest, which gets your hopes up, the trail again shoots steeply uphill. Steepness is followed by moderation and steepness and moderation and swamp.

At the marshy area, the trail becomes faint while the mosquitoes become strong. Of course, this would be the best spot for photographing magestic Mount Alice, to the west. A little pond here usually is still and provides a more dependable reflecting surface for Alice than does Lion Lake No. 1 a few yards farther ahead. It is very pleasant to sit a spell on relatively soft and dry meadows by the shore of Lion Lake No. 1.

But there is much to lure you on. A short walk along the northeastern shore presents good views of Tanima Peak rising behind a small rock- and tree-covered ridge. Very lush meadows border the stream between Lion Lake No. 1 and _Trio Falls_ Immediately beyond the falls is Lion Lake No. 2, which may have more snow on its shore than _Snowbank Lake_, a short way farther up the drainage.

From Snowbank you can veer left to the top of a ridge leading uphill to the saddle between Mount Alice and Chiefs Head Peak, to the north. Very fine photos of the east face of Alice are available from the ridge. Having hiking companions in the foreground of your pictures helps give an idea of the immensity of this sheer rock wall. From the saddle there is an interesting northern view looking down on Lake Powell in its cirque below McHenrys Peak. Chiefs Head is seldom climbed from this saddle because there is a shorter way to get there (see below, Sandbeach Lake Trail System).

To reach the summit of Alice, you turn left at the saddle and descend for a short distance along the continental divide on rocks that look more difficult to pass over than they really are. The route is easiest on the right-hand (western) side of the ridge. Actually, the rocks are quite interesting and definitely should be included as a frame for a photo of the North Inlet valley, to the west. A little ridgetop notch at the bottom of the descent is a cozy, pleasant place carpeted with patches of tundra.

From the notch, it takes a certain amount of will to begin the very steep ascent, over boulders, of the final long slope to Alice's summit. Again, the route is less awful than it appears. As you approach the top, bear to the right (west) to avoid a false summit on the left (east). From the summit, the bulk of Chiefs Head Peak diminishes the drama of Longs Peak and Pagoda Mountain; Mount Meeker, on the other hand, looks singularly pointed.

There is well over a mile of downhill tundra walking to Boulder-Grand Pass from the top of Alice. The alpine flowers can be magnificent. Half-sliding down loose pebbles past Lake of Many Winds leads to snowlilies and Thunder Lake, the goal of your lengthy descent. But unless you have a camp there, it is a long seven miles out to the trailhead. After a fine climb like Alice, you will have a lot to think about on the way.

The trail to _Box_ and _Eagle lakes_ leaves the Thunder Lake Trail a little more than a half-mile before Thunder Lake. Descending through subalpine forest and meadows, the path disappears in the vicinity of North St. Vrain Creek. You should keep going in the same general direction through narrow slanting meadows lying between cliff and forest, then climb a steep, narrow gorge that levels off to a marsh. Skirt the marsh on the left and climb through flowered subalpine meadows following the brook that flows from **Box Lake**. A final spurt of energy through Krummholz takes you to Box Lake, in a basin carved from solid rock by glaciers.

Eagle Lake was similarly carved in a shelf 70 feet higher than Box Lake. To reach Eagle, climb up the rocks on the left-hand (southern) side of Box. Make your way through the least dense Krummholz to the edge of the lake.

More trials in the Krummholz along the northern shore take you to Eagle's outlet stream. There, in early September, we found the largest arctic gentian we have seen. From the same spot you can take a good photo of Mount Meeker featuring Box Lake in the lower part of the frame.

The most unusual sight at Eagle Lake appears a few yards downstream from the outlet — a tunnel. Big enough to walk into, with dynamite-fractured rock at its mouth and on the floor, it leads straight through the granite back toward Eagle Lake. It evidently was intended to provide a means of draining the lake when water was needed on the plains. Fortunately the tunnel remains unfinished, and Eagle Lake undrained.

Peak-baggers may want to add _Mahana Peak_ to their list by climbing it from Eagle Lake, even though Mahana is bounded on three sides by taller peaks. Make your way around the eastern end of Eagle Lake and climb by the least steep route over rocks to the shelf overhead. Follow the border of alpine willows uphill to a broad expanse below the Mahana-Isolation saddle. From there you can turn right to _Frigid Lake_, which sits below the base of Eagles Beak, nearly a mile's hike from Eagle Lake. Or you can climb on to Mahana, more than 1.2 miles from Eagle Lake. Head first for the broad easy saddle, because an attempt to cut straight up the peak may lead to a bothersome false summit. The true top is on the right (southwest) side of Mahana.

Sandbeach Lake Trail System

The Sandbeach Lake Trailhead lies at the eastern end of Copeland Lake. (For driving instructions to this point, see the beginning of this chapter.) From the lake the trail ascends steeply through sunny woods on Copeland Moraine. After .4 mile you climb across the Rocky Mountain National Park boundary. Eventually, you reach a ridgetop after a short set of switchbacks. Here a trail from Meeker Park comes in on the right, when you are 1.2 miles from Copeland Lake.

Continue climbing straight ahead at a steady rate for 1.1 miles to the crossing of Campers Creek. Exactly one mile farther on you cross Hunters Creek. After almost another mile of steady uphill hiking you arrive at Sandbeach Lake, 4.2 miles from Copeland Lake.

If this description of the hike to Sandbeach Lake has failed to stir your interest, it may be because until you reach the lake the trail is not terribly fascinating. The lake itself is pretty, with the high peaks in southern Wild Basin rising beyond, somewhat subdued by distance. And it serves as a jumping-off point for the three highest mountains in Rocky Mountain National Park — Longs Peak, Mount Meeker and Chiefs Head Peak — plus the difficult Pagoda Peak.

The actual point of departure for all these summits lies a short way back up the trail, before it reaches the lake. At the point where the trail turns southwest and begins to descend to the lake, climbers must strike off through the woods. The first step in climbing _Chiefs Head Peak_ is to climb _Mount Orton_. From the trail keep walking northwest, in the same direction the trail was heading before it turned toward the lake. Then bear a little to the left to cross a rivulet that flows into the lake and climb out of the trees onto a ridge above the lake. Keep heading uphill until you reach the top of Orton, a jumble of rocks on the eastern end of a crest leading to Chiefs Head.

Mount Orton is not particularly high, but you will notice before you reach the top that it is strategically located. The Orton Ridge (also called North Ridge) juts into Wild Basin from the surrounding mountain wall. Thus it provides a relatively convenient platform from which to view the entire basin.

Fairyslipper (calypso) orchids

From the top of Orton, which you can bypass easily on the right, it is an uncomplicated hike over tundra to the summit of Chiefs Head. The way becomes steeper at the end, naturally. Nearby peaks such as Mount Alice, McHenrys Peak, Pagoda Mountain, Mount Meeker and Longs Peak fill the panorama with grandeur.

The Wild Basin route up _Mount Meeker_ (see "Longs Peak and Nearby Goals" for an alternative route) leaves the Sandbeach Trail as it begins to descend to Sandbeach Lake: Bear to the right and cross Hunters Creek. Ascend the gully on the south side of Meeker, keeping to the left of Dragons Egg Rock which stands out obviously in the middle of the gully. As you draw even with the rock, bear left to climb Meeker's southwestern ridge. The final stretch along the ridge to the summit is steep but uncomplicated.

Pagoda Mountain usually is climbed from Glacier Gorge (see "Bear Lake Road," Glacier Gorge Trail System). But if you are in Wild Basin and get the urge to do Pagoda, leave the Sandbeach Trail as it turns down to the lake. Keep walking in the same direction the trail was heading, into the valley between Mounts Meeker and Orton.

Cross Hunters Creek and pick your way up the valley until you can turn right without scaling cliffs. Climb up the steep valley between Meeker and Pagoda to masses of loose rock — scree — at the base of Longs Peak. Scramble up this scree toward the cliffs on the right-hand side. Keep climbing the right-hand side of a huge cirque in the southeast face of Pagoda to the lowest point in the saddle between Longs and Pagoda. Long after you have grown thoroughly sick of loose rock, you will reach the saddle and turn left toward the summit. The terrain will guide you below the crest of the ridge to the very small summit of Pagoda, which is just as pointed as a mountaintop should be.

To climb _Longs Peak_ by the difficult route of the first ascent back in 1868, follow the above route (from the Sandbeach Trail to Pagoda) as far as the scree slopes at the base of Longs. Then look up for the Notch, on the right-hand side of the peak, and a wall to the right of it. Climb up the fan of loose rock farthest to the right below the wall. When the fan narrows, bear left and follow a diagonal ledge to the left. This becomes a gully (filled with loose rock, what else?) which eventually takes you to a small shelf below the vertical columns — the Palisades — to the right of the Notch.

On ledges to the left of the gully, traverse a few hundred feet across cliffs. Then climb diagonally left to the base of the Homestretch. Follow the red-and-yellow painted bull's-eyes up the 45-degree slope to the summit.

This route up Longs was discovered by L.W. Keplinger, who scouted it for explorer John Wesley Powell. Nearby *Keplinger Lake* commemorates the intrepid scout. To reach Keplinger Lake, climb Mount Orton. If you wish, you can bypass the top of Orton and contour along its northern slope to Hunters Creek. The traverse will necessitate some steep side-hill walking and perhaps a slight loss in elevation, but it will keep you out of dense Krummholz traps that require magic to pass through. Follow Hunters Creek upstream past large boulders to its source, Keplinger Lake. A cirque hangs dramatically over the lake on the southwest face of Pagoda.

Finch Lake Trail System

The Finch Lake Trailhead is located about 1000 feet east of the bridge that crosses North St. Vrain Creek to Wild Basin Ranger Station. Look for an identification sign on the left-hand (south) side of the road.

From the road the trail climbs steadily eastward through heavy forest along a lateral moraine. The trees disappear at the top of the moraine where the path switchbacks toward the west, nearly a mile from the trailhead. The path passes on a level grade through aspens and lodgepole pines, then runs gradually downhill to an intersection with trails from Meadow Mountain Ranch (on the park's eastern border) and the little town of Allenspark.

Take the trail farthest right (north), continue on through an aspen grove and resume climbing via wide switchbacks. Visible to the north (right) across Wild Basin are Chiefs Head, Pagoda Mountain and Mount Meeker. The bulk of Meeker hides all but a corner of Longs.

Another intersection appears 2.3 miles from the trailhead. For its mysterious power to baffle hikers, this spot is dubbed Confusion Junction. The trail on the right winds down through subalpine forest for about 1.5 miles to Calypso Cascades (see above). The trail on the left starts out uphill but soon drops through thick woods to meet the Allenspark Trail, coming from the previous intersection. Allenspark is about two miles from Confusion Junction.

The middle path leads along a mostly moderate grade to Finch Lake. As the trail flattens about two miles from the second intersection, it crosses several streams. After the last crossing, it leads over a small ridge and down to Finch Lake, 4.5 miles from the trailhead. Finch often is calm and reflects Copeland Mountain. The best photo may be had from just off-trail on the eastern shore of the lake.

The trail goes around Finch Lake on the northern side. The two miles of uphill trail from Finch to Pear Reservoir are pretty but rather steep and sloppy in places. Snow there lasts far into the summer. When it finally does melt, excellent flower displays spring up in response to the abundant water.

The trail reaches Pear Reservoir at the best place for taking fine photos of the always-dramatic Ouzel Peak. A sheer-faced ridge of Copeland Mountain will also add a share of drama to the picture. Follow the path as it bears left at the dam along the southeastern shore. Among the rocks along the trail roughly 100 yards past the reservoir hide rare dwarf columbine.

The trail is not maintained beyond Pear, but it is obvious nonetheless. Passing between two unnamed ponds, and quite close to one of them, you leave Rocky Mountain National Park and enter Roosevelt National Forest. Soon you reach the lowest of the _Hutcheson Lakes_, in the Cony Creek drainage. These lakes can be reached also via the Middle St. Vrain Trail System (see "Indian Peaks East of the Divide," Middle St. Vrain Trail System).

Stay north of and higher than the lowest Hutcheson Lake and continue up the drainage. The way is marshy in places and lined with Krummholz in others. At the largest of the Hutcheson Lakes, you reenter the national park. The setting here at tree line is spectacular, with Ogalalla Peak rising in the background.

Cross the outlet of the largest Hutcheson Lake and angle uphill on the left-hand (south) side. Follow Cony Creek upstream from where it tumbles over a cliff into the lake. Circle with the creek around a buttress jutting from the south, and walk across rocks and tundra to _Cony Lake_. Situated high above tree line, Cony Lake is devoid even of bushes. Its shore is more tundra than rock. Glacier-sculpted peaks rise directly from the water. The entire effect makes a very fine photo; you will want to use a wide-angle lens. Rocks or hiking companions in the foreground will add interest to the rather plain shoreline.

Indian Peaks, East of the Divide (Roosevelt National Forest)

Indian Peaks east of the continental divide is in Roosevelt National Forest. For hikers, however, Indian Peaks trails form a unit with the trails in Rocky Mountain National Park, adjacent to the north. But hikers in the national park tend to be cosmopolitan, while hikers in this part of the national forest tend to be Colorado residents from the nearby Denver-Boulder megalopolis.

Because trailheads are situated relatively high on Indian Peaks' eastern slope, many destinations are close to roads. The combination of short easy trails to spectacular spots and a large urban area's proximity guarantee crowds at Indian Peaks.

There are two ways to avoid the crowds. First start hiking at dawn. This practice is less painful than it seems and yields benefits far too numerous to list. Second, get together with hiking friends and use two vehicles, leaving them at opposite trailheads. Thus, one group can start at each trailhead, rendezvous on the trail and exchange car keys. Alternatively, you can set up a complicated shuttle and have everyone begin at the same trailhead. Starting in one spot and ending in another is a logistical bother, however, so relatively few people do it. Somewhere between the two trailheads, the crowds begin to thin out. Of course, you also experience more terrain in this way.

Regulations for wilderness use in the national forest are not terribly different from regulations instituted to protect the national park backcountry. In the national forest you do not, at present, have to obtain a backcountry camping permit. But you should choose a campsite on a dry forest floor (not in a meadow) at least 100 yards from lakes, streams and trails. Campfires are permitted but

Indian Peaks, East of the Divide

discouraged in favor of backpacking stoves. Unlike in the park, leashed pets are allowed on national forest trails.

Pawnee Pass Trail

To reach trailheads in the *Brainard Lake* area, drive to the old mining town of Ward on State Highway 72. Just north of Ward, turn west at a sign that indicates the paved access road to Indian Peaks.

Early in the season (June) this road may be closed at a temporary trailhead a few miles from the highway. A short hike past this road closure takes you to *Red Rocks Lake*, which has a good view of striking peaks to the west. After 1.5 miles more you reach Brainard Lake, a highly developed but very scenic campground area. A paved road circling the lake runs one-way to the right, crossing a bridge at the outlet. The road is the shortest route on foot to the Long Lake and Mitchell Lake trailheads.

Once the access road is free of melting snow, the soggy subalpine soil presumably has dried enough to withstand the tramping of thousands of booted feet. Hoping that everybody will stay on-trail, the Forest Service then opens the access road all the way to Brainard Lake and the two trailheads. At a fork in the road beyond Brainard, 5.7 miles from Route 72, you can turn right to reach the Mitchell Creek Trailhead or left to reach the Long Lake Trailhead for the Pawnee Pass Trail, which connects Long Lake with Lake Isabelle.

Forest Service regulations reserve the parking area at Long Lake Trailhead for day hikers. Backpackers who wish to leave their car overnight should drop their gear at the trailhead (with a guard) and park the car at designated areas about a half-mile back down the road toward Brainard Lake. This practice makes for more efficient use of parking space and cuts down on the demand for land to be bulldozed and paved. Additionally, cars left overnight in areas designated for that purpose may be somewhat more secure than others because they are more closely watched by Forest Service personnel.

NATURE WALK TO LAKE ISABELLE (SUBALPINE ZONE)

The forest around the Pawnee Pass Trail is a good example of the subalpine zone of vegetation. Many hikers feel that a path in this zone provides the most pleasant walking found anywhere. The first stretch of the trail is particularly nice because it is flat.

The dominant growth along the way is Engelmann spruce and subalpine fir. Both are short-needled conifers whose needles grow individually from the twigs. Close examination reveals obvious differences between the two trees. The easiest test is to grab a branch; if it hurts, the tree is a spruce. Spruce needles are four-sided, stiff and sharp. Fir needles are flat, soft and blunt.

There are other differences as well. Engelmann spruce cones are brown, have parchmentlike scales and hang down from the branches. You probably can see some of these small (less than two inches long) cones that have fallen to the ground. Fir cones, on the other hand, are dark purple to black and grow erect in the top of the tree. When fir cones are ready to spread their seeds, the scales do not open as do those of spruce and pines. Rather, the scales merely fall off, leaving the cores of the cones standing bare and upright.

The trunk of a subalpine fir generally is smooth and gray in color; after it grows to a foot or so in diameter, it becomes furrowed near the base. Blisters containing pitch are scattered over the smooth bark. The bark of an Engelmann spruce begins to flake off while the tree still is young. With age the trunk becomes red-brown and develops a scaly texture.

The plant life along this section of trail is relatively lush because the subalpine zone, extending from 9000 feet to about 11,500 feet above sea level, gets more moisture than any other zone in Colorado. More than 22 inches of annual precipitation is normal here, almost double the amount expected down on the plains. Furthermore, snow is blown from the mountaintops and accumulates in this zone, providing additional moisture vital to luxuriant growth.

Protected by the trees from wind and hot rays of the sun, snow remains here far into the summer. Melting slowly, snowbanks serve as reservoirs, constantly watering the trees during their short growing season. Thanks to the steady water supply, the forest grows taller and denser, providing more shade to protect more snow to nourish more growth and so on in a circle of cooperation. There is a fascination in this system's efficiency that only water-starved westerners can appreciate fully.

The forest shade is not the only reason for a supply of water. The forest floor is rich with years' accumulation of rotting needles and other plant material. Their decay adds humus to the bits of minerals produced by disintegrating rock. The combination of organic and inorganic material creates fine-grained dark soil which retains water.

In drier areas in the mountains, where plant growth is much slower, little organic material is contributed to the soil. There the soil is light in color and consists of larger particles. It has no humus to hold it together, and water percolates quickly away. In the case of water so essential to plant survival, it is surely true that "Them that has, gets."

Forming a continuous ground cover over much of the damp forest floor is grouseberry, or broom huckleberry. This type of blueberry has small leaves which turn bright red in fall and tiny urn-shaped flowers which mature to small red berries. The berries are fairly tasty, although less so than some other members of the blueberry family. They are a favorite food of many species of wildlife, including the blue grouse.

Flowers common in shady areas along the trail include Jacobs-ladder, with sky blue blossoms and ladderlike leaves whose leaflets grow opposite each other on a central stalk, and arnica, which are totally yellow composites. Growing in sunny areas is the brilliant dark pink fireweed, named not for color but for a tendency to invade areas that have been opened up by forest fires or other disturbances such as avalanches.

Less conspicuous plants are the lichens, the gray-green splotches that you see on rocks next to the path. Lichens represent a relationship in nature called mutualism, or symbiosis — a partnership between algae and fungi. The algae, which contain chlorophyll, produce food for the fungi. The fungi, in turn, absorb and store water for the algae. They cooperate so well that lichens thrive where no other plants can survive. On bare rocks, in hot deserts, in the frigid Arctic, lichens of many varieties display the advantages of partners working together for their common good.

These crusty plants actually contribute to the disintegration of rocks and the building of soil. Lichens adhere very strongly to the rock surface. When they are wet, their colors (which can be far more varied than those here) are brilliant; but when they dry out and their colors fade, they shrink or curl up. This small movement tends to loosen the bits of rock to which the lichens are attached, causing some particles to fall away as sand.

Lichens further break down rock by secreting small amounts of organic acids, which, mixed with water, gradually dissolve the bonding material that holds the rock together. Such acids are comparatively weak, of course, and the wearing away of a rock is not noticeable in several human generations.

Soon after leaving the trailhead, you see the woods to your left opening up along the banks of South St. Vrain Creek. The name of St. Vrain is scattered all over the Indian Peaks and Wild Basin areas, and it has a colorful history. The brothers Ceran and Marcellin St. Vrain were nineteenth-century traders who swapped the goods of civilization with Indians in exchange for furs and hides.

The profit was vanishing from the beaver trade in 1837, when the St. Vrain brothers built Fort St. Vrain on the South Platte River. Yet they and their partners, the Bents, managed to do well. Experienced traders, they exploited the expertise of mountain men like Kit Carson who knew the trapping business well but had been reduced to picking the bones of a dying trade. Such men still operated efficiently in the Colorado Rockies, which had not yet been trapped out like the mountains farther north in Wyoming.

The site of the St. Vrain trading post was well chosen, being easily accessible to the Indians. The Bents and St. Vrains were the

Big-rooted spring beauty

fairest traders in a generally unscrupulous business. Soon their honorable dealings had gained them the entire business of the Southern Cheyenne and most of the Arapahos. By their unheard-of honesty, they were able to maintain a nearly permanent truce among the constantly warring customers in the vicinity of the post.

But mainly the St. Vrains were just smart businessmen: they diversified. Their economic base consisted of not only the very shaky beaver trade but of trade with Santa Fe, and a general retail business. Eventually, after gold was discovered, there was a St. Vrain trading post in the new town of Denver.

South St. Vrain Creek, which you see from the Pawnee Pass Trail, flows into a creek which in turn flows into the South Platte just upstream from the St. Vrain brothers' 1837 trading post. The peaks that surround you were named for the St. Vrains' Indian customers.

A quarter-mile from the trailhead a dam across the creek forms _Long Lake_. Here the trail divides. The left-hand branch crosses the dam and divides again: a turn to the left takes you back down to Brainard Lake at the Niwot picnic area. A turn to the right takes you on a loop trail that circles Long Lake, providing fine views of the jagged peaks rising overhead, and meets the Pawnee Pass Trail above the lake.

From the loop trail you can head uphill to the tundra slopes on broad _Niwot Ridge._ If you elect to go all the way to the ridgetop, you will arrive at the boundary of the Boulder Watershed. The city of Boulder is very diligent about keeping people out of this area, however, and you would be better off acceding to its wishes.

It is even more important to avoid disrupting the natural history experiments being conducted on Niwot Ridge by the Institute of Arctic and Alpine Research. Years of data collecting can be ruined by one careless step or handling of markers. It also is well to refrain from poking around inside the mountain research station building that IAAR maintains on the ridge.

Back on the Pawnee Pass Trail before the dam at Long Lake — the eastern end — follow the right-hand fork along a level grade roughly parallel to the lake's northern shore. Long Lake is long indeed, extending about a third of the way to Isabelle Lake. In several places the trail is built up above bogs. These are excellent spots to observe the results of plant succession.

Pools of water are formed by glacial action or by the blocking of drainages by beavers or human beings. Tiny algal plants are the first vegetation to invade these pools. Some algae float; others find a home on wet rocks at the water's edge. Among the rocks, moisture-loving mosses and liverworts (some species resemble lobed livers; "wort" is Old English for "plant") also establish plant communities. These pioneer plants help to create soil on the margin of the pond as do lichens on the surface of a rock. Although it is a small beginning, it is important.

The seeds of various plants land on the mud at the shoreline; others end up in shallow water; still others come to rest in deeper water. Then they germinate and grow according to specific adaptations to specific pond environments. Some species grow submerged entirely in deep water. Others are rooted in mud in shallower water, and their leaves float on the surface. There are no floating-leaf varieties along this path, but they are obvious in Red Rocks Lake, which you passed en route to Brainard Lake.

The most common and varied seed-producing water plants are the sedges, rushes and water grasses growing in shallow water along the pond's margin. Various willows and other deciduous shrubs spring up around the soggy shore. Farther from the water are dry land grasses, and then the coniferous forest. You easily can see most of these concentric zones of vegetation in the marshes next to Long Lake.

Year after year the plants grow and die, slowly depositing layers of dead organic material. The process of decay builds soil composed mostly of humus. Humus and other material carried by wind and running water gradually fill in the pond, lowering the water level and drying out the margins.

Plants that require drier habitat invade the filled-in edges of the pond. The ones that need water over their roots begin to grow in a ring closer to the pond's center as the entire body of water becomes shallower. Plants requiring deep water, which no longer exists, no longer can survive in the pond.

The plant life continues to change as the pool gradually shrinks and is succeeded by marsh, which is succeeded by meadow, which is succeeded by forest. In the subalpine zone, plant succession stops with Engelmann spruce and subalpine fir, the so-called climax plants. Of course, fire can destroy a spruce-fir forest, including its humus soil. In such a situation, lodgepole pine and quaking aspen tend to succeed. Centuries later, spruce-fir again will take over and will grow until beavers or people build another pond or until fire sweeps the area once more. Change is the most universal condition in nature.

The flowers that are obvious along this section of the Pawnee Pass Trail are typical of wet subalpine areas. White marsh-marigold is the first to appear after snow has melted in the sunny bogs. In midsummer, rose crown with its fleshy leaves is very conspicuous. The deep pink spikes of elephanthead (little red elephant) blossoms are beautiful from a distance and fascinating close up. Each blossom looks like the flower's name. Fireweed grows in drier areas, a brightly garbed herald of the encroaching forest.

Past the marshes, the trail once more enters pure subalpine climax forest. Frequently on grand old trees you will see burls, which are flattened hemispheres bulging from the trunks. A burl generally originates at the site of an adventitious bud — a bud that grows at an abnormal place, such as the side of a tree trunk, where the plant is not putting on any length. Such buds have no vascular system to carry water or minerals to nourish growth. The buds are eventually covered by trunk tissues — burls — having very dense, contorted, wild and disorderly grain structure. Analogous growths on humans are termed cancer.

We hope that the medical term will not uglify burls for you. Burls are benign in that they do no harm to the tree. And when trees are cut for lumber, burls themselves can be valuable. Their natural shape suggests their transformation into wooden bowls, which are much desired for their beautiful mottled grain. The grain makes burls appropriate as veneer, thin slices of wood used to overlay less attractive wood, particularly in furniture.

Furthermore, burls are beautiful growing on the tree. The way their round shapes contrast with the rough texture of the bark inspires some very fine photos. Often a tripod and a slow shutter speed are necessary for getting maximum depth of field in close-ups in less than bright forest light.

The philosopher of Ecclesiastes stated that God "has made everything beautiful in its time." That broad generalization is proven true in the forest, where even a cancerous deformity becomes a thing of beauty. Conservationist John Muir observed that all things in nature, "however mysterious and lawless at first sight they may seem, are only harmonious notes in the song of creation, varied expressions of God's love."

About three-quarters mile from the trailhead, and in other places along the trail, you may notice a familiar-looking plant, a clover. Its leaves and flowers are easily recognized. Although there are native clovers in the Rockies, the clovers growing alongside this section of trail are aliens. They were introduced here by horses that ate hay brought in from the plains. The hay had clover seeds in it. The seeds passed through the horses' digestive systems and were deposited along the trail, fertilized and ready to grow.

No horses have been permitted on the Pawnee Pass Trail since 1965. Therefore it seems that these alien plants have been maintaining their population for a significant length of time without the help of any new seeds. So far as is known, the alien clover does not have a serious impact on the local ecosystems. But man's accidental introduction of alien organisms into natural areas often has been catastrophic. Water hyacinth clogs waterways in the South; alien insects have caused the destruction of chestnuts and elms in the East. Many more horror stories emphasize that we must be extremely careful not to introduce chaos into a delicately balanced system.

Past the western end of Long Lake, the trail divides. The left-hand fork is the loop trail around the lake. The right-hand fork begins, gradually at first, to climb toward Lake Isabelle and Pawnee Pass.

Soon the way levels out, and you will notice more marshland on the left. This is a classic example of plant succession, showing almost all the stages. There still remains a central pool, but it has been taken over almost completely by marsh.

This pool was considerably larger following the retreat of the last glacier 8000 years ago. The moving masses of ice carried rocky rubble to this point and dropped it when the ice melted. The ridge or moraine thus formed was piled up next to an older land form, and the depression between them filled with water.

Plant succession began very slowly at first because there was little time for plant development in the short growing season, and little or no soil for plant habitat. But succession picks up momentum, progressing at ever-increasing speed as more and more plants throw themselves into the task of creating soil. In terms of land formation, succession at the marsh is racing along at this time. Some change might be observable within one human generation.

As you walk past the marsh, high jagged peaks that have been hidden from sight for the last mile come into view to the west, supplying new drama and awesomeness. The sculpting power of snowflakes becomes immediately impressive.

About 27,000 years ago, the climate in this area cooled to the extent that snow at the top of the mountains failed to melt in summer. Snow began to accumulate in the low places between the peaks, where wind from the west dumped extra amounts and where it was protected to some extent from the sun. As more and more snow piled up, the bottom layers were crushed by the weight of the upper layers. The compacting pressure squeezed out all the air spaces, creating a solid mass of ice under perhaps 100 feet of snow. Eventually, the weight of snow and ice became so great that it forced the ice at the bottom to flow downhill, like molten plastic.

As a glacier flows, it carves the surrounding mountains in several ways. At the headwall, where the glacier first forms, summer meltwater seeps into cracks in the rocks, only to refreeze at night or

Pygmy nuthatch on Engelmann spruce

when winter returns. As it freezes, water expands, forcing the cracks to widen and eventually wedging off chunks of rock. The chunks are frozen into the glacier's mass and carried away in its flow.

Through the centuries this quarrying action forms steep cliffs, many of them shaped like bowls. The cliff-sided basin at a glacier's headwall is called a cirque. A part of a cirque is visible on the left side of Shoshoni Peak, the main double-pointed summit that dominates the view from the trail. The cirque's distinctive shape is not obvious from here, though. You will be able to pick out two classic cirques from Lake Isabelle.

As a glacier moves downhill, it quarries the rock beneath it, too. In this way it widens the floor and steepens the walls of the valley through which it flows, giving the valley a typical U-shape. Simultaneously, the ice carves away at softer areas of bedrock, forming giant ledges or stairs on the valley floor. The tons of rock carried by the ice act as the rasps on a file, enabling the glacier to scour basins on the ledges. When the ice finally melts, the basins become glacial lakes, or tarns. _Lake Isabelle_ is a tarn sitting on such a shelf.

To reach _Lake Isabelle,_ you must leave the nearly level grade where you have been walking and turn onto switchbacks that climb through the forest. It may seem easier to bypass the switchbacks and head straight uphill. This course may be quicker, but presumably you are having a good time and are in no big hurry to finish your walk. You would save absolutely nothing in total expenditure of energy by short-cutting the switchbacks.

And what is more important, short-cutting switchbacks does great harm. It causes unnecessary wear to the vegetation and soil, setting up a perfect path for destructive erosion. In one area along these switchbacks the Forest Service is trying to restore land severely damaged by short-cutting hikers.

Many folks are surprised to learn that trails are designed not so much to be easy on hikers as to be easy on the terrain. It is a happy arrangement that trails which protect the land also follow the easiest way to walk.

At the top of the switchbacks you traverse a steep meadow with a brook tumbling down it. The meadow is lush with colorful wildflowers. Particularly eye-catching is the dark pink Parry primrose, which grows right next to the water or on a cushion of soil atop rocks in the middle of the stream.

Ford the stream and bear left. (Heading right will take you over Pawnee Pass, see below.) Lake Isabelle is situated on the other side of a low ridge facing you to the west. Very likely you will have to cross a short patch of snow to get there.

Lake Isabelle has been enlarged by a small dam and converted to a reservoir. When the water is drawn down (as happens more and more frequently), the lake becomes an ugly mud flat, commemorating the corruption of what could be one of the loveliest tarns in Colorado. In any case, the mountains always are fine. As you face the lake, the long ridge rising behind you on the left is Niwot Ridge. The conical peak is Navajo; the double-humped peak to the right of Navajo is Apache. Shoshoni, on the far right, was pointed out earlier. There is a cirque with a permanent snowfield between Navajo and Apache. There is a second one between Apache and Shoshoni; in this cirque lies Isabelle Glacier, the source of South St. Vrain Creek.

Isabelle Glacier is the most easily accessible glacier described in this book. Like all the other glaciers in the area, it was born just 3,000 years ago during a slight cooling following a period when the climate was warmer than today. It is not a very active glacier; it is barely holding its own against the sun.

To reach Isabelle Glacier follow a path along Lake Isabelle's northern shore. At the western end of the lake, follow South St. Vrain Creek upstream from the inlet until Krummholz forces you to the right. Ascend over rocks and through small gullies, surmounting a series of glacial ledges toward the eastern end of the glacier, roughly two miles from the eastern end of Lake Isabelle.

An irresistible urge to climb up the glacier and slide down comes over some hikers at this point. That is unfortunate, because

sliders who splat down against them at high speed. The glacier is especially steep on the Apache Peak side. There have been serious injuries and at least one fatality here. Be careful.

No marked path exists up _Apache Peak_, but the least difficult route is obvious from the glacial shelves above Lake Isabelle. Bearing southwest of the South St. Vrain Creek drainage, pick your way over the boulders and head for the saddle on top of Apache between the left (lower) and right summits. Note a very steep slope covered with large loose rocks, called talus, to the right of the permanent snowfield between Navajo and Apache. This talus slope is the least difficult way past the cliffs that guard Apache's east face. Please do not kick the loose rocks down on the heads of climbers below you.

The most popular route for climbing _Navajo Peak_ begins in the same way as the route up Apache, on the glacial shelves above Lake Isabelle. On the level, bouldery floor of the cirque below Navajo's permanent snowfield, turn left to head up "airplane gully," which is the left-handmost of two obvious ravines on Navajo's flank. It is marked by the wreckage of a late-forties plane crash scattered throughout its entire length and at its base.

Airplane gully is full of small loose rocks, called scree. This stuff is extremely difficult to walk on (wade through) because it keeps slipping underfoot and carrying you back downhill. Even worse, it presents the real threat of accidentally bombarding climbers below with dangerous rocks.

A group's best method of overcoming this gully is to climb very close together so as to catch bounding rocks before they can pick up momentum. Stay very alert to what is happening above. No stolid concentration on your feet here; you'd miss a lot of scenery that way, anyhow. Short gaiters are nice for keeping rocks out of your boots.

At the top of the gully, turn right onto a tundra saddle. Continue west straight up the southeastern shoulder of Navajo toward the cliff-bounded summit tower. At the base of the southeastern section of the tower, look for a vertical gully, or chimney, that provides an interesting but easy climb to the summit.

Back in the meadow before Lake Isabelle, the trail to _Pawnee Pass_ turns to the right. It climbs upstream for a short way, then veers left (west), following a contour above the lake. About three-fourths of the way along the northern shore, it runs through a series of switchbacks which climb to a bench situated about 1000 feet above Lake Isabelle. There is a good overlook of the lake and excellent views of Navajo Peak as the trail winds up this bench toward Pawnee Pass. At a final series of switchbacks you leave the tundra of the bench and climb through boulders to more tundra at the pass.

West of Pawnee Pass, the trail goes downhill to _Pawnee Lake_. The slope is very steep and rocky, and the path is the most masterful example of sinuous, switchbacking trail construction in the entire area covered by this book. (For description of Pawnee Pass Trail beyond Pawnee Lake, see "Indian Peaks, West of the Divide," Cascade Trail to Pawnee Pass). The spire-decked western cliffs of Pawnee Peak are certainly worth a photo themselves, and they make a dramatic frame for a picture of Pawnee Lake. Photos of the spires need a hiker in the distant foreground to provide size perspective.

Turning right from the trail at Pawnee Pass, you can follow the continental divide over easy terrain, given the nearly 13,000-foot altitude, to the top of _Pawnee Peak_. Continuing north along the divide from Pawnee Peak is considered by many to be the easiest way up _Mount Toll_ (see below, Mitchell Creek Trail).

To climb _Shoshoni Peak_, strike left (south) from the Pawnee Pass Trail just before the final set of switchbacks east of the pass. Traverse the steep, rocky slope to the saddle between Shoshoni and an unnamed rise south of Pawnee Pass. Once on the saddle, you face a gentle tundra walk almost to the summit. The last 10 or 20 feet up the summit knob requires an easy rock scramble which might make acrophobic folks nervous.

Mitchell Creek Trail

To reach the Mitchell Creek Trailhead, drive to the road junction beyond Brainard Lake, 5.7 miles from State Highway 72 (see above, Pawnee Pass Trail). A right turn there takes you to the trailhead parking area, which is reserved for day use only. Backpackers should leave their car at the designated parking places close to Brainard Lake.

The Mitchell Creek Trail begins on the left-hand (south) side of the parking lot. (The Mount Audubon Trail System, covered below, begins on the north side.) Mitchell Creek is less than a half-mile away; the path runs fairly level through fine subalpine woods. After crossing the creek, the trail bears to the left, winds uphill to the level of _Mitchell Lake_ and meanders through more open woods to the lake itself. You may want to compose a photo of Mount Audubon rising from behind the trees on the opposite shore. At the outlet end of Mitchell Lake you can take a picture of Mount Toll, prominent behind a relatively low ridge at the side of Audubon.

From the lake, follow a recently constructed trail directly uphill parallel to Mitchell Creek. Bear east around a small tarn near tree line. Contour along the northern slope of an east ridge of Pawnee Peak until the trail descends into the Mitchell Creek drainage to cross the creek at the outlet of an unnamed lake.

From this tarn you climb northwest as the trail passes through sparcer spruce. Near tree line a large snowbank covers Mitchell Creek far into the summer. The stream's channel-cutting underneath the snow and tumbling over rocks make an interesting photo, with Toll rising over a ridge in the background. The trail passes to the right of this snowbank (over it, earlier in the season) and continues over rock slabs and around outcrops to reach _Blue Lake_ at tree line, 2.5 miles from the trailhead.

Mount Toll soars more than 1600 feet right out of the water. The lake is frozen well into the summer, thawing first at the spot where Mitchell Creek cascades over a waterfall into the northwestern end. The stream tumbles from a shelf 500 feet above Blue Lake,

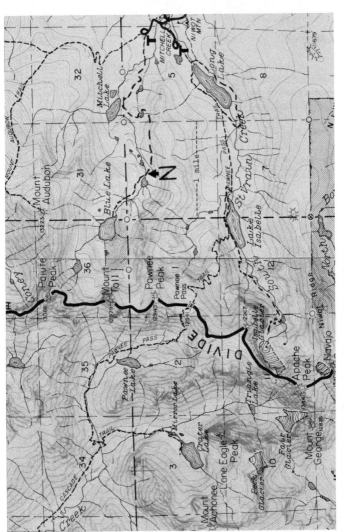

Mount Audubon, Mitchell Creek, and Pawnee Pass trail systems

on which is located a fairly good-sized tarn unofficially called *Little Blue Lake*. Little Blue Lake is the source of Mitchell Creek.

To reach this tarn follow a faint path around Blue Lake's northern shore as far as the waterfall. Be careful there. It is farther — straight down — to the lake than you would imagine; the frigid water will paralyze instantly anyone who falls in; boots and cameras are heavy; the lake is 100 feet deep. From the falls, follow Mitchell Creek very steeply upstream to Little Blue Lake.

To climb *Mount Toll* from Blue Lake, circle to the waterfall via the track on the northern shore. Then climb to a glacial shelf above the lake and traverse south along the base of Toll. Below the saddle between Toll and Pawnee Peak, the mountain to the left, head straight uphill by whatever route looks least steep to reach the saddle. From there it is an uncomplicated boulder hop to the summit. This route is less popular as an ascent than as a descent for climbers who have reached the saddle by traversing the top of Pawnee Peak from Pawnee Pass (see above).

Similarly, you can climb *Paiute Peak*, located north of Mount Toll, from Little Blue Lake. Ascend an extremely steep energy-sapping gully filled with loose rock to the low point in the ridge between Paiute and Mount Audubon, to the northeast. But the preferred route is to climb Mount Audubon first, follow the ridge to Paiute and then use the steep gully for the descent.

Mount Audubon Trail System

The Mount Audubon Trail begins at the north (right-hand) side of the Mitchell Creek Trailhead parking lot. The path climbs steadily to the northwest through typical subalpine forest for more than a half-mile to a long set of switchbacks. From the western end of the second switchback, you get a fine view of Mount Toll rising behind a steep rocky slope of Mount Audubon. As the trail switchbacks, the trees change to limber pines, then back to scrubby spruce-fir as you near tree line.

A short distance above tree line, the trail divides. The right-hand fork takes you to the Buchanan Pass Trail via Beaver Creek Trail (see below). The left-hand fork bends up a gradual tundra slope which has excellent displays of wildflowers in July and August. The uncommon alpine pedicularis exhibits its deep pink blossoms here.

The trail winds across tundra toward a large snowbank, then switchbacks up some distance to the right of it. The terrain is very rocky in the switchbacks; it is an excellent place to see cushion plants such as moss campion. Once above the switchbacks, the trail levels on tundra. Follow the tundra uphill into the saddle immediately north of the main bulk of Audubon. Turn sharply to the left and climb steeply, following cairns and snatches of trail to the summit. Watch for big-rooted springbeauty; it has white blossoms tinged with pink blooming around a large rosette of fleshy leaves which turn brilliant red in autumn. This plant seems to be much more common on Audubon and the rest of Indian Peaks than on the mountains farther north in the national park.

You can descend from Audubon by the same route you ascended. Or you can descend the southwestern ridge to climb *Paiute Peak*. From the saddle between Audubon and Paiute, the easier route tends toward the northern side of the ridge and up to Paiute's summit.

Descend Paiute from the low point in the ridge between Audubon and Paiute, via a very steep gully to the Mitchell Creek drainage. There is much loose rock in this narrow couloir; be careful not to kick it down to batter the body of a fellow climber. When you finally reach Blue Lake, an easy tramp of 2.5 miles lies ahead to the Mitchell Creek Trailhead parking lot where you began hiking. This is an excellent and exciting circle trip — one of the very few with no worries about shuffling cars.

The *Beaver Creek Trail* basically is a connecting link between the trails of the Brainard Lake area and the Buchanan Pass Trail (see below, Routes from Beaver Reservoir). It leaves the Mount Audubon Trail just above tree line, climbing straight ahead where the trail up Audubon veers left. After a few yards it begins to descend by relatively easy grades and a few wide switchbacks. It soon is surrounded by trees — mixed limber pines, Engelmann spruce and subalpine fir.

This path is a pleasant walk which crosses branches of Beaver Creek and passes the junction of the Stapp Lakes Trail, so-called. Actually, the Stapp Lakes Trail goes nowhere near Stapp Lakes, which are on private property visible from above tree line on Mount Audubon. The Stapp Lakes Trail comes out on a four-wheel-drive road connecting a broad open area on Coney Creek called Coney Flats with Beaver Reservoir.

The Beaver Creek Trail also goes to Coney Flats. If you lack a four-wheel-drive vehicle, it is a three-mile hike from Coney Flats through lodgepole pines down to Beaver Reservoir and a road passable by normal passenger cars.

Routes from Beaver Reservoir

To reach Beaver Reservoir drive 7.4 miles on State Highway 72 south of its junction with State Highway 7, or 5.8 miles north of the town of Ward, to a sign marking the Boy Scout Camp Tahosa. Turn west on the unpaved Camp Tahosa road and drive 2.5 miles to a trailhead on the northern shore of Beaver Reservoir.

This is the beginning of a three-mile four-wheel-drive road to *Coney Flats* — a wide, open area made marshy by beaver activity around Coney Creek. This road definitely should not be attempted in a normal passenger car. There is room to park a few cars at the spot where the four-wheel-drive road leaves Beaver Reservoir. Additional parking is available on Forest Service land bordering the road immediately before you reach the reservoir. Walking up the four-wheel-drive road takes you through easy grades in lodgepole pine forest with an occasional beaver-made marsh.

If you are driving a four-wheel-drive vehicle, you can ride almost a mile closer to *Buchanan Pass* via the road following Middle St. Vrain Creek (see below). But this road is much rougher than the road connecting Beaver Reservoir with Coney Flats. Additionally, the trail you follow after leaving your vehicle on the Middle St.

Vrain road is much steeper than the trail from Coney Flats.

If you are driving a passenger car, Beaver Reservoir is unquestionably the best place to begin walking for Buchanan Pass. The reservoir is 523 feet higher and a little closer to the pass than the more popular starting point at Camp Dick on Middle St. Vrain Creek (see below). Also, the terrain covered from Beaver Reservoir is easier than that from Camp Dick. The trail from Camp Dick is prettier but not, in our opinion, enough so to be worth the extra effort.

Past where it is permissible to drive, you must ford Coney Creek on the south (left-hand) side of the wide trail that heads toward Buchanan Pass. The pass is the low saddle with a permanent snowfield below it and to the left, directly west of Coney Flats. It is three miles from the ford to Buchanan Pass. The trail is good, running first through quaking aspens and limber pines, then through Engelmann spruce and subalpine fir. Ultimately, trees give way to tundra and tundra to rocks as the trail snakes steeply through switchbacks uphill to the pass. A left turn at Buchanan Pass leads across a half-mile of tundra, gaining 500 feet of elevation to *Sawtooth Mountain*, which marks the easternmost point on the continental divide.

From the ford at Coney Flats you can follow a trail upstream along Coney Creek drainage to *Coney Lake* and *Upper Coney Lake* (about two and three miles, respectively). Beyond the lower lake the route becomes less distinct and more rugged. Upper Coney Lake has a very dramatic setting in the cirque between Paiute Peak and Mount Audubon.

Especially around Upper Coney Lake, the steep slopes covered with loose rock are ideal habitat for the pika, also called the cony or coney. This little round-earred cousin of the rabbit has caused a certain amount of confusion about locations. For instance, nearby to the north in the Wild Basin Trail System is Cony Lake, the source of Cony Creek. The slightly different spellings of the animal's name — both correct — are no help in alleviating the confusion.

Another four-wheel-drive road, a little less than a mile long, connects Coney Flats with the Middle St. Vrain road. The Middle St. Vrain road is a trial, but the connecting track to Coney Flats is for folks who enjoy repairing their vehicles. It has deteriorated to the point that only hikers can get much pleasure out of the thick spruce-fir forest through which it passes.

Middle St. Vrain Trail System

To reach the Middle St. Vrain Trail System, turn west from State Highway 7 at Peaceful Valley onto an unpaved road. Peaceful Valley is situated four miles south of the junction of State Highways 7 and 72, or 9.2 miles north of the town of Ward. Follow the unpaved road for a mile to the second campground, Camp Dick.

The road beyond Camp Dick is a severe trial even for high clearance four-wheel-drive vehicles, so hikers riding in a normal passenger car must begin to walk. It is a very pleasant four miles from Camp Dick west along lovely Middle St. Vrain Creek to the spot where the trail to _Buchanan Pass_ strikes off to the left, perpendicular to the road. (The trail to St. Vrain Mountain and Rock Creek climbs very steeply from the right-hand side of the road; it is described below as St. Vrain Mountain Trail.)

South of Middle St. Vrain Creek, the trail to Buchanan Pass forks. The right-hand branch heads up to _Red Deer Lake_, passing two more trails on the way. The first of these bears right and back down to the road. The second cuts left to connect with the trail that branched left by Middle St. Vrain Creek, the trail to Buchanan Pass.

Red Deer Lake, about a mile from the road, is a rock- and Krummholz-rimmed tarn which has been enlarged by a small dam. "Red deer" is the European name for the animal that Americans call elk. From the place where the trail reaches the lakeshore, you can see a mountain called Elk Tooth peeking over the top of a ridge on the opposite side of the lake. In the entire area covered by this book, these two features are the only ones named for the most spectacular animal you are likely to see along the trails.

Leaving Middle St. Vrain Creek road, back at the beginning of the trail to Buchanan Pass, the way is fairly steep for a half-mile. Then you meet a trail on the right that connects with Red Deer Lake. After another half-mile your trail joins the trail from Coney Flats and climbs to Buchanan Pass, about 2.5 miles from Middle St. Vrain Creek (see above, Routes from Beaver Reservoir).

The Middle St. Vrain road is closed to all vehicles about a mile beyond (west of) the trail to Buchanan Pass. From this closure, a trail to Red Deer Lake crosses the creek and passes the site of an old sawmill to head south up a moderate grade. It connects with the trail to Red Deer Lake described above.

Hiking farther west along the road, you find that it very soon evolves into a good trail. Open subalpine forest covers the narrow valley floor, while the steep valley walls display fewer trees and more rock. More than two miles beyond the road closure, the trail bends left to climb a half-mile into the cirque containing _Lake Gibraltar_, the source of Middle St. Vrain Creek. The outlet from Lake Gibraltar flows at once into a smaller lake unofficially called _Little Lake Gibraltar_. Over a low ridge to the east of the trail at Lake Gibraltar there is another cirque, which contains _Lake Envy_. Towering above all these lakes are spectacular cliffs on which hang _St. Vrain Glaciers_.

For those who can drive to the road closure, the Middle St. Vrain Trail System offers shorter, but not necessarily easier, routes to two Wild Basin destinations. To reach _Hutcheson Lakes_, leave the trail about 1.5 miles beyond the road closure. Climb over loose rock up the very steep north wall of the Middle St. Vrain Valley wherever it looks least difficult. From the top of the ridge between Middle St. Vrain and Cony Creek drainages, descend with care over more loose rock to Hutcheson Lakes.

A shorter approach to _Ogalalla Peak_ leads to a much more difficult final climb than do the approaches from Ouzel Peak or Cony Pass. When the trail bends south to Lake Gibraltar, keep going west, uphill, to a small tarn unofficially called _Pika Lake_. Continue on to the head of the Middle St. Vrain Valley and climb into the cirque containing the largest and northernmost of the St. Vrain

Glaciers. Ogalalla lies straight north of this body of ice. Between the cliff above the glacier and the peak there is a very steep slope covered with loose rock. Climb this talus slope to the lowest point on the skyline southwest of Ogalalla. This spot is on the continental divide. Once there, you have a short walk east over relatively level tundra to the summit of Ogalalla.

St. Vrain Mountain Trail

The trail to Meadow and St. Vrain mountains begins near the town of Allenspark, which is on State Highway 7, more than 13 miles south of Estes Park. To reach the less than distinct trailhead, drive on the main road through, not bypassing, Allenspark. A short way downhill from town, at the base of the roadbed of Route 7, take the first unpaved road on the right. This is called the Ski Road. Follow the Ski Road as it twists uphill, then heads in a southerly direction.

The Ski Road forks 2.2 miles from the paved road. The left-hand fork goes downhill to Rock Creek and deteriorates to logging roads passable only with four-wheel drive (see below). The right-hand fork goes uphill about .1 mile to the vicinity of the St. Vrain Mountain Trail. The trail materializes among the pines on the south (left-hand) side of the road.

To reach _Meadow Mountain_, follow the trail as it switchbacks through a wide and long slope cleared by forest fire for more than two miles up to Krummholz. Once above tree line, strike off for the rounded hump of Meadow to the north whenever it looks convenient. The final scramble up Meadow is very rocky. But, logically enough, the top is covered by alpine meadow, thick with tundra flowers in July and August. The summit is just inside Rocky Mountain National Park.

The St. Vrain Mountain Trail levels below Meadow Mountain and heads south through mixed tundra and Krummholz. Another rounded hump, which rises ahead to the southwest, is _St. Vrain Mountain_. From a saddle east of the mountain, leave the trail to walk over boulders and patches of tundra to the summit, 700 feet

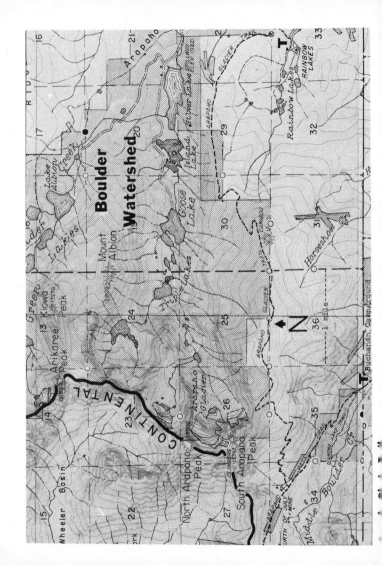

above. The summit of St. Vrain is about four miles from the trailhead. From there you get good views north to Longs Peak, Mount Meeker and the eastern end of Wild Basin. To the southwest are many fine but nameless peaks overlooking Middle St. Vrain Creek.

From the summit you may see hikers laboring up the St. Vrain Mountain Trail from the four-wheel-drive road next to the creek. Folks who manage to force their vehicles clear to the south end of the St. Vrain Mountain Trail have an ascent which is a mile shorter than the approach you have taken. They also have a much steeper ascent. From where you are standing, the trail appears to simply drop into the Middle St. Vrain Valley. And it does.

The map indicates a trail heading from the St. Vrain Mountain Trail, a short distance south of the saddle below the summit, downhill into the valley of _Rock Creek_. The Rock Creek Trail soon wanders through a maze of elk paths in marshes and Krummholz at the creek's source. Below tree line, it enters another maze, this one of logging roads cutting through the forest. These roads can be driven only with four-wheel-drive vehicles, but they are easily walked. Follow your feet downhill; they will naturally take you on the logical road along Rock Creek, away from St. Vrain Mountain. The euphemistic description of this trail is "unimproved." It is used mostly by people out for a walk from lovely unimproved campsites they have discovered beside Rock Creek.

Arapaho Glacier Trail

Rainbow Lakes Campground is the northern trailhead of the Arapaho Glacier Trail. To reach the campground, drive on State Highway 72 for five miles south of Ward or eight miles north of Nederland. Turn west on an unpaved county road identified as the road to the University of Colorado Mountain Research Station. The road forks after .8 mile; take the left-hand fork for a bumpy five-mile drive uphill to the campground. Drive all the way through the campground and park at its west end.

A trail to _Rainbow Lakes_ begins at the very end of the road. It is a short, easy walk up to these ponds, which are connected by a web of fishermen's trails. From the highest lake you can look up past subalpine forest to a small cirque and the long tundra ridge of Caribou (Mountain, Peak, Ridge, Bump?).

A few dozen yards from the beginning of the trail to the lakes, the Arapaho Glacier Trail leaves the northwestern side of the campground. A sign may still be in place marking it as the Glacier Rim Trail.

The trail begins by climbing steeply through the forest, then moderates its grade along the fence marking the border of the Boulder Watershed. Numerous signs will inform you as to which side of the fence you should travel. More than a mile from the trailhead, the path turns left away from the fence and switchbacks nearly to tree line.

From the crest of a ridge above the trees you can look down on the beautiful valley of the south fork of North Boulder Creek. Again the edge of the Boulder Watershed is marked; occasional signs may name the reservoirs below. At the head of the valley, to the west, a line of grand but unnamed 12,000-foot peaks follows the continental divide. The "thirteeners," North Arapaho and Arikaree, are high points on the left and right of your view. Mount Albion stands out massively across the gorge.

Be sure to photograph the valley and the peaks before you follow the trail in a sharp left turn up the ridge. As you climb higher past the switchback, the lake-filled valley will drop below your view. The peaks still will be magnificent but will rise out of a tundra slope somewhat less dramatically than from the depths of the valley.

The tundra where you walk is well carpeted with flowers; alpine sunflowers may be the most prominent. Through wide switchbacks the trail winds up the slope north of Caribou, then flattens on top of the ridge. Peak-baggers may wish to walk a few dozen yards to the left (east) of the trail to the cairn marking the top of Caribou. Since several bumps on the same ridge are hundreds of feet higher than this point, we speculate that it was singled out to be named because it was visible from some point below. Try to step on rocks and avoid trampling the rosettes of fleshy leaves that belong to big-rooted springbeauty.

Past Caribou the trail crosses to a south-facing slope and switchbacks on up the ridge. Above 12,600 feet the path undulates gradually across the tundra for a few miles. The view of colorful alpine flowers at your feet competes with the view of rugged peaks and hanging lakes across the valley to the south. Six miles from Rainbow Lakes Campground, the trail joins another coming up from the valley of North Fork Middle Boulder Creek. (Yes, the watercourses around here have confusing names.)

From the junction walk uphill a few yards to the viewpoint for *Arapaho Glacier*, the southernmost glacier in the Rockies. The dramatic conical mountain rising directly above you is *South Arapaho Peak*. The route to the top is easy to follow over boulders on the south slope, to the left of the east-face cliffs. A bronze peak finder is cemented into the summit to elaborate on the fine view, especially to the south and west as far away as Mount of the Holy Cross.

The climb over to North Arapaho Peak is somewhat more challenging. It is a half-mile trip — farther than it appears. The route involves boulder scrambling and a little easy climbing. Before you have gone far on the southwestern side of the ridge extending between the two Arapahos, splashes of red paint appear on rocks, marking the route. (These are camouflaged in autumn, however, when the abundant rosettes of the big-rooted springbeauty turn bright red.)

It seems to us — and we are not avid rock climbers — that the route to North Arapaho is interesting without being scary or exposed to dangerous falls. Yet we have met enough wide-eyed folks returning from the peak and exclaiming that they had stared death in the face to suggest that our assessment is wrong. Or perhaps some of the climbers, bothered by exposure to long falls, got off-route too far to the right and too close to the east-facing precipice above the glacier.

Anyone who has had enough climbing experience to use a rope effectively probably will be experienced enough not to need one on North Arapaho. But a rope in the leader's hands, belaying a nervous member of the party, may be useful psychological protection. At any rate, all climbers should be extremely careful.

There is a huge cairn on the summit of North Arapaho — from far and wide a visible monument to the activity of the human species, *Homo constructus*. You can climb the cairn to have your picture taken on the tip-top of the mountain, or hold a square dance on the monument, if you like. But the best subject for a dramatic photo is a secondary promontory south of the true summit. The photographer stands on the true summit, focusing across at fellow climbers atop an absolutely sheer cliff that juts over Arapaho Glacier with South Arapaho behind them. Do not get too daring as you shoot. It is fatally far to fall.

From the Arapaho Glacier viewpoint below South Arapaho it is only 3.5 miles down to the trailhead at Buckingham Campground. This is about half the distance of the hike back to Rainbow Lakes Campground. Moreover, the trail to Buckingham, on the banks of North Fork Middle Boulder Creek, is very pleasant. It winds over rock and tundra down a steep 1.5 miles to the site of the old Fourth of July Mine, which once yielded silver and a little gold.

From a trail junction at the mine site, a path cuts steeply uphill for a mile across the rocky slope east of Arapaho Pass. From the pass it is an easy walk over tundra and boulders to *Lake Dorothy*, hanging below Mount Neva. You can continue beyond Lake Dorothy along a fine trail to Caribou Pass. Or you can descend steeply along a sinuous path from Arapaho Pass to Caribou Lake; it is a long way back up (see "Indian Peaks, West of the Divide," Caribou Pass Trail).

Buckingham Campground is situated two miles below the mine site. Many streams cross the trail, and the subalpine flowers are spectacular from June through late August. Near the end of the trail, when it begins to evolve into a road, two other roads cut sharply right from the main path. Don't take either. Keep walking east to the parking lot of the campground, where presumably you have transportation waiting.

Driving instructions to Buckingham Campground begin at the town of Nederland, west of Boulder at the junction of State Highways 119 and 72. From the south side of Nederland, a half-mile from the road junction, turn west toward the Lake Eldora Ski Area. At the spot where the road forks uphill (left) toward the ski area, continue on the lower (right) fork through the town of Eldora. Its pavement ends shortly. A mile past Eldora the road forks again. Again you should head right, driving up a rough but passable road, (for all cars) for four miles to the campground.

Snowlilies

Indian Peaks, West of the Divide (Arapaho National Forest)

Indian Peaks west of the continental divide has only one destination that is close to a road. Although you must walk a ways to get to most hiking goals, the effort is worth it. To exaggerate the splendor of the west side of Indian Peaks is difficult. The entire area defies hyperbole. Yet most of the hiking traffic funnels into one trail system.

Four of the five Indian Peaks trail systems west of the divide are reached from an unpaved road south of Lake Granby. To reach this road, drive along U.S. Highway 34 to a point 11 miles south of the town of Grand Lake and six miles north of the town of Granby. From that point the unpaved road winds generally east along the south shore of Lake Granby to Arapaho Bay Campground and Monarch Lake.

After about nine miles, the unpaved road crosses a bridge over the narrow neck of the southernmost tip of Lake Granby. Past the bridge, a mile-long road branches left (north) past Arapaho Bay Campground and dead-ends at the beginning of the Roaring Fork Trail System (see below). Past the left-hand branch to Roaring Fork, the unpaved road from Highway 34 bends right (south) and dead-ends after about a mile at a parking lot a short distance from Monarch Lake (see below, Buchanan Pass Trail, Cascade Trail to Pawnee Pass, and Arapaho Pass Trail).

Regulations for wilderness use in the national forest are not terribly different from regulations instituted to protect the national park backcountry. In the national forest it is unnecessary, at present, to obtain a backcountry camping permit. But you should

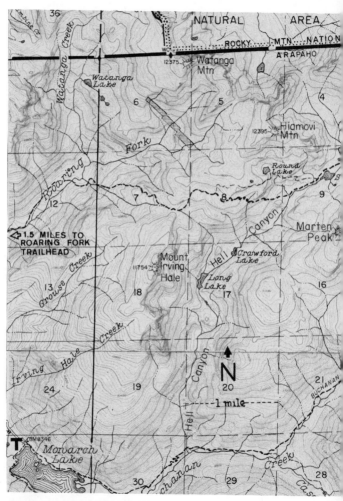

Roaring Fork Trail System

choose a campsite on a dry forest floor (not in a meadow) at least 100 yards from lakes, streams and trails. Campfires are permitted but discouraged in favor of backpacking stoves. Unlike in the park, leashed pets are allowed on national forest trails.

Roaring Fork Trail System

The parking lot for the Roaring Fork Trail System is near the National Park Service's Arapaho Bay Ranger Station. If you plan to leave a car in the parking lot overnight, it would be well to place a note on the dashboard saying when you expect to return. Thus, when a ranger looks over the cars in the parking lot, he will know that yours is not abandoned or in other need of official attention. (For driving instructions to Roaring Fork Trailhead, see above.)

The Roaring Fork Trail heads northeast out of the parking lot and climbs immediately through steep switchbacks above Arapaho Bay to a welcome level stretch that leads to Roaring Fork. (Roaring Fork was a fork of Arapaho Creek until Lake Granby backed up to convert Arapaho Creek to Arapaho Bay.) In easy grades the trail follows the broad Roaring Fork Valley upstream, sometimes in marsh, sometimes in lodgepole pine. In a wide meadow about two miles from the trailhead, turn right to cross Roaring Fork. From the crossing, the trail climbs steeply along an unnamed stream flowing from the Irving Hale Divide, a broad saddle north of _Mount Irving Hale._

This section of trail has only a few switchbacks to lessen the grade. It is a real lung-popper until you reach the Irving Hale Divide. Here displays of wildflowers — tall chiming bells, yellow senecios, various colors of paintbrush — can be spectacular, especially when the trail sloshes through bogs. Paintbrush are abundant also in the drier subalpine meadows, along with some alpine flowers extending their range down from the tundra.

Mount Irving Hale is an easy climb up a tundra ridge from the Irving Hale Divide. On the double-humped top of Irving Hale are two large cairns. From a distance, they look like two mountaineers standing watch over Hell Canyon. The summit is about two miles from the crossing of Roaring Fork.

Vistas from the top of Irving Hale are magnificent. To the west, Lake Granby stretches out in Middle Park, and the Gore Range defines the horizon. Mount Toll, Paiute Peak and Mount Audubon tower on the southeastern skyline. Hell Canyon extends to the east with Long and Crawford lakes far below your feet at the base of craggy cliffs on Irving Hale.

Back down at the Irving Hale Divide, the trail descends slightly to the east past ponds and puddles. Early in the season, abundant snowlilies testify to heavy snow accumulation. In a particularly lovely meadow with a fine view east to the continental divide, a tumbledown log cabin can add a romantic element to your photos.

Descending past the cabin, the path reenters thick Engelmann spruce-subalpine fir forest. Various informal tracks lead downhill from the Irving Hale Divide to several lakes. To the right, informal paths descend to _Long_ and _Crawford_ lakes. To the left, another unmaintained trail leads to the little pond called _Round Lake_.

But the only maintained trail drops through switchbacks on the wall of Hell Canyon to the canyon floor between Crawford and Stone lakes. On the way, flower displays compete with rugged scenery for your attention. Below the switchbacks, you traverse rocky open areas before descending the final stretch to the bottom of the canyon.

Bending to the left around a large glacial knob, the path continues up a stream to _Stone Lake_. Stone Lake lies in a stone basin which was scoured out by a glacier roughened into a rasping tool by the tons of rock it carried. Unlike many such tarns, Stone Lake is not particularly deep. Interspersed among the rounded rocks that form its shoreline are patches of subalpine meadow and trees of the forest's upper margin.

A narrow track leads up the valley over meadow and rock slabs to _Upper Lake_. The trail stops at Upper Lake, but you can continue upstream over flowery tundra meadows to a pass overlooking Paradise Park. From lake to pass there is a rise of 800 feet in about a mile; the terrain makes for easy walking.

The pass is in a unique position between Paradise and Hell. But it is difficult to feel like Dante in a spot where both places are covered with tundra flowers and where Paradise and Hell are sublimely similar. Paradise Park lies within Rocky Mountain National Park and has been set aside as a research natural area. It is a preserve for scientific study; horses and camping are prohibited so as to maintain this remote mountain valley in a totally pristine condition. If you continue into Paradise Park, please be extra careful to leave no trace of your passing.

From the pass above Paradise Park, you can climb east over a steep narrow ridge and broad tundra slopes to *Ogalalla Peak*. Ogalalla is 1.2 miles away and 1600 feet higher than the pass. Climb on the southern side of the ridgeline.

Buchanan Pass Trail

To reach the Buchanan Pass Trail drive to Monarch Lake. (Driving instructions are at the beginning of this chapter. Hiking around the lake is a trip of more than three miles.) The trail along the left (north) shore is the western end of trails traversing both Buchanan and Pawnee passes. These trails run together for about 1.5 miles along the lakeshore and beyond to a junction where a spur trail branches right. The spur connects with the Arapaho Pass Trail (see below) to continue on around Monarch Lake's opposite shore.

The trail to Buchanan Pass and Pawnee Pass bears left from the junction and follows Buchanan Creek up to *Shelter Rock*. This large boulder with overhanging ledges is an easy four-mile walk from the trailhead at Monarch Lake. A few hundred yards beyond Shelter Rock is another trail junction. The right-hand fork leads up Cascade Creek to Pawnee Pass (see below).

The left-hand fork is the Buchanan Pass Trail and climbs steeply through lodgepole to a more moderate grade at the edge of beaver-made meadows along Buchanan Creek. Continuing to climb gradually, the trail crosses outlet streams of Island Lake and Gourd

Lake. About 1800 yards past the brook flowing from Gourd Lake, you arrive at the junction with the _Gourd Lake Trail_.

The 1260-foot difference in elevation between the trail junction and the top of the Gourd Lake Trail is gained in a long two miles of twisting through switchbacks without number. Along the way the views of Paiute Peak are extremely dramatic. Oddly enough, the best shot can be had from near the bottom as you approach the eastern end of a switchback amid aspens. To frame Paiute with aspen leaves, continue walking a few more yards east, off-trail, from where the switchback turns west. Afternoon light is best; a short telephoto lens with polarizing filter will be helpful. Farther up the trail the view expands to include double-topped Mount Toll and, across the valley, Thunderbolt Peak.

When you finally reach Gourd Lake, follow a faint trail around to the right (east) shore for the best photos. The surface of the lake's deeply indented bays frequently is still enough to reflect Cooper Peak for photos.

At the base of Cooper Peak the large tarn called _Island Lake_ hangs above tree line. Patches of Krummholz around its rocky shores do little to soften the austerity of the setting. The ascent from Gourd to Island Lake calls for a rise of 600 feet in about a mile. Follow the eastern shore of Gourd Lake to that part of the northern shore having the least steep slope above it. Scramble up this slope to a glacial shelf where there is a small unnamed pond. Bear northwest across this shelf and climb the least steep route to a higher bench where there are more nameless ponds. Then contour along the outlet stream past even more small tarns to Island Lake.

The Buchanan Pass Trail continues past the Gourd Lake Trail at an almost level grade until it meets the valley of Thunderbolt Creek. The same glacier that so dramatically sculpted the tower of Paiute carved deep and steep down the Thunderbolt Creek Valley. It cut faster than a tributary glacier flowing from farther north on the divide at the head of Buchanan Creek. Thus the valley of the tributary glacier was left hanging 700 feet up on the mountainside, overlooking Thunderbolt Creek.

Fox Park lies on the floor of this hanging valley. To get to it, the Buchanan Pass Trail climbs, climbs, climbs through switchbacks distressingly reminiscent of those on the Gourd Lake Trail. Yet if you happen to be at Gourd Lake and want to reach Fox Park (or vice-versa), you do not have to lose and regain 1000 feet of elevation and walk two extra miles between these two points. What you do is follow an unimproved but marked and mostly distinct trail that extends directly down to a meadow just above Fox Park from the southeastern slope of a low forested ridge adjacent to the lake's southeastern shore. This route is not appropriate for horses. In a couple of places, the path heads straight uphill to avoid traversing steep rock. In others, it crosses obvious avalanche slopes which can be very dangerous in early spring. Sometimes it fades away in sheltered places where snowbanks remain into autumn.

But most of the trail is a pure joy of subalpine flowers and magnificent views up Thunderbolt Creek toward Paiute and Toll. Finally, the track fades away completely in a marshy meadow with a good view that will be unavailable in Fox Park, only a short way down a tributary brook to Buchanan Creek.

Buchanan Pass rises in plain sight 1400 feet above Fox Park. The climb for the next two miles promises to be tough. But it looks worse than it turns out to be. The steepest part climbs through classically beautiful subalpine forest which gives way abruptly to alpine tundra. Farther uphill the trail steepens somewhat again on a rocky slope below Buchanan Pass.

From the pass, you can leave the trail and climb to the south over tundra slopes to the top of _Sawtooth Mountain_, the easternmost point on the continental divide. Sawtooth is a half-mile from Buchanan Pass and 467 feet higher. To the east there are three downhill miles of rocky trail to a four-wheel-drive road at Coney Flats and another three miles along this road to a road for passenger cars at Beaver Reservoir (see "Indian Peaks, East of the Divide," Middle St. Vrain Trail System and Routes from Beaver Reservoir).

Cascade Trail to Pawnee Pass

The trail along Cascade Creek is the most heavily used trail on the west side of Indian Peaks, despite relatively long distances to the most popular destinations. Although the dramatic scenery in Cascade Creek's drainage can be equaled on other trails, it cannot be surpassed. If you have a choice, make every effort to enjoy this trail at times other than obviously crowded holidays and weekends.

The Cascade Trail to Pawnee Pass branches right from the Buchanan Pass Trail at the trail junction four miles from Monarch Lake, just past Shelter Rock (see above). A short level walk takes you to Buchanan Creek, which is spanned by a substantial bridge. From there a short and rather steep stretch moderated by one switchback leads to the edge of a canyon cut by Cascade Creek. The grade moderates from the canyon edge as you continue up the valley through lodgepole pines.

About a mile from Shelter Rock, the trail bends to the right and crosses the creek on a bridge that has a beaver dam foundation. The open marshy area here is in a middle stage of plant succession from beaver pond to forest. Located upstream from the old beaver workings is your first clear example of how Cascade Creek got its name. Falls like this, too numerous to be named individually, make the trail itself a hiking destination, rather than merely a route to the lakes at the base of the peaks.

Twisting through many tight switchbacks, the trail climbs along the cascades onto the next highest glacier-cut shelf. The views of rushing water will slow you down even more than the steepness of the climb. Various spur paths branch off to viewpoints of the cascades. If you are in a rush, keep to the right — on the main trail. Near the level of the next shelf, the trail bends to the left to recross the creek over water-smoothed rock above a particularly fine falls.

A bit more climbing takes you to another broad level area where Cascade Creek meanders lazily through old beaver ponds, seemingly resting before its spectacular rush down the falls. Amid the rock-covered slopes overhead on the left, groves of quaking

Cascade Trail to Pawnee Pass and North Section of Arapaho Pass Trail

aspens have pioneered a place to live among the boulders. Leaving the creek on the valley floor, the trail traverses uphill along a sunny south-facing slope. Peaks in the vicinity of Mount George, to the east, draw your attention as you climb.

The trail reenters deep spruce and fir forests before crossing Pawnee Creek. A short winding way uphill is a trail junction, about seven miles from Monarch Lake. The right-hand fork continues up Cascade Creek to Mirror and Crater lakes (see below).

The Pawnee Pass Trail branches left and recrosses Pawnee Creek. Switchbacks just past the crossing wind up through quaking aspens and narrow spires of Engelmann spruce. These trees are good frames for effective photos of Lone Eagle Peak flanked by Peck and Fair glaciers (see below, Crater Lake Trail).

Variations on this spectacular view continue as the trail climbs east parallel to Pawnee Creek. Lone Eagle and its glaciers are last seen from an open avalanche slope covered with large boulders. The trail continues ascending through spruce-fir forest into the cirque containing _Pawnee Lake_. The lake is a little more than a mile from the junction of the Crater Lake Trail.

Pawnee Lake is extremely grand. Spires on the slopes of Pawnee Peak, east of the lake, are picturesquely jagged. The glacier-quarried peaks on the north and west, although unnamed, are nearly as spectacular. A wide-angle lens will be very helpful in composing photos in which spruce and fir trees along the eastern shore lead your eye into this picture.

Beyond Pawnee Lake, the 1.5 mile ascent to Pawnee Pass is very steep. The path, however, is a remarkable example of superb trail construction. In tight switchbacks, it snakes up terrain that must approach the maximum limit of steepness and ruggedness for trail building. If you climb it, be sure to use your rest stops to photograph over the switchbacks to Pawnee Lake, using rock spires on Pawnee Peak for a frame. East of Pawnee Pass there are various trail systems in the vicinity of Brainard Lake (see "Indian Peaks, East of the Divide," Pawnee Pass Trail).

The Crater Lake Trail branches from the Pawnee Pass Trail

Chipmunk and golden-mantled ground squirrel

about seven miles from Monarch Lake. As you ascend the sometimes wet, sometimes rocky, path to Crater Lake, the impossibly pointed spire of Lone Eagle Peak comes into view above the trees, echoing their sky-etching quality. The classic view of Lone Eagle is from _Mirror Lake_, a shallow, rock-rimmed tarn a few hundred yards past the third crossing of Cascade Creek. Fair Glacier is on the left of Lone Eagle, Peck Glacier on the right. A wide-angle lens is needed at Mirror Lake to include Lone Eagle and its reflection in one photo.

Less than a half-mile past Mirror is _Crater Lake_, where the view of Lone Eagle is more believable. But the setting of subalpine forest, large deep lake, spires and cliffs of Mount Achonee on the right, incredibly jagged ridge on the left, and the sheer face of Lone Eagle rising straight up to a point is a scene of extravagant grandeur. The one-time occupants of a tumbledown old cabin perched atop glacially smoothed bedrock at the lake's western end had quite a view when they arose each morning.

If you can stop staring at Lone Eagle, there are several interesting hikes to take from Crater Lake. To reach _Peck Glacier_, circle Crater Lake to the right (west) and climb along the base of Lone Eagle's western flank. It is a steep mile from the lake's northern shore to the glacier.

The spire of _Lone Eagle Peak_ that is seen from Crater Lake is not a true summit. Lone Eagle really is a jagged ridge extending north from Mount George. The highest point on the ridge (12,799 feet; the spire above the lake reaches 11,950 feet) can be climbed from the east. Cross the outlet stream of Crater Lake to the slopes of loose rock below Lone Eagle ridge. Scramble up this rock, following the base of the ridge.

Eventually, you will come upon snatches of faint trail and cairns that lead south and up rock slabs at a relatively moderate grade for more than a half-mile. Watch carefully for cairns and do not try to cut uphill too soon, or cliffs will block your way. After you are well south of the high point on the ridge, the route cuts back to the north and begins to climb ramps to the ridgeline at a point south of the summit. From here you must descend a few feet over slabs on the western side of the ridge, circling a small spire. This spot is exposed to a long drop and, though not difficult, might unnerve the acrophobic.

Climbing back over the ridgeline toward the summit spire, you ultimately must head to the right (east) side of the ridge and then ascend to the very top from the northeast. The summit is not so sharp that it hurts to sit on it, but there is room for only a few climbers at a time. The entire climb is exciting, dramatic and less difficult than it appears from below. On the other hand, Lone Eagle has claimed its share of lives, so be very careful.

Triangle Lake is an aptly named tarn lying in the valley below the route to Lone Eagle. To reach Triangle, cross the outlet of Crater Lake and ascend the valley through forest and meadow. Clamber up a short steep barrier of boulders to the lake, about a mile from Crater. Triangle's water is milky, which indicates that powdered rock is being carried into the lake in meltwater from _Fair Glacier_. Evidently, enough ice still is flowing in the glacier to keep it actively grinding rocks.

Arapaho Pass Trail

The Arapaho Pass Trail begins by following the southwestern (right) shore of Monarch Lake. (For driving instructions to Monarch Lake, see the beginning of this chapter.) About 1.5 miles from the parking-lot end of Monarch Lake, the High Lonesome Trail branches off from the Arapaho Pass Trail. Eventually, the High Lonesome Trail connects with trails along the continental divide south of Indian Peaks.

Bear left at the High Lonesome junction and follow the Arapaho Pass Trail across a bridge over Arapaho Creek. Just past the bridge, the trail divides. The left-hand branch continues on around Monarch Lake by connecting with the Buchanan Pass Trail (see above). The Arapaho Pass Trail turns sharply right and, after a series of switchbacks, climbs a steep slope forested by lodgepole pines. Above the switchbacks, the trail follows a more moderate grade, paralleling Arapaho Creek. Most of the creek is out of sight behind trees and willows, but now and then side trails lead down to the water. The main trail runs south along the base of a steep ridge.

In occasional open spaces, wet habitat subalpine flowers such as tall chiming bells and monkshood grow thickly. Before long, the lodgepole pines mix with Engelmann spruce and subalpine fir. Gradually pines become less common and spruce and fir more so until the last lodgepole is left behind in a field of boulders. Except in areas opened up by avalanches, the trail passes through a thick spruce-fir forest which provides shade and beauty for a pleasant walk up the long valley. Should you desire to climb _Mount Achonee_, pick one of the avalanche-cleared slopes for the best route to the tundra slopes below the summit.

Just past an avalanche slope about 3.5 miles from the last trail junction, the path climbs away from Arapaho Creek in a series of long switchbacks. Then it proceeds on a gentle uphill grade for less than a half-mile to meet the creek again at a point where a throne-shaped rock has been frost-wedged from the cliff. You might as well rest here; you rarely will find a rock more suitable for sitting.

Past the chair rock, the trail climbs through more switchbacks in forest of increasing density. After crossing various creeks at the mouth of Wheeler Basin, it steepens somewhat, and wildflowers begin to become more abundant. Then the path meanders through the meadows of Coyote Park. Early in the season the ground is yellow with snowlilies. Uphill from Coyote Park, the woods are less thick, and the open spaces are multihued with flowers. Switchbacks keep the grade moderate until you reach _Caribou Lake_, at tree line.

Caribou Lake lies in a cirque walled in by cliffs between Arapaho and Caribou passes. A walk along a narrow trail on the marshy western shore presents superb views across the lake of jagged Apache and Navajo peaks. Patches of Krummholz, willow and alpine flowers add nice details to the lakeshore in the foreground.

Clearly visible from the lake is the continuation of the Arapaho

Pass Trail; it climbs remarkably in many tight switchbacks up the very steep slope of loose rock below Arapaho Pass. From a distance, the rock looks like the last word in sterility. But the actual ascent reveals patches of richly blooming tundra flowers growing in loose gravel seemingly devoid of soil. Especially impressive are perfect spheroid cushions of moss campion and broadleaved or dwarf fireweed, the latter rarely found this far south in the Rockies. The tenuous hold that these heroic plants maintain on the scree is easily destroyed by a careless step. Cutting through switchbacks is bad anywhere, but it would be especially damaging and disgusting on this delicate terrain.

From Arapaho Pass you can descend to the Arapaho Glacier Trail (see "Indian Peaks, East of the Divide," Arapaho Glacier Trail) or head west up gradual tundra and rock slopes to Lake Dorothy and beyond that to Caribou Pass. Actually, Caribou Pass is the easiest and most enjoyable gate to Arapaho Pass and Caribou Lake. If you can work out the car shuttle, hiking the Caribou Pass Trail to Lake Dorothy, going downhill to Caribou Lake and exiting via Monarch Lake, is by far the best way to travel the magnificent Arapaho Pass Trail.

Caribou Pass Trail

The trailhead for the Caribou Pass Trail is located on an unpaved road overlooking Meadow Creek Reservoir (on old maps the lake occupies a site called Sawmill Meadow). Begin by leaving U.S. Highway 40 about a half-mile east of the town of Tabernash or 3.5 miles north of the town of Fraser. Turn east onto an unpaved road immediately south of the spot where Route 40 crosses a railroad track via an overpass. Very soon the road forks; take the left-hand fork and stay on the main road going to Meadow Creek Campground. Continue past the campground, along Meadow Creek, then follow the main road uphill through switchbacks almost to Meadow Creek Reservoir. Just before you reach the dam, bear left; the road climbs through forest past a great pile of sawdust left from

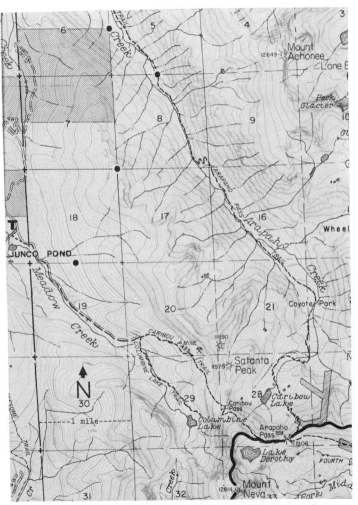

Caribou Pass Trail System and Southern Section of Arapaho Pass Trail

lumbering operations. (Note: Meadow Creek Reservoir can be reached on foot via the High Lonesome Trail — see above, Arapaho Pass Trail.)

About three road miles from the dam (12 miles from the highway), above the reservoir, the road forks again. The main road goes to the right through an open grassy area. The left-hand fork, obviously the road less taken, climbs slightly into another grassy meadow. We recommend that you take the right fork for a few yards, park your car and start walking along the left-hand road to the southeast past little Junco Pond. Four-wheel-drive vehicles or trail bikes can go considerably farther but only at the cost of unconscionable tearing up of the wet subalpine terrain. All mechanized travel should be barred east of Junco Pond.

Hike up the old roadbed along Meadow Creek past two fallen-down log cabins; the footing is sloppy in places. After about 1.5 miles there is a trail junction. The Caribou Pass Trail goes to the left, and the _Columbine Lake Trail_ branches off to the right.

The Columbine Lake Trail follows a gradual grade for about 175 yards to the forest edge and increased steepness. A level meadow appears about a half-mile from the trail junction, and a third smaller meadow above the second. The trail climbs steeply along Meadow Creek before bending to the left to wander amid boulders and trees, soon meeting the creek again and crossing it. A short climb past the creek crossing takes you to the level of the shelf on which lies Columbine Lake, at tree line. The trail mucks around in marsh, half losing itself, before reaching the lake several hundred yards past the stream crossing and three miles from the trailhead.

Columbine Lake has numerous slabs of granite along its shoreline that serve well for lunch and relaxation. Glacier-quarried cliffs rise overhead, but the summit of the nearest prominent peak, Mount Neva, sits back out of sight to the south.

To climb _Mount Neva_ from Columbine Lake, circle a short way to the right around the western shore and climb to an obvious pass in the ridge south of the lake. From the pass climb steeply up the ridge to the summit. It is a long mile from the lake.

Back at the Caribou-Columbine Lake junction, the Caribou Pass Trail heads steeply uphill to the left. It climbs through thick subalpine forests and sunny flower-filled meadows. It crosses rivulets and passes bogs and old mine sites — all without benefit of a single switchback. But the surrounding wilderness beauty supplies ample inspiration to offset any weariness caused by the direct ascent. Soon you find yourself above tree line and then at Caribou Pass, 1.5 miles from the junction.

It is a vast understatement to say that the view to the east from Caribou Pass is spectacular. Your eye will be drawn particularly to the double-humped summit of Apache Peak and the adjacent cone of Navajo Peak, on the right. Caribou Lake lies at tree line, 850 feet below your boots. Uphill from the lake stretches as perfect a terminal moraine as you will ever see. There is a tiny pond behind it — a memento of the melted glacier.

From Caribou Pass a half-mile walk north along the ridgeline takes you to the top of _Satanta Peak_. South of Caribou Pass, the Caribou Pass Trail follows a dramatic route carved in the face of a cliff. Large mats of moss campion grow amid rock slides at the trail's edge. After a half-mile of trail bordered by cliff and campion, you find _Lake Dorothy_ hanging in a cirque below Mount Neva. A short way down the path beyond Dorothy are Arapaho Pass and the trails to Caribou Lake and Arapaho Glacier (see above, Arapaho Pass Trail, and "Indian Peaks, East of the Divide," Arapaho Glacier Trail).

Sky pilot, alpine sunflower (Rydbergia), fairy primrose, wandlily, alplily

Trail Ridge Road

Trail Ridge Road is the highest continuous highway in the United States. Hikes from this road cover every type of ecosystem in Rocky Mountain National Park.

Old Ute Trail

The Old Ute Trail stretches across the national park from Beaver Meadows to Timber Lake Trailhead. But since most of the trail rarely is out of sight or sound of Trail Ridge Road, only two relatively remote sections are described here. The rest of the trail is little used because of its proximity to the road. Nevertheless, if you want to walk it, the entire trail is well marked and easy to follow. It can be reached conveniently from every parking area along Trail Ridge Road except Forest Canyon Overlook.

One section of the Old Ute Trail that is removed from the highway is the 2.9 miles between Gore Range Overlook and Milner Pass. The ideal way to walk this section is to park one car near the continental divide sign at the southwestern end of Poudre Lake (Milner Pass) and hike down to it from Gore Range Overlook, the parking area midway between Lava Cliffs and Fall River Pass. The return to Gore Range Overlook from midway down at Forest Canyon Pass is not terribly steep, however.

NATURE WALK TO MILNER PASS (ALPINE ZONE)

Vandalism and theft, lamentably, are nothing new in national parks. But maintenance personnel and rangers in Rocky Mountain National Park thought it unusual for the lid of a trash can to be missing. They did not realize how bizarre and tragic the loss really was.

In this national park, as elsewhere across the nation, litter receptacles are 20-gallon cans topped by hemispherical lids with doors hinged at the top to swing back into place after trash is pushed inside. The device is windproof and as danger-free as anything imaginable. But of course, nothing is absolutely danger-free.

A particular cow elk adopted the very unusual habit (for an elk) of raiding trash cans. The quarter-ton animal was not subtle in her scrounging. She simply poked her head through the doors on the trash can lids and ate whatever was appealing. But the last time she put her head in, she went too far. The door swung down on her neck, and she was stuck. Lifting her head in fear, the cow jerked the lid from the trash can. But she could not pull the accidental burden from around her neck.

It greatly hampered her normal grazing of alpine tundra vegetation. It made drinking from tundra ponds and gurgling brooks a difficult process. The lid weighed several pounds and wore down the elk's considerable strength. It rubbed her neck raw and bleeding, further sapping her vitality.

In a natural ecosystem, wolves or a grizzly bear would have put the elk out of her misery relatively quickly. But Rocky Mountain National Park is too small to contain these predators. Lack of predators, however, does not mean lack of danger. The winter range of this elk was the alpine tundra on Trail Ridge and nearby mountains — one of the harshest environments south of the Arctic.

The animal died, of course, on the absolutely unforgiving tundra. She died of starvation and exposure to the elements, on the windy ridge between Gore Range Overlook and Mount Ida. The missing trash can lid was discovered by hikers early the following summer. The park's research biologist got the less than romantic task of retrieving the lid from the elk's carcass.

This was not the only elk to die in the normal bitter cold that winter. But the freakish circumstances of her death dramatize how even the slightest, most innocent, altruistic actions of man can tip the extremely fragile balance between life and death in the alpine zone.

The path from Trail Ridge Road down the tundra slopes below Gore Range Overlook first felt the wear and tear of human beings a couple of millennia after ice barriers melted from the glaciated valleys below this high tundra ridge. Perhaps 6000 years ago, ancient Indians used Trail Ridge as a route from one side of the mountains to the other. They eventually were followed by bands of people later called Utes. The Utes were accompanied by dogs that dragged platforms — travois — which gouged parallel ruts in the tundra.

Tundra vegetation is very slow to heal; probably these ruts never healed. Rather, they were obliterated by Utes and later by Arapahos hauling bigger travois, making wider ruts with horses introduced to North America by Europeans. Indians were followed by Europeans themselves in horse-drawn wagons. Wagons were followed by automobiles.

Given the clarity of the route beaten across the tundra by these generations, today's hikers on the Old Ute Trail should have no trouble staying on ground that already is beaten bare. There is no need for modern walkers to do further damage. The rule for responsible tundra travel is simple: since there already is a trail, stay on it.

The most obvious flower to a walker starting downhill from Gore Range Overlook may be the yellow composite variously called alpine sunflower, Rydbergia, or old-man-of-the-mountain. It has the largest blossom on the tundra, two to four inches in diameter. These blossoms are all the more prominent because every alpine sunflower always points its face to the east, a worshipper of the rising sun.

Most tundra flowers cannot spare the time or energy to produce such large blossoms in the six-week interval between winters at this elevation. Alpine sunflower achieves relatively gargantuan blooms by growing only root, leaves and short stem for several years. When it has stored enough food in its large taproot, it will expend it all in a glorious splendor of flower and seeds. Then the entire plant dies.

A massive display of alpine sunflowers may indicate that the previous summer was a good one for building food reserves. Additionally, large numbers indicate two things about the local soil. First, it is soil in transition. It contains much sand and gravel and a little organic material. Water drains away easily. The soil is still evolving, and decaying alpine flowers contribute to the formation of rich humus that eventually will support different types of plants. Second, this species flourishes where the transition soil has been disturbed either by people or by burrowing rodents.

If not the largest, then by far the most common tundra flower along the Old Ute Trail is alpine avens (*Geum rossii*). This diminutive member of the rose family grows in a wide range of habitats although, like alpine sunflower, preferring churned-up soil. Alpine avens has a five-petaled yellow flower and blooms throughout the short summer. The flowers mature to feathery seedheads, and ultimately the fernlike leaves color the autumn tundra red. Alpine avens tend to attract tiny black flies rather than bees to their nectar. Like many other fly-pollinated flowers, these have scant scent.

Quite strong in fragrance is sky pilot, a flower with bell-shaped blossoms growing close together in spheroid formation. Bright orange pollen contrasting with royal blue flowers may be sky pilot's main attraction for bees. But the skunklike aroma of the leaves certainly adds to the plant's distinctive lure.

When checking the aroma of tundra flowers, be careful. The most serious mountaineering accident either of us has suffered befell Donna while she was smelling alpine flowers a few yards below Trail Ridge Road. The injury came from a sedge. Sedges, a family of grasslike plants, make up the largest proportion of vegetable matter on the tundra. Easy to distinguish from grasses, most sedges are three-cornered and solid. Some grow erect and have sharp tips.

One of these pierced Donna's left eye as she crouched low to smell a ground-hugging flower. The injury was very painful and totally incapacitating. Had it occurred on a tundra slope far from any road, the accident could have been very serious indeed. As it was, Donna was bedridden for days. The lesson seems to be that to avoid injury in the mountains, it does not always pay to keep one's eyes open.

Nevertheless, do keep your eyes open for tiny willows creeping along the ground beside the Old Ute Trail. These are woody plants growing far above tree line. Some have "trunks" measuring more than an inch in diameter which often are buried in the ground while the branches lie on the surface. Only twigs less than three inches high can stand erect before the desiccating blasts of winter wind.

Wind is the ever present, most important, least ignorable factor in the tundra environment. Even in summer you cannot walk far along Trail Ridge without commenting — at least mentally — about the wind. The eastern end of the Old Ute Trail passes through Windy Gulch (see below), a section of trail no windier than a good many other sections.

The higher you climb in the mountains, the faster the wind blows. The average wind speed increases also with height above the ground. When you begin to feel the chill and pressure of the wind on the Old Ute Trail, try lying down for a graphic not-to-be-completely-understood-until-you-try-it lesson in how alpine plants survive by being small.

Plants are tiny on the tundra because the growing season is short, because food for growth often is in short supply and because hugging the ground provides protection from winter wind, which quite simply kills anything that dares to stand upright against it. Wind drastically lowers the chill effect of temperature that already is quite cold. It sucks moisture from plant tissues at a time when it cannot be replaced because all water is locked up as ice. Winter winds that frequently surpass 100 miles per hour carry bits of gravel and ice, sandblasting anything that gets in the way.

But wind can be beneficial, too. It scatters pollen and seeds of willows, sedges and many other plants. It piles up snow in some places while sweeping other areas bare of cover. This action creates variety in the life of the tundra, where some plants have adapted to heavy snow cover while others live without protection of snow.

Hikers feel ambivalent about the wind. It is exciting, for it adds a touch of adventure and romance to mountaintop experiences. A well-known quotation from the writings of America's most well known conservationist, John Muir, states that on mountains, "the wind will blow its own freshness into you and the storms their energy."

Perhaps. But the wind also saps your energy if you have to walk into it. It chills your body and dries it out, necessitating the carrying of extra clothing and water. It "burns" exposed skin, brings tears to your eyes and is more than an inconvenience to contact lens wearers. Although experienced mountaineers can predict what the wind will do, local variations caused by the shape of nearby terrain destroy the usefulness of such predictions.

With its predictability subject to unpredictable whims, with its power to both benefit and harm, wind is more human than any inanimate aspect of nature. It is not surprising that people throughout history have tended to think of wind as a living force. In fact, the original New Testament Greek of the Bible uses the same word for both wind and spirit.

West of Trail Ridge, the larger effects of prevailing winds can be seen on the Never Summer Range. Originally called *Ni-che-be-chii* by Arapahos chasing and being chased by their enemies, the Utes, this wall of peaks translated into English as Never Summer. The basis of its name obviously is the number of perpetual snowbanks that deck its eastern slopes. Prevailing westerly winds sweep the snow from western slopes and pile it on the eastern slopes. In summer the resulting huge drifts never disappear completely before winter returns to replenish them.

Between Trail Ridge and the Never Summer Range a rounded ridge rises to its highest elevation at a double-humped mountain to the north. This is Specimen Mountain, so named because its volcanic origin resulted in unusual rock specimens being deposited on its slopes. The heavily eroded western side of Specimen Mountain draws bands of mountain sheep to lick its mineral deposits. Because of its unique qualities, the western slope receives special protection from disturbance as a research natural area. (See below for the hike on Specimen Mountain.)

There is nothing unusual about sighting mountain sheep along Trail Ridge. Far more common, though, are elk, which you quite likely can see with binoculars, especially in early morning or late evening, in the marshes to the left of the trail (east) at tree line. These marshes are typical elk habitat. The abundance of water allows the lush growth of vegetation necessary for supporting a herd of the largest animals in the park. Elk love forest edges where they can feed on herbaceous vegetation but still be near the cover of trees.

To the right and overlooking the marshes, broad open tundra slopes contrast dramatically with steep cliffs leading left to the summit of Mount Ida and other crags to the east. Similarly, the rugged eastern slopes of the Never Summer Range are radically different in appearance from the rounded contours on Specimen Mountain. The craggy areas were carved by glaciers; the rounded slopes followed by the Old Ute Trail remained ice-free.

At the height of the last (Pinedale) glacial period, about 15,000 years ago, the valleys on either side of Trail Ridge were filled with ice. Although deep drifts did occur in some protected areas on the ridge, most of it was cleared of snow by wind. Without insulation from snow, the cleared ground froze permanently during that cold age.

When the climate began at last to warm, ice, snow and frozen ground all began to thaw. The meltwater seeped into cracks in the rock. In winter, the water refroze, expanding as ice and widening the cracks. Years of freezing and thawing broke up rock and mixed it with the overlying soil. The result was the mixture of large rocks and sandy soil over which the Old Ute Trail winds today.

The climate of that dying glacial era was a good deal more frigid than today's. Frost heave — the expansion and contraction of the ground from successive freezing and thawing — tilted rocks on

White-tailed ptarmigan

edge. On steep slopes, gravity pulled rock debris downhill, shaping the slopes in a descending flowing pattern. The abundant water from thawing ground and melting snow completely saturated the ground so that large sections of soggy soil began to slide downhill. This process, called solifluction, formed terraces on the slopes of Trail Ridge.

As the climate became drier and warmer, the surface of Trail Ridge began to stabilize. Plants pioneered bare areas and with their roots added to the stabilization. Today much of the evidence of postglacial instability has been overgrown by tundra with only larger boulders protruding from the surface. But signs of frost heaving, solifluction and rock breaking still are easy to find along the Old Ute Trail.

The trail below Gore Range Overlook has a fairly mild grade and is easy to walk. The slope becomes even less steep where the first skirmishers of tree line dare to advance above the front ranks. These trees (subalpine fir in this case) may not look very magnificent. Yet in the war between woods and wind for control of the heights, these dwarfed and battered Krummholz trees are aboreal heroes.

Krummholz is a German word which translates aptly as "elfinwood." These trees, usually Engelmann spruce or subalpine fir, sprout from seeds that blow up from tree line. (Krummholz are too busy surviving to produce cones and seeds themselves.) The seeds land in some spot protected from the wind. After several years of growth in this sheltered outpost, a tree peeks above the level of its protection, usually a rock. Almost at once the wind kills the top of the tree by desiccating and sandblasting it. But lateral branches fill the protected area and take root where they touch the ground. Gradually, the Krummholz expands its beachhead by growing into the shelter of its own increasing bulk.

There is, of course, a limit to how far this tactic can expand the tree's living space. The wind prunes off every shoot that extends into its blast. No gardener with active shears could be more zealous or thorough in shaping the Krummholz into a living sculpture.

Some trees may gain enough erect posture so that their trunk becomes a windbreak for branches growing on the lee side. All twigs on the windward side are killed, while the leeward branches are flung out like flags on a staff. This distinctive shape has earned the name of "banner tree." Indeed, these trees are the forest's banners of defiance against the mighty wind.

After the trees establish their positions, they provide shelter for other forms of life. Wildlife, such as various birds, snowshoe hares or even elk, find refuge from the wind under Krummholz branches. Subalpine flowers can extend their range upslope if their seeds chance to land within the Krummholz sphere of influence. More often than not, however, hikers find that dense stands of Krummholz are impassable barriers to walking, frustrating to the point of being proverbial.

Between patches of Krummholz and willows there are large open areas of tundra where the wind continues to dominate. One animal affected by it only indirectly is the northern pocket gopher. The chance of seeing one of these subterranean burrowers lies somewhere between slim and zero. But along this trail, evidence of their activity is easy to find: long mounds of dirt, looking rather like a jumble of heavy rope cable.

In winter, when the soil is frozen, pocket gophers tunnel through the snow where it meets the ground. They dig up tundra plants to eat and dump the dirt behind them in the snow tunnel. When the snow melts, the core of dirt remains to mark the route of the tunnel.

We never have seen a pocket gopher, but they generally are described in less than flattering terms. Usually the first statement is that a gopher is a little larger than a rat and has constantly prominent yellowish orange incisors. Its eyes and ears are small; its tail is short and hairless; it has cheek pockets lined with hair which are open to the outside rather than the inside of the mouth. The critter is said to have a grouchy disposition and generally lives alone in unforested habitats at all elevations in the mountains. (In the montane zone, Richardson's ground squirrels are hard to miss and often are incorrectly called gophers.)

As burrowers, pocket gophers have no peers in the Rockies. Their strong, heavily clawed front limbs can dig through the rockiest soil. Their lips close behind their prominent front teeth, which they use to carry rocks and dirt. The burrow of a single gopher can be as long as 500 feet, running from four to 18 inches beneath the surface. This represents about three tons of excavated soil. Side tunnels and galleries are stuffed with roots and other plant parts stored for future gopher meals. Additional chambers are filled with feces or are used for nesting.

All this digging has a profound effect on the tundra environment. Pocket gophers churn up the soil and enrich it with their droppings. On the other hand, the mounds of dirt from their tunneling cover up and kill many plants besides the ones they eat. The dirt dries out and blows away eventually, leaving bare spots where soil rebuilding may take centuries. But before the erosion takes place, the disturbed soil nurtures for decades some of the most spectacular flower displays on the tundra. Relatively tall large-blossomed plants like alpine sunflower and many other colorful blooms grow thickly in these "gopher gardens."

About a half-mile from Gore Range Overlook two small ponds come into view on the left of the trail. These remnants of surface instability during the period of dying glaciers are surrounded by marsh, the richest plant community on the tundra. White marsh-marigold is the most conspicuous, abundant flower; the brilliant magenta of Parry primrose looks like fire when the sun shines through the petals. Willows are the dominant plants of the marsh, and their vivid green, fed by a constant and abundant supply of water, stands out on the tundra when drier areas fade to yellow and russet.

Soon after you become aware of the lush vegetation around the ponds, the barrenness of an old road branches to the right. The Old Ute Trail follows this wide track most of the way down to Milner Pass. The road dates from 1918, when it was built to Fall River Pass; it served as an adventure in transmountain motoring until 1932. That year it was abandoned with the completion of the new western section of Trail Ridge Road between Poudre Lake and Fall River Pass.

After a half-century, the tundra has made a negligible recovery over and around the abandoned unpaved road. Gravel quarries and borrow pits look as though the road machinery left only yesterday. Here is one of the best places along the Old Ute Trail to see moss campion and other cushion plants — pioneers growing on sterile gravel above tree line.

The classic shape of cushion plants is a flattened hemisphere. It presents the minimum possible amount of leaf surface exposure to wind and cold, and the maximum possible exposure to sunlight for photosynthesis. Also, the low streamlined profile is best suited for offering the least amount of resistance to the wind. The shape may be varied to suit particular conditions. You may have seen cushion plants as soon as you left Gore Range Overlook. There heavy foot traffic and construction of the parking lot destroyed significant amounts of soil on the upper portion of the trail, and cushion plants have moved in to help rebuild the soil. On the old road, however, the soil destruction was complete and absolute. Here cushion plants are large and abundant as though having massed their forces to begin the centuries-long process of tundra repair.

Moss campion (resembling but not truly a moss) is the most common and typical cushion plant. It also is one of the prettiest and fastest growing. Under relatively favorable conditions, it may grow to half an inch in diameter in five years. At ten years it begins to produce dainty pink blossoms; at 20 years blooms cover the cushion. At 25 years the cushion may be seven inches in diameter.

A brief search along the old road turns up some good-sized moss campion that appear to be growing right on schedule. Some of the cushions are being invaded by grasses and other flowers that have taken root in the little mound of wind-blown soil captured and hoarded underneath the cushions' many-branched stems. In another thousand years or so, all signs of the road may be gone — except for the excavated gravel pits.

Of all the tough tundra flowers, moss campion probably arouses the most admiration. It manages to survive the rigors of mountaintop living, yet would die quickly if transplanted to a milder climate.

Similarly, a small alpine grouse, the white-tailed ptarmigan, is the toughest animal adapted to life above the trees. This bird is the only species in its clan to sport white feathers on the edges of its tail. In winter the rest of the feathers also are white, providing perfect camouflage in the snow. The camouflage continues into summer: white plumage is replaced by mottled gray and brown feathers which blend in with the rocks protruding everywhere from the tundra.

Ptarmigan are quite common along the Old Ute Trail, but hikers rarely notice them. Holding every feather still, they trust their protective coloration completely to disguise them as rocks. Sometimes, though, close approach will cause them to flush and run away. To have inanimate granite transformed into a scurrying bird always is startling, no matter how many times the trick is repeated. After fleeing on foot, ptarmigan may take flight if they feel closely pursued.

The invisibility of a ptarmigan hen on her nest defies belief. She probably will expose her eggs to the elements only if she is actually touched. If she does not move, a passing hiker is more likely to hear her pounding heart than to see her. Finding a ptarmigan nest is a very rare privilege, even though they must be relatively common.

Spotting ptarmigan at any time of year is a thrill and joy to mountaineers, who seem to identify with the alpine birds. One reason may be their down jackets. Ptarmigan, too, use down but can control its insulating capacity by raising or flattening their feathers. Widespread toes are covered with feathers in winter to keep the birds' feet warm and to support them, just as snowshoes support humans. Mountain climbers may even recognize in ptarmigan a heroic stubbornness to survive and enjoy life on the high peaks.

At 1.5 miles from Gore Range Overlook, the Old Ute Trail levels in Forest Canyon Pass. Looking southeast down Forest Canyon of the

Big Thompson River conveys the impression that Estes Cone sits at the end of the canyon. Actually, that small peak is situated several valleys beyond the mouth of Forest Canyon, just north of Longs Peak. From Estes Cone, it appears that Specimen Mountain sits at the northwestern end of the canyon, which, as you can see from this pass, is equally untrue.

Although Forest Canyon is not quite as long as it appears, 15,000 years ago it did contain the longest glacier — 13 miles — on the east side of the park. The canyon's U-shape, which is quite noticeable from Forest Canyon Pass, is typical of valleys carved by ice 1000 to 1500 feet thick. Today, the steep walls of this trackless canyon help make it the national park's most difficult wilderness to penetrate (see below, Routes to Gorge Lakes).

A short and very gentle uphill walk from Forest Canyon Pass takes you to trees — genuine, upright, erect, undistorted Engelmann spruce and subalpine fir. You have left the tundra behind. Your trail now traverses the subalpine zone, where wind is a friend, for it piles up precious water in reservoirs of snow stolen from the alpine zone. The old road is a wide aisle enclosed by spruce and fir. Smaller spruce and fir are making a good beginning toward reforesting the road itself.

The path is built up over bogs in openings that explode with the colors of lush subalpine flowers after the snow melts. Where it passes through forest, the old road becomes more and more overgrown by trees the lower you go. In a few spots, it and the invading trees are totally obliterated by what appear to be annual avalanche runs.

Yet the Old Ute Trail remains clear as it follows the route of the old automobile road. Poudre Lake and Trail Ridge Road appear through the trees below. The trail continues on, eventually leaving the old highway and descending in easy switchbacks to the parking lot at the south end of Poudre Lake.

The _east section of the Old Ute Trail_, like the Gore Range Overlook-Milner Pass section, is removed from proximity to roads. It runs from the upper end of Beaver Meadows for six uphill miles to Trail

Ridge Road. On the way, it passes through all the life zones in the park and every stage of plant succession.

To reach the trailhead at Beaver Meadows, drive past the park headquarters building on U.S. Highway 36 and into the park through the Beaver Meadows Entrance. Continue straight, bypassing the Bear Lake turnoff, to an unpaved road that meets Route 36 from the left (west) at .7 mile from the Beaver Meadows Entrance. (If you are approaching from the opposite direction, the unpaved road is 2.7 miles south of the joining of Highways 36 and 34 at Deer Ridge Junction.) Turn onto the unpaved road and drive 1.5 miles to a picnic area at the end of the road.

The Old Ute Trail begins on the south side of the parking lot at a crossing of Beaver Brook. The way is very wide and obvious through a grassy meadow into an aspen grove. A fenced-in area is an elk "exclosure," an experiment to determine how vegetation reacts to protection from brousing elk herds. The difference in plant growth inside the exclosure is obvious.

Soon a jeep track branches off to the right to a water filtration plant. Follow the path to the left, to a trail junction. From the junction the left-hand fork, which is used mainly by horse riders, extends for a mile to Moraine Park. The Old Ute Trail follows the right-hand fork.

The Old Ute Trail winds through a classic — that is, open — montane zone forest of ponderosa pine, aspen, juniper and Douglas-fir. About a mile from the trailhead (after passing a spur trail to the left that goes to Moraine Park), the path climbs a bit more steeply through thick Douglas-fir forest on the northern side of a lateral moraine.

Below an interesting rock prominence the trail levels in a very narrow gulch. Aspens predominate at first, but soon Engelmann spruce and subalpine fir take their place in the forest. This delightful cool gulch is the result of the lateral moraine (on the left) having been dumped beside Beaver Mountain (on the right). Here and there to the left along the trail you can see faint spur paths where hikers have climbed to the ridgeline of the moraine to look down into Moraine Park.

Young bighorn

The gulch is easy and comfortable to walk. It is filled with beautiful trees and flowers and seems to have a rather hidden, secret mood. But the unique way in which it was formed probably contributes most to its special charm.

Too soon the trail climbs from the gulch onto a sunny, south-facing slope. The grade moderates amid alder bushes and quaking aspens at a boggy stream crossing. Another short steep stretch follows; then the trail levels again before descending slightly to the top of _Windy Gulch Cascades._

Windy Gulch Cascades are about two miles from the trailhead and make an excellent destination for a short easy hike. The top of the cascades overlook the Big Thompson River Valley. Standing on an open rock ledge and looking southwest up the drainage, you get excellent views of glacier-sculpted Notchtop, Knobtop and Gabletop mountains. The rounded green summit of Mount Wuh, on the opposite side of the valley, blocks views any farther south along the continental divide. But Longs Peak and its neighbors stand out well, defining the horizon to the southeast.

All in all, the view from this easily reached high point is quite good — despite the fact that you cannot see Windy Gulch Cascades. Here the wall of the valley is so steep that from the top of the cascades, they are out of sight below.

A few steps from the viewpoint the trail enters cool charming woods where the stream flows from Windy Gulch, which is uphill from the Cascades. This is a good spot to watch for dippers, stream-loving birds resembling large gray wrens which do a funny bobbing dance on spray-splashed rocks.

Windy Gulch represents another interesting feature of glacial geology: a hanging valley. Water draining from Trail Ridge eroded the gulch; there has been no glacier between its walls. But a series of very large glaciers did move down the Big Thompson River Valley between 160,000 and 15,000 years ago. They broadened the valley floor and steepened the walls. The steepening left Windy Gulch and its tributary stream hanging 1000 feet above the valley floor. Windy Gulch Cascades are the result of the stream's tumbling down the clifflike, glacier-carved valley wall.

A short walk through lodgepole pines leads to an opening unofficially called Ute Meadows. The Old Ute Trail skirts the northern edge of the meadow area, dodging old beaver-made marshes. Past Ute Meadows, the route is marked by cairns as it climbs very steeply through picturesque limber pines to Krummholz at tree line and then on to tundra.

Above the trees, the trail heads through Timberline Pass and levels on the south side of Tombstone Ridge. The two-mile walk across tundra below the monolith-lined ridge probably will reveal many fine tundra flowers and possibly a ptarmigan. The trail is easy to follow from cairn to cairn as it descends to cross Trail Ridge Road at a point two miles west of Rainbow Curve, or .8 mile east of Forest Canyon Overlook.

Most hikers who travel this end of the Old Ute Trail start on Trail Ridge and walk down to Beaver Meadows. Of course, this necessitates a helpful chauffeur for dropping them at Trail Ridge. Or you can shuttle cars back and forth to both ends of the trail. Cars can be parked in a paved turnout a short way west of the point where the Old Ute Trail crosses Trail Ridge Road.

Deer Mountain Trail

Oddly enough, there are quite a few mule deer on Deer Mountain. You also might see a fairly uncommon flower. But virtually certain is an enjoyable view of dramatic peaks. The hike is more comfortable if you carry a quart of water per person, because the trail is sunny and dry.

The Deer Mountain Trailhead is at Deer Ridge Junction, where U.S. Highways 34 and 36 join inside Rocky Mountain National Park. Park your car somewhere along wide road shoulders and begin hiking uphill east of the road junction.

The trail proceeds along a level grade in an open parklike stand of mature ponderosa pines. Be sure at this point to bear right; do not get off on a trail that drops downhill into Horseshoe Park and Aspenglen Campground.

As you begin to climb gradually to the east, notice the wildflowers typical of open montane zone forest: wild geranium, Indian paintbrush, penstemon, miners candle, harebell, sulphurflower, wallflower and Brittons skullcap. The last named is not as common as the others. It can be recognized by its blue-purple blossoms, each of which has a protruding lip shaped like a cap. Brittons skullcap is a member of the mint family; its leaves grow opposite each other on a square stem. It grows from four to six inches tall.

Quaking aspens soon begin to appear at trailside, their white bark scarred black by nibbling elk. The aspens frame lovely vistas of Longs Peak and other high mountains along the Front Range. Closer by are lateral moraines — glacial ridges — bordering Moraine Park and Beaver Meadows.

From the view of Longs Peak and the Front Range, the trail switchbacks to the left to a view dominated by Ypsilon Mountain, in the Mummy Range. Ypsilon is named for vertical snow-filled gullies that form a Y on its face. For the first two miles, the path maintains a fairly moderate grade by following switchbacks which take you from the view on one side of Deer Mountain to the view on the other.

Eventually, you reach a broad level area on Deer Mountain, where limber pines and aspens block long vistas. The natural tendency of limber pine to drama, especially in death, is obvious here. Forest fires have left enough picturesque twisted snags of burned pine to keep photographic artists busy for days. Despite its relatively low altitude, Deer Mountain seems to be a preferred target for lightning, which probably started the fires. Remember this when thunderheads start to build; a hasty retreat back down the mountain may be wise.

For more than a half-mile, the trail meanders up and down on the mountain until you suspect that you are headed down the other side toward Estes Park. About the time your suspicion matures to certainty, you reach a trail junction where a spur branches sharply south (right) to the summit. The final few yards to the top are steeper than most hikers like, but the reward is a good view in nearly every direction.

Beyond the junction, the trail switchbacks downhill to the east in the same fashion by which it climbed. Following this path across the park boundary will lead you to mazes of horse trails, roads, homes and eventually an ice cream cone in downtown Estes Park.

Routes to Gorge Lakes

Gorge Lakes are the nine named tarns and a scattering of unnamed pools on the other side of Forest Canyon when viewed from Rock Cut, on Trail Ridge Road. Because Gorge Lakes are so visible and in such a dramatic setting, many hikers are struck with a desire to visit them. But there is no trail, and they are difficult to reach.

Most hikers take the longest route, which crosses the least difficult terrain. Beginning at Gore Range Overlook, they follow the Old Ute Trail southwest 1.5 miles to Forest Canyon Pass (see above, Old Ute Trail). There they leave the old road and climb to the south along the side of the long ridge leading up to Mount Ida. From Forest Canyon Pass it is four miles of up-and-down hiking with some unavoidable marsh sloshing to reach a ridge overlooking lovely meadows in the vicinity of _Love Lake_. Then they continue on to _Arrowhead Lake_, the largest of the Gorge Lakes and one of the closest. From Arrowhead the uphill terrain to _Inkwell_ and _Doughnut lakes_ is not terribly steep. Reaching the higher lakes involves steep climbing over rock ledges.

The trail that approaches closest to Gorge Lakes is a trail to Timber Lake (see below, Timber Lake Trail). From Timber Lake, it is less than a mile as the raven flies to _Azure Lake_, among the highest Gorge Lakes. That would be fine if you could fly 1800 feet up and over Mount Ida and down 980 feet to Azure. Alas, to follow this route, mere hikers must climb Mount Ida twice in one day. The terrain is steep and arduous.

Yet the route from Timber Lake is less steep and arduous, and involves less loss of elevation, than the shortest (by proverbial bird flight) route. This least-recommended way drops from a parking area east of Rock Cut into Forest Canyon, struggles through dense subalpine forest, fords the Big Thompson River and fights uphill through more thick woods and marsh to _Little Rock Lake_ and _Rock Lake_. These are not the most scenic of the Gorge Lakes, and returning to Trail Ridge is much harder than the descent. This route combines most of the problems of the other two and throws in some of its own. It is a challenge.

Trails from Milner Pass

Milner Pass is a low point on the continental divide. From Poudre Lake, on the east side of the pass, the Cache la Poudre River flows into the Mississippi River drainage. Beaver Creek, on the west side, flows into the Colorado River drainage. The pass is the focal point of several trails.

The _Poudre River Trail_ begins on the west side of Trail Ridge Road just north of Poudre Lake. The path passes up and down through subalpine woods but soon drops into willows along the river and is very sloppy. Occasionally, it loses itself in a maze of elk trails. The chances of seeing deer and elk in the valley are excellent.

The valley widens a bit, and the trail dries out considerably 5.6 miles downstream, where Chapin Creek and the Chapin Creek Trail join the Poudre River and its trail from the right. From this point on, the Poudre River Trail is much easier to walk, avoiding beaver swamps and willow thickets. Running north, it follows an easy grade for 3.4 miles to a junction with the Mummy Pass Trail (see "Mummy Range," Mummy Pass Trail).

The trail on _Specimen Mountain_ is the most popular trail beginning at Milner Pass. Parking space for Specimen Mountain Trailhead is situated on the west side of Trail Ridge Road at roughly the midpoint of Poudre Lake. The damp meadow beside the parking area can be very colorful with subalpine flowers in July and August.

Specimen's western slope has been given special preservation status as a research natural area. The entire mountain is closed to hiking from May 1 to July 1 to protect bighorn sheep from disturbance during lambing season. And at any time of year it is a poor practice to try approaching the sheep closely for photography. The animals will not tolerate close approach, and the futile chase will cause harmful stress to both sheep and erstwhile photographer. The photographer's friends will suffer unpleasant stress later if they are forced to view a dot reputed to be a mountain sheep in nontelephoto pictures of acres of rocks.

The trail up Specimen Mountain climbs steeply through mature subalpine forest to tree line. At the forest's upper edge there are classic banner trees and many Colorado blue columbine and Indian paintbrush. Well onto the tundra, a mile from the trailhead, you arrive at the edge of _The Crater_. This area was named in the belief that it was the eroded crater of a long extinct volcano of Specimen Mountain. Subsequent geological study, however, established that the heavily eroded western slopes of Specimen are not the crater of an ancient caldera. Additional investigation showed that Specimen Mountain is not a volcano, extinct or otherwise. Rather, it is formed of ash from the flow of an eruption that took place elsewhere, perhaps in the Never Summer Range.

The mountain itself was named for the variety of interesting rock specimens deposited by volcanic eruptions. It need not be said, of course, that collecting specimens is strictly forbidden in a national park.

Forbidden, too, is hiking by the public in The Crater or west of the continental divide along the mountain's ridgeline. This closure protects bighorn sheep that use the mineral licks in The Crater. From The Crater, they climb to tundra slopes along the divide to graze. These mineral and vegetation resources benefit the sheep only if hikers are not close at hand to disturb them.

Besides protecting the sheep, the closure of The Crater and the continental divide gives more hikers the chance to see bighorn in a dramatic setting. If the first hiker who sees the sheep each day were permitted to attempt an always futile stalk, he would scare the sheep away. The bighorn would be undernourished, and subsequent hikers that day would not have the pleasure of seeing them. But with the first hiker restricted to binoculars or long telephoto lens for a close view, the sheep do not feel harassed and will stay around most of the day. Thus the literally scores of hikers who daily climb Specimen in summer all get a chance to see the sheep.

The scores of hikers, however, have caused severe impact despite the closure. An obvious trail from The Crater leads straight up a very steep puff-and-pant slope to a false summit far below the true top of the mountain. The sheep would like to graze on the entire tundra slope east of the divide, but hikers tramping doggedly up the steep trail tend to keep the bighorn confined to a narrow strip just east of The Crater. Even hikers who stay on the trail can disturb the sheep enough to cause them to retreat into the rocks, where they have little or no food.

The tundra has taken a beating from tramping feet. The scenario of tundra destruction on a heavily used peak begins with a beaten path that goes straight up and down. Water runs down the path, eroding it and making it hard to walk on. Therefore, hikers walk on the tundra on both sides of the path, also straight up and down. More wear and erosion follow. Gradually (or not so gradually where there are as many lug-soled hikers as on Specimen) the path becomes a broad, eroded road.

The erosion problem can be solved by building a well-designed trail that does not shoot straight up the mountain and erode like a beaten path. But trail construction damages a specific, although confined, area of tundra and is very visible from a distance. For instance, a constructed trail on Specimen would mar the side of the mountain seen by literally millions of people from Trail Ridge Road.

Hikers can help solve the erosion problem by not climbing all the way to the top of Specimen Mountain. If you want only to see bighorn, take your binoculars to The Crater and just sit. The Crater offers both alpine and subalpine wildflowers, and the vistas from there are hard to beat. Besides sheep, the wildlife includes marmots, golden-mantled ground squirrels and pikas.

A nice alternative to climbing Specimen is to ascend *Shipler Mountain*, an easy 1.5 miles from The Crater. To reach Shipler, head left (south) from The Crater to follow the contour around the east side of the ridge. Once around the large bump south of The Crater, descend slightly into an open saddle bordered by Krummholz. Bear right out of the saddle to bypass another bump on the ridge. Past the second bump, climb directly to the top of Shipler. The view of the Never Summer Range from the summit is similar to that from The Crater or the summit of Specimen. Additionally, Shipler offers unique perspectives of The Crater and of the Kawuneeche Valley.

Another trail from Milner Pass begins at the continental divide sign at the southern end of Poudre Lake and goes to *Mount Ida*. You ascend the Old Ute Trail to the abandoned section of old highway on Trail Ridge. Continue uphill on the road through one bend to the road's southernmost point. Where it switchbacks sharply north along a road cut, leave the old highway and keep climbing south toward Ida.

Less than a mile from Milner Pass, you climb above the trees. Continue climbing steadily south, bypassing a bump on the ridgeline and ascending to a saddle on the continental divide above Forest Canyon. Hike up the divide, keeping to the right (west) of minor promontories. After more than three miles of steady uphill walking on tundra, you think that surely the summit of Ida must be close, just up that last hill. But you reach a false summit first. Descend a bit to climb a quarter-mile farther over large flat rocks. The summit of Ida is about 4.5 miles from Milner Pass.

The view from the top of Ida is well worth the moderately tiring walk it takes to get there. The Never Summers are fine to the west, but even more dramatic, scattered among rugged precipices, are Gorge Lakes, hundreds of feet straight down from your boots. Less rugged but nevertheless grand is the view to the southwest of Julian Lake, Big Meadows and Lake Granby.

From Ida you can descend with ease to Timber Lake and the 4.8 mile path to Trail Ridge Road at Timber Creek Trailhead. From the picnic area, a three-mile switchback connection of the Old Ute Trail leads uphill to Milner Pass. More appealing, perhaps, is to arrange for vehicular transportation. Timber Lake is also a common route of ascent for Ida (see below, Timber Lake Trail).

From the saddle southeast of Ida, on the divide, it is a relatively easy descent to Azure Lake and other Gorge Lakes. Climbing back out is another matter (see above, Routes to Gorge Lakes).

Another possibility is to hike southeast from the saddle, climbing or skirting the next unnamed summit on the divide, to look down on Highest Lake, highest of the Gorge Lakes. To reach *Cracktop*, circle around the top of the cirque containing Highest Lake and head northeast toward the summit of *Mount Julian*. Cracktop is the last bump before you reach the ragged knife ridge that leads from the divide to Julian. Continuing on the one-half mile to Julian necessitates finding a way around the huge boulders blocking the rugged ridgeline. Try to stay on the less cliffy side, away from Gorge Lakes.

Three-fourths mile past Julian, at the end of the ridge, is *Terra Tomah Mountain*. It is an uncomplicated walk, but after Ida, Cracktop and Julian, the up-and-down trudge to Terra Tomah is wearing, and once there, you retrace your steps. The only alternative is to descend into Forest Canyon, which is a good deal harder to traverse than the peaks.

Timber Lake Trail

The *Timber Lake Trail* is advocated by some hikers as the best route up Mount Ida, despite the fact that the route from Milner Pass (see above) is 1.5 miles shorter and has 1750 feet less elevation gain. Nonetheless, the route to Timber Lake is an interesting hike, worth doing on its own merits.

The parking area for Timber Lake Trailhead is located on the eastside of Trail Ridge Road, 9.6 miles north of the Grand Lake Entrance to the national park and 10.7 miles southwest of Fall River Pass. From the trailhead, Timber Lake Trail heads east across a level meadow to a junction where the Old Ute Trail heads to the left uphill to Milner Pass. The Timber Lake Trail continues to the right through open woods to cross Beaver Creek on a substantial bridge. Past the crossing, the trail climbs fairly steeply along the flank of Jackstraw Mountain. Still close enough to Trail Ridge Road so you can hear the traffic, the trail is enclosed by dense stands of lodgepole pines.

A few miles from the trailhead and 400 feet above the valley floor, the path begins to parallel Timber Creek, going upstream. Then the grade is gentle until you arrive at the junction of the Timber Lake and Timber Creek trails, 3.1 miles from the trailhead. Here, where a tributary flows into Timber Creek, the landscape is filled with moisture-loving flowers — marsh-marigold, senecios, tall chiming bells, Parry primrose.

The *Timber Creek Trail* crosses the creek a few yards south of the junction, then climbs steeply to moderate its grade parallel to the creek, going downstream, along the south valley wall. But after .6 mile, the path disappears in the marshes of Long Meadows. It reappears 1.5 miles later at the southern end of Long Meadows and proceeds rather obscurely for another 1.5 miles to meet the Onahu Creek Trail. The least swampy way to traverse Long Meadows is anybody's guess. The Park Service terms Long Meadows a "cross-country experience."

Back on the Timber Lake Trail, the grade steepens past the junction and climbs through a series of very short switchbacks. Finally you emerge into a meadow at the base of Jackstraw Mountain. Wetland subalpine flowers — paintbrush, kings crown (roseroot), tall chiming bells — line both sides of the trail as it parallels Timber Creek through the meadow.

The trail reenters pleasant subalpine forest but soon leaves again to wind across a very rocky area. A final set of switchbacks takes you to the marshy land around the outlet of Timber Lake. The northern shore of the lake bears some trees, but the southern end has only rock, some tundra and snowfields that last far into summer.

Timber Lake is not as spectacular as many lakes in the park; no sheer cliffs rise above it. But the terrain is rugged enough to hide the summit of _Mount Ida_. To climb Ida, head up not terribly steep tundra to a low point on the ridge south of the lake. From this saddle it is an uncomplicated walk to the summit.

From this saddle you can also go to _Julian Lake_, about a mile southeast of Timber Lake, although most hikers merely view Julian from the summit of Ida. Julian can be reached also via an unmaintained path from the lower (south) section of the Timber Creek Trail, which too is rather vague in places.

Jackstraw Mountain is an easy climb from the flowery meadow you encountered on the way to Timber Lake. Various game trails, typically quite steep but short, lead up to the broad summit. Jackstraw was named for the view of its fire-cleared slopes as seen from Trail Ridge Road. Had the namers seen the massive spread of elk excrement on top of the peak, the name chosen might have been even more colorful.

Trails from Holzwarth Homestead

Holzwarth Homestead, which became part of Rocky Mountain National Park in 1974, greatly benefits all park visitors by providing the opportunity to experience a living history exhibit. Moreover, the acquisition opened new routes for hikers to _Mount Stratus_ and _Green Knoll_.

The parking area for Holzwarth Homestead lies (well marked) on the west side of Trail Ridge Road, 7.2 miles north of the Grand Lake Entrance to the park and 13.1 miles southwest of Fall River Pass. From the parking area, you walk to the homestead along an unpaved road which is closed to public vehicles.

At the homestead, pass through the corral gate and continue walking until you reach a fork in the road. Take the right-hand fork, which is a service road for the Grand Ditch, a water diversion project in the Never Summer Range to irrigate the plains east of the Rockies. Follow the road uphill to the level of the ditch, about three miles of walking from the parking area.

Where the grade flattens beside the ditch, cross the water on an antiquated bridge providing access to routes up Mount Stratus and Green Knoll. Walk north along the west side of the ditch for a short way, while watching for a faint path that takes off straight uphill to the left through the trees on the southeastern slopes of Green Knoll. Blazes on trees as well as the track on the ground make the path uncomplicated to follow, but very steep.

As it climbs through the forest, the track bends left around the mountain, zigzagging its way above tree line onto tundra. Eventually, it reaches the ridgeline between Green Knoll and Mount Stratus. There the path becomes faint. It does not matter if you lose it, though, because the choice of routes at this point is limited.

Turning left leads to pyramid-shaped Mount Stratus, which, prior to the opening of access through Holzwarth Homestead, was one of the most remote summits in the Never Summer Range. Narrow, crumbly ridges lead to it from Baker Mountain, Mount Nimbus and Green Knoll; the ridge from Green Knoll is by far the shortest and the easiest to reach. Additionally, it is the ridge with the most exposure to falls. Be very careful here; do not cause rocks or your body to bombard campers exploring in Red Gulch, on the north side of the ridge.

Turning right on the ridgeline between Green Knoll and Mount Stratus leads to the summit of Green Knoll, less than five miles from Trail Ridge Road. This mountain is not high but is well situated for excellent views of the Colorado River drainage all the way north to La Poudre Pass. Various informal trails lead back down to the Grand Ditch via more northerly slopes than those you ascended. Locating and walking these trails is an interesting experience in route finding.

The route-finding adventure could begin long before you leave the summit of Green Knoll if the bridge over the Grand Ditch finally collapses, for the bridge probably would not be rebuilt. In that event, you would face an unbelievably cold wade across the ditch. Alternatively, you could walk a short way south on the road paralleling the ditch to another crossing. It probably would be best to climb the Green Knoll ridge directly from this crossing, because the west side of the ditch is very precipitous and the footing is bad. Following the west side in an attempt to reach the path described above, to Green Knoll and Mount Stratus, you could easily fall into the ditch's icy water.

Baker Gulch Trail System (Arapaho National Forest)

The Baker Gulch Trail is the easiest approach to a lake or peak in the Never Summer Range. Baker Gulch has felt the heavy hand of man, but the area remains beautiful and well worth visiting.

Access to the Baker Gulch Trail begins at a picnic area on the west side of Trail Ridge Road, 6.4 miles north of the Grand Lake Entrance to the park and 13.9 miles southwest of Fall River Pass. From the picnic area, an unpaved road extends west for three-fourths mile nearly to the boundary of Arapaho National Forest. Since this road may be closed to public vehicles during the summer, you should park at the picnic area and walk along the road.

Staying overnight in Baker Gulch entails parking your car inside the national park. Thus, even if not backpacking in the park, you need to leave the stub of a backcountry camping permit on your car's dashboard. This helps Park Service rangers, who check the parking lot daily, to keep track of who is in the park's backcountry and to check on your car while you are gone. You can pick up backcountry camping permits at park offices located north of Grand Lake or west of Estes Park.

From the picnic area, the unpaved road crosses the Colorado River and meadows in the Kawuneeche Valley. As meadow gives way to forest, the road divides. Take the right-hand fork, which bends around to the beginning of the Baker Gulch Trail, just short of the national forest boundary.

Once inside the national forest, the trail runs upstream on a ridge above the creek flowing down Baker Gulch. Lodgepole pines block all distant views until you reach clearings created by beavers about 1.5 miles from the forest boundary.

Just past the beaver workings, a series of short switchbacks

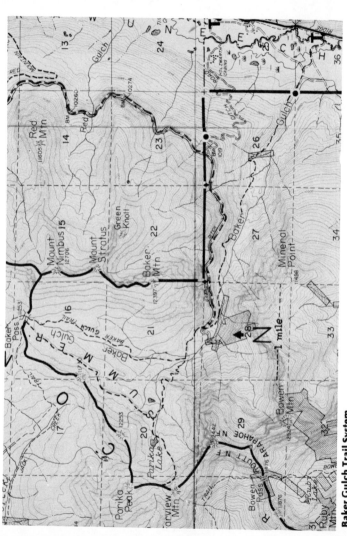

Baker Gulch Trail System

leads to rocky rubble cast down from excavation for the Grand Ditch. Views open here across the narrow valley to Mineral Point and uphill into Baker Gulch. After you walk a half-mile along fractured rock slopes below the ditch, new vistas appear to the southeast, all the way to the back of the Front Range. Chiefs Head Peak presents a very pointed aspect from this angle. From farther up the trail, Longs Peak comes into sight, looking very boxy.

You may not notice the distant peaks if your attention centers on the raspberry bushes growing among the rocks. At the right time of a good year, these bushes produce abundant and excellent fruit.

After walking for a long, hot mile over the foot-bruising rubble of ditch excavation, hikers are relieved to reenter subalpine forest. Soon the trail climbs steeply a short distance uphill to the ditch. When you cross the ditch via a substantial bridge, you enter a different world. Here no water has been diverted, and the subalpine growth is luxuriantly beautiful.

The trail becomes less distinct as it passes through three marshy meadows and enters cool, mature subalpine woods. Traveling on an easy grade, you feel real soil underfoot — dirt well laced with organic matter made available by adequate water. It is almost springy to walk on.

About a half-mile from the ditch, you enter a subalpine meadow and cross the stream flowing down Baker Gulch, from the right (north). Past the stream crossing, there is a trail junction. From the junction the Baker Gulch Trail cuts right to head uphill toward Baker Pass on the continental divide (see below). _The Parika Lake Trail_ continues straight ahead and soon crosses the stream flowing from Parika Lake. It climbs directly upslope and away from the stream. There are a few switchbacks to help, but this stretch seems very steep in comparison with that below.

After a final switchback to the left, the path opens into a marsh where you see a brook tumbling down a ravine from Farview Mountain. It is a nice setting, with little waterfalls and a pond surrounded by meadow.

The final quarter-mile to Parika Lake is very steep. But rest stops offer views of the wall of the Never Summer Range, especially Baker Mountain and Mounts Stratus and Nimbus. Longs Peak still is visible far to the southeast down Baker Gulch. After a trail runs off to the right (see below), it is just a few hundred yards farther to Parika Lake.

The lake lies in open tundra, with an unnamed 12,253-foot bump to the north, _Parika Peak_ directly west and Farview Mountain to the southwest. In the vicinity of the lake's outlet, a few stunted trees have been vandalized by an active ax directed by a small mind. Other unfortunate evidences of ignorant and/or malicious visitation appear here and there amid the Krummholz, but the lakeshore itself remains relatively unspoiled.

From the outlet a trail climbs southwest across shelves overlooking the lake before angling north uphill to a broad saddle on the continental divide situated between Farview Mountain and Parika Peak. The trail runs to the left along the divide toward Farview. From the saddle it is a fairly easy climb to the right to the double-humped top of Parika. The summit cairn is located on the northwestern part of the peak, but deciding which point really is highest is tough.

Views from the divide are similar to those from Parika Lake except that Jack Creek drainage is visible to the north, North Park to the west, and Bowen Gulch and Bowen Mountain to the southwest. You can follow the divide down the eastern slope of Parika Peak to a saddle between Parika and its unnamed neighbor. There you meet a trail that ascends south from the Jack Creek drainage and continues vaguely through marshy terrain downhill to the northern shore of Parika Lake.

Back at the junction a few hundred yards short of Parika Lake, the trail branching to the north goes to the vicinity of _Baker Pass_. This route runs directly uphill to the pass without losing any elevation; you would have to lose elevation from here if you wish to reach Baker Pass via the Baker Gulch Trail.

Back at the earlier junction just after the stream crossing, the Baker Gulch Trail heads north and away from the Parika Lake Trail, climbing gradually through a maze of elk trails and marsh. When the trail passes into forest, Engelmann spruce and subalpine fir are large, and subalpine flowers — monkshood, larkspur, tall chiming bells — are abundant. Eventually, the route becomes considerably less distinct and crosses a stream to climb to another track on the side of _Baker Mountain_. If you desire, you can keep on climbing very steeply to the east to the summit of Baker.

From the Parika Lake Trail, it is a little more than two miles of exploration on the Baker Gulch Trail to Baker Pass. The overall grade is not difficult and the terrain is lovely, especially above the trees. A beautiful chartreuse tundra extends from tree line to what appears to be the pass. Actually, the top of the pass is on the continental divide and cannot be seen from tree line.

The trail crosses the divide into the Michigan River drainage. To the east, the Never Summer Range is a high wall of broad tundra slopes, except for the black cone of Mount Richthofen and the sharp ridge of Lead Mountain at the northern end of the wall. The gentle tundra slopes of Mount Cindy are to the northwest.

To descend from the pass to Parika Lake, you may have to hunt around a bit for a trail that materializes downhill and south of the pass. Head southwest below the ridge of the continental divide past mine tailings and an old cabin. Stay above tree line and watch for a distinct path that descends into the trees. It ends about 1.5 miles later at the junction with the Parika Lake Trail a few hundred yards east of the lake.

Onahu Creek-Green Mountain Circle

The Onahu Creek and Green Mountain trails form a very convenient circle hike. The trailheads of Onahu Creek and Green Mountain trails are near enough to each other that car shuffling is unnecessary. And the 6.5 miles of trail are interesting, pleasant and pretty.

Begin by dropping packs and a guard at Onahu Creek Trailhead, 3.3 miles north of the Grand Lake Entrance to the park

North Inlet and Tonahutu Creek trail systems and

Onahu Creek-Green Mountain Circle

and 17 miles southwest of Fall River Pass. The driver then takes the car down the road (south) for slightly more than a mile to the parking lot at Green Mountain Trailhead. It is a very easy walk back to Onahu along a trail bordering the west (left) side of the road. In August this procedure gives the person guarding the packs just enough time to pick a handful of wild strawberries.

Starting out through willows that show signs of heavy elk browsing in winter, the Onahu Creek Trail maintains a nearly level grade through marshy meadow to forest of lodgepole pines and quaking aspens. As the grade steepens, aspens begin to be crowded out. Young Engelmann spruce and subalpine fir growing in indicate that absence of forest fire in this area is allowing plant succession to proceed toward a climax spruce-fir forest. Spruce and fir already have achieved dominance along the water courses, where extra moisture speeds their growth.

Nevertheless, as the trail steepens considerably, lodgepole pines continue to prevail. There are enough brooks to create pleasant variety in what otherwise would be a monotonous lodgepole forest. Chickarees (red squirrels) seem to be the dominant animals here, angrily cursing every hiker who dares to trespass into their domain. The familiar buzzing calls of mountain chickadees are friendlier greetings. Wild strawberries and blueberries offer a special treat to hikers in late summer.

After only one moderately steep section, the trail levels along the main drainage of Onahu Creek. Passing from forest into meadow and back into shade along the broad valley floor, the path recrosses the creek for the last time at a distance of three miles from the road. Past the bridge, Timber Creek Trail runs in vaguely from the left. (Timber Creek Trail is obscure in some sections and non-existent in others. See above, Timber Lake Trail.)

From the creek, the well-constructed trail slants up a northern slope where the surrounding forest is classic mature spruce-fir. But on the sunnier ridgetop, lodgepole pines take over again. The trail, now running south, winds on a level grade overlooking a swampy depression and is crossed by several faint elk trails before descending fairly steeply to a junction with Tonahutu Creek Trail at Big Meadows.

From the junction, follow Tonahutu Creek Trail south along the side of Big Meadows for slightly more than a half-mile. Take time to examine a couple of log ruins at the edge of the forest. These are the remains of a turn of the century haying operation run by Sam Stone. One structure was a barn, the other a human habitation. Stone plowed part of the meadows, but little came of his attempt at development. He eventually fell under the influence of a woman spiritualist who divined that there was gold to be found in Paradise Park, on what is now the national park's southern boundary. Together she and Stone went off to look for a rich lode. Fortunately, the crystal ball was wrong; Paradise Park remained unmined, unspoiled and true to its name.

Today, little remains of Sam Stone's ranch in Big Meadows. His buildings are slow to decay because of the chilly, dry climate, but they are at least in an advanced state of disrepair. Elephantheads (little red elephants) have replaced his livestock in the meadows.

The Tonahutu Creek-Green Mountain Trail junction is broad and obvious. Green Mountain Trail once was a wagon road along which Sam Stone's hay was hauled from Big Meadows to Green Mountain Ranch. The way still is wide, singularly free of rocks, not very steep and easy to travel. Relatively plentiful water on this northern slope makes possible a greater variety of vegetation than on the rest of the circle hike. You will reach Trail Ridge Road 1.8 miles along Green Mountain Trail from Big Meadows.

Mountain chickadee on lodgepole pine

Phantom Valley

Phantom Valley is a singularly appropriate name for a valley that does not exist. The guest ranch that formerly stood at the trailhead for most routes into the Never Summer Range was called Phantom Valley Ranch. Perhaps it was named for the ghosts of trappers, miners and irrigation ditch diggers who all figured prominently in the history of the area. The National Park Service purchased and obliterated the ranch to restore the setting to a more pristine condition.

To reach the trailhead for the Red Mountain and Luly City trail systems, drive along Trail Ridge Road for 10.2 miles west of Fall River Pass or 10.1 miles from the Grand Lake Entrance to the national park. At this point, turn west down the road that ends after a few hundred yards at Phantom Valley picnic area.

Red Mountain Trail System

The Red Mountain Trail begins on the west (left-hand) side of the parking area. Immediately past the trailhead, the path bridges the Colorado River and continues across a meadow. The grade steepens somewhat after entering lodgepole pine woods, then steepens considerably just before crossing Opposition Creek. Past the creek, a climb to the south up an open rocky slope reveals views downhill to the meadows and marshes of Kawuneeche Valley. Raspberry bushes growing among the rocks produce delicious fruit in late August.

When you reenter the woods, the grade becomes less steep. A

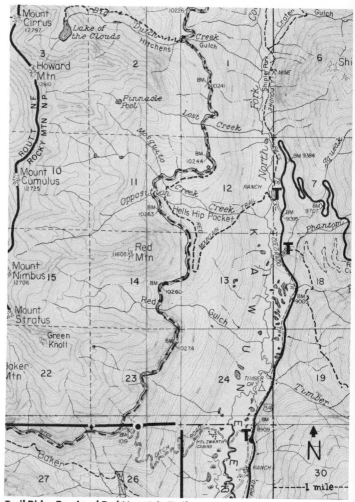

Trail Ridge Road and Red Mountain Trail

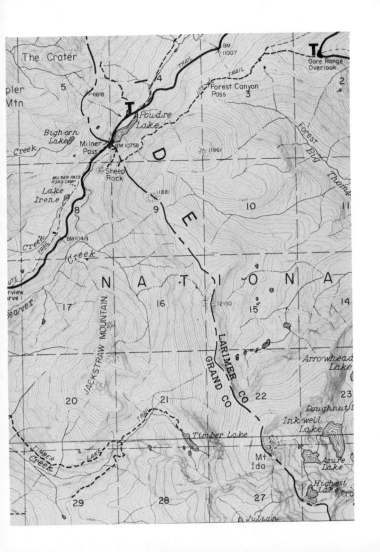

switchback turns you in the opposite direction (north) along a level walk through subalpine forest. Blueberries take over the wild edibles role along this section of trail, where there is little other ground cover. A few openings among the trees reveal occasional views to the east, and a large rocky gap in the forest gives another perspective of Kawuneeche Valley.

The way heads slightly downhill to cross Opposition and Mosquito creeks, then climbs up to the service road that follows the Grand Ditch. The ditch is a water diversion project irrigating crops on the plains east of the Rockies. The road, 2.8 trail miles from Phantom Valley picnic area, is closed to public vehicles and provides hiking access to many destinations in the Never Summer Range. The most popular may be _Lake of the Clouds_.

To reach the lake, take the very easy walk to the north (right) along the ditch. Red Mountain rises behind you and Mount Cumulus to the left. Directly ahead are the massive ridges of Howard and Lead mountains. Hitchens Gulch, which leads to Lake of the Clouds, is out of sight behind Howard. Clumps of subalpine flowers — Parry primrose, tall chiming bells, senecios, brookcress — grow nicely in some spots along the ditch.

The flowers are especially fine 1.7 miles along the road at Hitchens Gulch, where Big Dutch Creek flows east toward the Colorado River. Cross the creek and then the ditch, on a bridge, and follow the Lake of the Clouds Trail uphill through switchbacks in Hitchens Gulch. The trail ascends steeply into beautiful subalpine forest where Engelmann spruce and subalpine fir grow to huge size, well watered by runoff from melting snowbanks. The runoff flows down to the Grand Ditch.

At a small clearing, which is the site of long-ago mining activity, the grade becomes less steep. Hikers in June may find the trail hidden by snow in some places. The forest opens a bit, and the trail crosses wet meadows here and there. Continuing west toward Hart Ridge between Mount Cirrus and Lead Mountain, you reach a meadow with a small, marshy pond at its southern end. Keeping just inside the woods, skirt the southern shore and continue west to a short, steep slope 5.7 miles from the trailhead.

The path ends at the top of the slope by the edge of a boulder field below Lake of the Clouds. This debris is an obstacle course of large, shaky, angular rocks, among which live a healthy population of large black spiders. Looking south (left), you can see a waterfall which drops from the cirque containing Lake of the Clouds, below Mount Cirrus.

The rest of the route to the lake is supposed to be marked with cairns. In any case, do not try to follow Big Dutch Creek all the way to the lake. Rather, fight your way southwest through cobwebs across the jumbled boulders to a very steep slope. There is no good way to climb this barrier. Cairns indicate the least difficult route over tundra ledges to the basin containing Lake of the Clouds, 6.3 miles from Phantom Valley picnic area.

After the grade levels in the basin, walk over the tundra and bedrock to the shore of the lake. This is the only really solid rock around Lake of the Clouds; the other shores are bounded by steep, loose rock and ice fields.

Photos taken from the solid rock are not particularly impressive. But good shots can be had from the eastern or western shore. Be careful of the snowfield on the northwest; an uncontrolled slide there would land you in water where ice still floats in July.

You might try for photos of the marmots and pikas that live around the lake. If they are feeling unfriendly, attach close-up equipment to your camera and photograph the excellent examples of tundra cushion plants among the rocks.

To ascend _Lead Mountain_, bear right from the Lake of the Clouds Trail at the spidery boulder field. Crossing the boulders, climb to tundra slopes below the saddle situated between Lead and an unnamed summit to the east (right). Continue uphill to the saddle, staying west (left) of snowfields wherever possible. From the saddle make your way over tundra, rock and sometimes snow to the knife ridge that leads to Lead's summit.

This is the part of the climb that sticks most firmly in everyone's memory, for the ridgetop is about three feet wide. The footing on top, however, is reasonably solid, while loose rock makes for awful going below the ridge on the south side. The north side is precipice. We recommend walking steadily along the ridgeline to the summit.

A variation on the return route is to go back down the knife ridge as far as the saddle and then descend to the north. A snowfield on the north side of Lead can be an easy way down for those equipped for and experienced in climbing on snow and ice. But after approximately mid-July, the lower and less steep part of the snowfield melts and exposes rocks. These could bring an unpleasantly sudden and painful stop to an uncontrolled slide from the steeper upper part of the snowfield, which takes longer to melt. Therefore, you may wish to descend later in the season via rocks along the edge of the snowfield, traversing carefully from time to time to reach easier rock. Failure to be careful on the snow could add another grisly incident to the history of _Skeleton Gulch_, which is situated below the snowfield. Descend into the gulch and catch a trail back to the Grand Ditch service road.

You can cross a bridge over the ditch and walk down a trail on the other side to the Thunder Pass Trail, Lulu City and finally Phantom Valley picnic area. From the Skeleton Gulch Trail-Grand Ditch road junction to the trailhead, it is 4.7 miles via Lulu City and seven miles via the Red Mountain Trail.

To climb Mount Howard from the Red Mountain Trail-Grand Ditch junction, walk south along the ditch service road .2 mile to Mosquito Creek. Cross the ditch on a bridge and continue up the east side of Mosquito Creek on an unmaintained trail for about a mile to _Pinnacle Pool._ The pinnacle is a ridge extending east from the continental divide.

Turn left past Pinnacle Pool and ascend between the pinnacle ridge and the ridge leading east from Howard. About a half-mile up the valley, you can turn right and begin climbing a tundra slope toward the top of Howard's east ridge. Too soon tundra is replaced by loose rock. Scramble up this stuff carefully; avoid kicking it down on those below you. Turn left at the ridgeline, skirt a bump on the ridge and proceed to the summit, a little less than five miles from Phantom Valley picnic area. They are interesting and spectacular miles; Howard is a worthwhile climb.

If time and weather permit, you can continue for an additional half-mile to _Mount Cirrus_. Follow the continental divide northwest and downhill to a bump on the ridgeline between Howard and Cirrus. Skirt the bump on the left (west) and continue downhill to the saddle between the two peaks, above Lake of the Clouds. Then climb a tundra slope to the top of Cirrus, dodging to the left around rock-filled gullies near the summit.

Descend from Cirrus via the ridge extending east from the summit, overlooking Lake of the Clouds. Loose rock covering the ridge and some exposure to falls while clambering over and around obstacles require care while you descend. On the lower end of the ridge, bear left (north) to avoid cliffs above Lake of the Clouds. Follow the route from Lake of the Clouds down Hitchens Gulch to the Grand Ditch, back to the Red Mountain Trail and then to the trailhead. Howard, Cirrus and Lake of the Clouds are about 12.5 miles, round trip.

Mounts Cumulus and _Nimbus_ are the peaks immediately south of Howard. They usually are climbed together and are easier to surmount than their neighbors. From the Red Mountain Trail-Grand Ditch junction, turn left and hike .4 mile along the ditch road to Opposition Creek. Cross the ditch on a bridge and continue west, upstream. Above tree line the trail you have been following, which has been growing gradually less distinct, disappears altogether. Continue climbing up tundra and rocks to the saddle on the continental divide between Nimbus, on the left, and Cumulus, on the right. At the saddle turn left and follow the ridgeline to the top of Nimbus, a little more than five miles from Phantom Valley picnic area.

Cumulus is located about a mile from Nimbus. To reach it, go back to the saddle and climb north along the divide. Circumventing loose rock along the ridgeline requires dropping down a bit in places.

To descend from Cumulus, you need not follow the divide all the way back to the saddle. Merely leave the ridgeline to hike down a ridge extending east and follow the least steep route down to tree line in the valley of Opposition Creek. This same route can be used to ascend Cumulus, if you wish to skip Nimbus. It is about five miles from Phantom Valley picnic area to the top of only Cumulus. Round trip for both peaks is about eleven miles.

The peak for which the Red Mountain Trail is named sits east of Mount Nimbus. To climb _Red Mountain_, turn left at the trail's junction with the Grand Ditch and walk 1.2 miles along the ditch service road to Red Gulch. Cross the ditch on a bridge and follow a trail to the west and up the gulch. The path begins to grow less distinct after about one-third mile, but it can be followed in bits and pieces.

After about a mile, turn right and climb steeply through struggling trees and over tundra to the ridge between Red Mountain and Mount Nimbus. Turn right to follow the ridgeline to the bare summit, about 5.5 miles from Phantom Valley picnic area. Although Red Mountain is not very high, it is strategically located as an excellent platform from which to view high mountains to the west and the Colorado River drainage.

Green Knoll is the next projection south of Red Mountain. However, there is a closer approach to Green Knoll than from the Red Mountain Trail — the approach from the Holzwarth Homestead (see "Trail Ridge Road," Trails from Holzwarth Homestead).

Lulu City Trail System

The Lulu City Trail probably is the most popular hike on the west side of Rocky Mountain National Park. It is an easy 3.1 mile walk to the site of an old mining community. Many hikers may expect to find a ghost town; all they see when they reach the site is a meadow with a few barely distinguishable remains of log cabins. To adventurers seeking mineral wealth in 1879, Lulu City was a disappointment. It is a disappointment, also, to modern hikers

seeking tangible historic relics. But if the pay dirt you seek is
wilderness beauty, the trail to the site of Lulu City and beyond is a
sure path to success.

The trailhead for Lulu City and La Poudre Pass is at the north
end of the Phantom Valley picnic area parking lot. The grade starts
out on the level, following the floodplain of the Colorado River
almost due north. Willows and other water-loving flora line the trail,
and beaver workings are obvious. The workings of humans also are
evident in an 1880 mining site to the right of the trail.

The trail follows the east bank of the Colorado, sometimes
closely, sometimes at a distance, over an easy grade for 1.4 miles to
some tailings below *Shipler* Mine. The mine, an unsuccessful effort of
the 1880s, is uphill to the right. Occasionally, hikers looking up at
the remains of the mine see bighorn sheep as well. Two log cabins
associated with the mine are situated .4 mile farther along the trail.
These ruins are in a remarkable state of preservation, considering
that the larger cabin was built in 1876.

Continuing on the level past the cabins, the trail follows a stage
road that used to run through Lulu City and then northwest over
Thunder Pass to Walden, Colorado. When you at last begin to
climb above the valley floor, the shade of subalpine forest through
which you walk is especially welcome. The trail forks at a junction
2.9 miles from the trailhead. The right-hand fork goes to Little
Yellowstone Canyon and La Poudre Pass (see below). The left-hand
fork heads back downhill through switchbacks to the site of Lulu
City, about .2 mile farther. The *Thunder Pass Trail* continues
through the meadow of Lulu City and past a connecting trail that
leads steeply uphill to La Poudre Pass Trail.

Heading left toward Thunder Pass, you soon cross the Colorado
River amid water-loving shrubs and rocks. On the other side of the
river there is another fork. The right-hand fork is yet another trail to
La Poudre Pass.

To continue on the Thunder Pass Trail, take the left-hand fork
for one very steep mile through subalpine forest to a road associated
with the Grand Ditch. Here the way levels out. Cross the road and

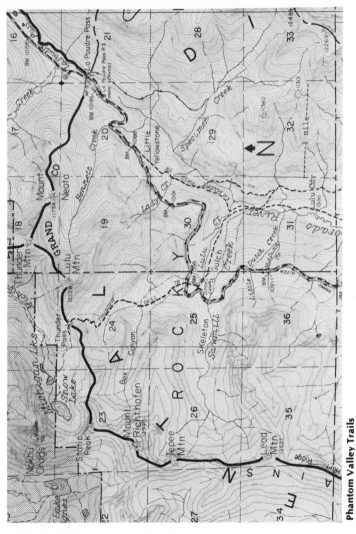

Phantom Valley Trails

walk .3 mile through lovely alpine meadowland to the ditch.

Cross the ditch on a bridge and then walk through subalpine woods and along the edge of marshland. At the mouth of Box Canyon you will reach a pleasant meadow through which Lulu Creek flows, .6 mile uphill from the ditch. Past the meadow, the trail climbs at a very steep grade. Only a few moderating switchbacks remind you that stagecoaches once were pulled up this remarkable slope. Below Thunder Pass, subalpine flowers often put on a spectacular display. A final short steep climb takes you to Thunder Pass and the national park boundary, 6.3 miles from the trailhead.

On the other side of the pass, the valley of Michigan Lakes, to the west, is very lovely with Static Peak and Nokhu Crags towering dramatically on the left. The highest and largest of Michigan Lakes, Snow Lake, is hidden in the basin below the crags.

From Thunder Pass, you can climb the three tundra-covered, rounded slopes of _Lulu_ and _Thunder mountains_ and _Mount Neota_. All these peaks provide good views of the Colorado River drainage and Never Summer Range. Turn right from the pass and climb uphill steadily past the upper limit of Krummholz for half a mile to Lulu Mountain.

On top of Lulu, the hardest part lies behind you. It is an easy stroll downhill to the saddle below Thunder and a steep but short walk uphill to Thunder's summit, three-quarters mile from Lulu. It is an even easier walk for another three-quarters mile along the continental divide down and back up slightly to Neota.

Descend from Neota by heading southeast to tree line, then downhill through forest to the Grand Ditch. The ditch presents something of a problem here, for the nearest dry crossing is at La Poudre Pass. If the day is warm and the water low, you may want to try wading or taking advantage of some other opportunity to reach the service road on the other side of the ditch. Once on the road, exit south via La Poudre Pass Trail to Phantom Valley picnic area (see below). Or you may have arranged for transportation to the northeast at Long Draw Reservoir, which is a third as far as Phantom Valley picnic area. (For driving instructions to Long Draw, see "Mummy Range," Mummy Pass Trail.)

From Thunder Pass, you can climb _Static Peak_ and _Mount Rich-thofen_, too. Turn left (west) from the pass and head along the north side of the divide in Routt National Forest. Your immediate goal is a saddle between Static and an unnamed lower peak east of it that rises above Thunder Pass. Once around this peak, cross the saddle and contour below the cliffs on Static to a shelf extending between Static and Mount Richthofen. You can reach this point without going all the way to Thunder Pass by leaving the Thunder Pass Trail about a mile before the pass and walking up Box Canyon. This more direct route necessitates climbing onto the shelf via the north (right-hand) canyon wall.

From the shelf, pick the least cliffy route, again to the north, over loose rock to the saddle between Static and Richthofen. From there the way is relatively simple to either summit. Beyond Static, the ridge to _Nokhu Crags_ is a much more challenging climb, crossing jagged and potentially dangerous terrain.

Mount Richthofen can be climbed, also, from the south, via the trail in Skeleton Gulch (see above) or a ridge extending east from Richthofen. But by far the shortest approach is from the west, via Lake Agnes. This route, which begins in Colorado State Forest, is about two miles long; the route from Phantom Valley picnic area is seven miles long.

To reach the starting point of the Lake Agnes route, take State Highway 14 from Walden or Fort Collins to a point about three miles southwest of Cameron Pass. Turn south there on an unpaved road passable by normal passenger cars and follow it to the end — two miles to a parking lot and trailhead. The parking lot holds about 15 cars. More than 15 would put enough hikers into the Lake Agnes area to seriously disturb the area's bighorn sheep and reduce their already uncertain chances for survival.

It is very important that hikers who are fortunate enough to see bighorn sheep do not bother them by trying to stalk them closely. Nearly 100 percent of the photos attempted by hikers pursuing sheep across the mountains results in dismal failure. And the stress that the animals undergo as a result of being chased from their feeding grounds gravely affects their health.

On one of our climbs up Mount Richthofen, we encountered a herd of ewes and lambs near Skeleton Gulch. Not wishing to disturb them, we immediately sat down — and rested quietly so the sheep could go on their way. To our surprise, the ewe leading the herd brought them over to look at us! We took excellent photos while seated in comfort, and the sheep placidly grazed and went about their usual business.

Admittedly, this event is unlikely to be repeated. But you will get no bighorn photos worth looking at in any other way. And it is *vital* not to pressure the sheep. Too much pressure from hikers will drastically reduce their numbers.

From the Colorado State Forest parking area, a trail extends for a little more than a half-mile to Lake Agnes. Once at the lake, continue around its western shore to the stream flowing into it from the slopes of Richthofen. Follow this stream to the south, ascending over boulders toward a saddle situated between Richthofen and an unnamed peak to the west. You must fight small loose rocks to get to the saddle. After scrambling carefully over this stuff, pick your way from the saddle up the ridgeline to Richthofen's summit. The angular rocks are fairly solid compared with those just climbed, but care must be taken to avoid kicking anything down on other climbers along this popular route.

From the west ridge of Richthofen, you can climb along a very rough knife ridge for a half-mile to the much lower *Tepee Mountain*. The rock is loose, and there is exposure to long drops when climbing around barriers on the ridgeline. Be very careful.

Back at the trail junction 2.9 miles from Phantom Valley picnic area, *La Poudre Pass Trail* heads to the right while the trail to Lulu City drops to the left. Soon La Poudre Pass Trail begins a gradual descent. At one point the trees open to reveal the meadow where Lulu City once stood. After .6 mile, you reach a trail that drops to the Colorado River on the northern edge of the same meadow.

Bear right again and continue along an easy grade, eventually leaving heavy forest and traversing rocky slopes to descend gradually to the Colorado River. Follow the riverbank upstream for a bit before crossing the river's channels on bridges. The trail then bears to the right as it climbs past the mouth of Little Yellowstone Canyon. In dense lodgepole forest, a connecting link with the Thunder Pass Trail comes in from the left. As the grade becomes less steep, the trees open a bit and allow blueberries to flourish as a ground cover.

At the rim of _Little Yellowstone Canyon_, about a half-mile past the Thunder Pass Trail connection, walk a few feet off-trail to the right. From the top of rock pillars overlooking the river you can see the canyon's resemblance on a diminutive scale to the Grand Canyon of the Yellowstone in the world's first national park. This viewpoint is an excellent platform from which to photograph the eroded volcanic rock that gave the canyon its name.

Uphill past the viewpoint, La Poudre Pass Trail crosses a brook and climbs up switchbacks through open areas before shooting straight up to the service road paralleling the Grand Ditch. A level 1.1 miles in the sunshine along the ditch road take you to La Poudre Pass, a broad, low and wide-open point on the continental divide, 6.8 miles from Phantom Valley picnic area. From the pass you have several options for your return route: back along the ditch 4.2 miles to the Thunder Pass Trail; back the way you came, with detours to Lulu City; or ahead two miles to prearranged transportation at Long Draw Reservoir.

Grand Lake

Grand Lake is the largest natural lake in Colorado. Yet it is considerably smaller than the adjacent man-made reservoir, Shadow Mountain Lake, or the nearby Lake Granby. In other words, there is a lot of water sloshing around this part of the Rockies. Precipitation is relatively heavy here. Streams are spectacular during most of the summer; trails are blocked by snow long into the hiking season. The forests are denser and seem more primeval than in the eastern part of the national park. Coincidentally, most approaches to various hiking goals are longer in the Grand Lake area than elsewhere.

North Inlet Trail

The North Inlet Trail and the Tonahutu Creek Trail start in almost the same place north of Grand Lake. By different routes they run east and climb to the summit of Flattop Mountain, where they come together and descend to Bear Lake. Most of the length of these trails is described under "Bear Lake Trailhead." Some goals, however, are more appropriately reached from Grand Lake, so they are described below.

To reach the North Inlet Trailhead, drive east from U.S. Highway 34 toward Grand Lake on State Highway 278. One-third mile from Route 34, Route 278 forks. Take the left-hand fork, which bypasses the village of Grand Lake and leads eventually to the West Portal of the Adams Tunnel of the Big Thompson Irrigation Project.

Leave Route 278 at .8 mile from the fork, turning left on a narrow unpaved road. A short distance along the unpaved road there is a parking lot on the left which is the best place to park for the Tonahutu Creek Trail. Continue past the parking lot, go over a hill, turn right and cross Tonahutu Creek on a bridge uncomfortably narrow for most cars. There is a parking lot just beyond the bridge.

From the parking lot walk east along a mostly level road with a few minor ups and downs for 1.2 miles to Summerland Park. This road provides access to private land within the national park and is closed to driving by the public. Beyond Summerland Park, the route is an easily walked trail passing through lodgepole pines for a few miles while running upstream along the North Inlet, the creek that flows into Grand Lake from the northeast.

Below _Cascade Falls_, the trail forks; the two branches come together above the falls. To avoid conflicts with horse parties, take the right-hand (lower) fork now and the upper fork on your return. Cascade Falls is located a few yards to the right of the lower fork, 3.5 miles from the trailhead. The best viewpoint for photographers is reached by climbing steeply downstream over boulders. Be careful; some of the rocks are wet and slick; smashing your cameras, not to mention your body, in a fall could cast a pall over your entire hike.

The trail remains mostly easy and well shaded for more than 6.5 miles from the trailhead. Finally, a short set of switchbacks marks the beginning of a gradually steepening grade. You reach a junction with the _Lake Nanita Trail_ 7.5 miles from the trailhead. The North Inlet Trail continues on the left-hand fork to Flattop Mountain (see "Bear Lake Trailhead," Flattop Mountain Trail System). The right-hand fork climbs at an easy grade for .1 mile to a bridge over the small gorge that is the site of _North Inlet Falls._

Past the falls, the right-hand fork climbs steeply away from North Inlet. Heavy subalpine forest opens at the ends of switchbacks to reveal views of marshes and of Lake Solitude, on the North Inlet valley floor. Overhead, Chiefs Head Peak presents an oddly pointed aspect. After four long sets of switchbacks, you climb across bedrock uphill from fine subalpine gardens where the outlet stream of _Lake Nokoni_ flows.

At 9.9 miles from the trailhead, you reach Lake Nokoni itself, a classic tarn, lying in a basin carved from solid rock by a glacier. Little soil and few trees mask the stone bowl shoreline. On the south, the promontories of Ptarmigan Mountain are sheer but rather blocky. A long broad slope blanketed with loose rock tends to spoil photographic composition. All in all, Nokoni is not as photogenic as might be desired. Or perhaps it suffers by comparison with Lake Nanita, a larger tarn over the ridge.

Lake Nanita is one of the most photogenic lakes in Rocky Mountain National Park. Admittedly, its attraction may be enhanced because you must work to get here. Past Lake Nokoni, the trail rises steeply before leveling in heavy subalpine forest on the ridgetop. You get a few glimpses of Nanita as you descend to a marshy meadow. The lake is forgotten briefly as incredibly ragged and dramatic spires on the south face of Ptarmigan Mountain saw across the skyline. Then you pass through trees to ledges overlooking Nanita, 11 miles from the trailhead. Andrews Peak rises on the opposite side of the lake; it is every first-grader's impression of exactly what a mountain should look like.

Scrambling down the rocky slope, you may be lucky enough to photograph Andrews reflected in Nanita. Afternoon or evening light is best for this shot. Should you arrive in the morning, Ptarmigan Mountain makes an even more dramatic subject from the other side of the lake.

A third tarn in the heavily glaciated vicinity of Ptarmigan Mountain is _Pettingell Lake_. It is a fairly easy hike of three-quarters mile from Lake Nokoni. Walk to the right from the bedrock lip of Nokoni's basin and climb steeply uphill to a low point on the ridge north of Nokoni. From the ridge, drop down a gradually steepening slope to the basin of Pettingell.

If you are in the vicinity of Nokoni and want to climb _Ptarmigan Mountain_ and _Andrews Peak_, you can start from the ridge separating Nokoni and Pettingell. You follow the ridgeline steeply uphill and climb along the edge of the Nokoni cirque to the summit of Ptarmigan, about 1.5 walking miles from Nokoni. Andrews Peak is

1.5 miles farther across tundra slopes. With unbeatable views of glacial lakes in North and East Inlet valleys and of the 13,000-foot peaks to the east, Ptarmigan and Andrews certainly are worth the climb. They are reached more easily, however, from the East Inlet Trail (see below) than via the long North Inlet Trail approach to Lake Nokoni.

Ptarmigan Creek, contrary to what you might expect, flows south down the north wall of North Inlet valley *opposite* Ptarmigan Mountain. It drains a magnificent basin where there are three named tarns — *Bench, Snowdrift* and *Ptarmigan lakes* — and many unnamed ones. Ptarmigan Creek crosses the North Inlet Trail at a point 6.7 miles from Grand Lake. From the trail you can follow the stream very steeply uphill through thick subalpine forest to *War Dance Falls*. Bench Lake is located in a hanging valley about a half-mile and 760 feet above the North Inlet Trail. Typically for a glaciated landscape, the hanging valley has a broad marshy floor and steep walls. Both are barriers to hikers wishing to explore the large tarns hanging in their cirques more than a thousand feet above the hanging valley containing Bench Lake and Ptarmigan Creek.

Tonahutu Creek Trail

The approach to the Tonahutu Creek Trail is the same as the approach to the North Inlet Trail (see above). Many folks park their cars beside Route 278, at .8 mile from the Grand Lake fork, and walk along the unpaved road to the trailhead. But there is a parking lot at the trailhead, on the left of the road. From the parking lot, the Tonahutu Creek Trail follows moderate grades to the north through lodgepole pines. After .9 mile it reaches a junction with a half-mile spur that originates at the western headquarters of Rocky Mountain National Park. The path steepens somewhat past the junction but remains moderate as it parallels Tonahutu Creek uphill to the beginning of *Big Meadows*, more than two miles from the trailhead.

The trail skirts the edge of Big Meadows, keeping in the shade and out of marshy grassland, which is more easily trampled than is the forest. The shade is welcome, for the 4.4 miles of trail between the trailhead and a junction with the Green Mountain Trail often is hot. We recommend skipping the first part of the.Tonahutu Creek Trail and hiking to the junction via the more interesting, more comfortable and 2.6-miles shorter Green Mountain Trail (see "Trail Ridge Road," Onahu Creek-Green Mountain Circle).

Big Meadows seem to go on and on, even if you reach them at the midpoint, at the Green Mountain-Tonahutu Creek junction. From the junction you hike north on an excellent trail and pass log cabin ruins. More than a half-mile north of the junction, the trail divides. The left-hand fork continues running north to Onahu Creek. The right-hand fork, the Tonahutu Creek Trail, bends to the east around the upper end of Big Meadows. Cutting between a forested hill and the northern bank of Tonahutu Creek, the trail follows an easy grade upstream most of the way to _Granite Falls_, 7.8 miles from the Tonahutu Creek Trailhead and 5.2 miles from the Green Mountain Trailhead. An afternoon with a clear sky is the best time for a photo of Granite Falls.

More than 1.5 miles past Granite Falls, the trail crosses a stream flowing south from _Haynach Lakes_, just below a pretty cascade. A little farther, around a bend, a narrow trail branches steeply left up a forested ridge to the beautiful Haynach Lakes, numerous marshy ponds and one large tarn at the base of _Nakai Peak_ (see "Bear Lake Trailhead," Flattop Mountain Trail System for further description of Haynach Lakes). The lakes are an excellent 7.5-mile hike from the Green Mountain Trailhead.

Nakai Peak can be reached in an uncomplicated ascent from Haynach Lakes. Walk uphill along the drainage flowing into the largest lake to a saddle on the ridge between Nakai and the continental divide. Turn left at the saddle and, skirting right (west) around a bump on the ridge, follow the ridgeline to Nakai's summit. The summit is about nine miles from the Green Mountain Trailhead.

East Inlet Trail

The East Inlet Trail runs uphill in the valley of the creek that flows into Grand Lake from the east. Its trailhead is located at the West Portal of Adams Tunnel, a point of some confusion.

To reach the trailhead, turn east from U.S. Highway 34 toward the village of Grand Lake on State Highway 278. After one-third mile, the road divides; take the left-hand fork, which bypasses the town of Grand Lake and heads directly toward Adams Tunnel, a link in the Big Thompson Irrigation Project. Follow more than two miles of paved road to the West Portal and continue driving, bearing left on an unpaved road to the trailhead parking lot.

The parking area is large, for the easy .3 mile to _Adams Falls_ attracts many walkers. The falls is attractive; a rainbow shines from the spray in the morning. The surrounding rocks are smooth, steep and wet. Parents should take care that children do not slip into the water and get washed over the brink.

Past Adams Falls, the trail runs on the level through lodgepole pines to a marshy meadow much loved by mosquitoes. With urging from the bugs, you tend to make excellent speed along the meadow's edge. Then there is more flat walking through lodgepole pines to a much larger meadow filled with obvious beaver workings. Bugs are not shy in this meadow, either, but there is some compensation ahead of you in the nice views of Mount Craig.

After crossing two streams in quick succession, the trail rises and falls through more lodgepoles, but each downhill pitch is a little shorter than the previous uphill pitch. You gradually gain altitude in this fashion until emerging on a rock shelf perched on one side of Mount Cairns. Switchbacks over the rocks reveal fine views to the east of the craggy walls of Mount Craig.

The trail resumes its up-and-down progress, occasionally approaching East Inlet. Along the stream, Parry primrose, globeflower, marsh-marigold and chiming bells are common. At 4.4 miles from the trailhead, the Paradise Park Trail branches to the right over level ground (see below). The East Inlet Trail climbs steeply northeast via switchbacks through thick subalpine forest. Through the trees you can catch glimpses of Mount Craig, on the opposite side of the valley, and of the tundra slopes of Andrews Peak, straight ahead.

Eventually, the trail circles a forested hill and climbs switchbacks to _Lone Pine Lake_, 5.5 miles from the trailhead. The lake is named for a single lodgepole pine that once took root in a crack in a rock island in the lake. Since the naming, that pioneer has succumbed to the extreme rigors of the trying environment. The tree has been replaced, however, by several young pines and by a subalpine fir, all growing on the same island. The mountain vistas surrounding Lone Pine Lake are unspectacular to the jaded eye so easily acquired in Rocky Mountain National Park, where remarkable views are normal.

East Inlet Trail curves to the right and follows the southeastern shore of Lone Pine Lake to a slope of large boulders. Traversing the slope, it reenters woods and winds uphill to several interesting crossings of streams cascading down Andrews Peak. Braided courses of brooks weave among trees and rocks, while the trail stays dry atop long bridges — a unique and very lovely area.

Past these streams the path turns right and traverses the upper end of the rocky slope crossed previously just before the streams. Having bypassed more boulders, the trail angles to the left above the gorge of East Inlet. The generally rocky character of the terrain is relieved occasionally by ponds and small meadows decorated with snowlilies. More than a mile from Lone Pine Lake, at a pond just below Lake Verna, climbers heading for Andrews Peak and Ptarmigan Mountain may wish to cut left over boulders and pick their way to the top of Andrews, more than 2300 feet higher.

The East Inlet Trail reenters subalpine forest, then leaves it on an interesting rocky ridge overlooking _Lake Verna_, 6.9 miles from the trailhead. Verna is a mysterious lake — so long and thin that it is difficult to see the entire tarn from anywhere on the north shore, which the trail follows. The best view, portraying the lake's fiordlike quality, is from the rocks above its outlet.

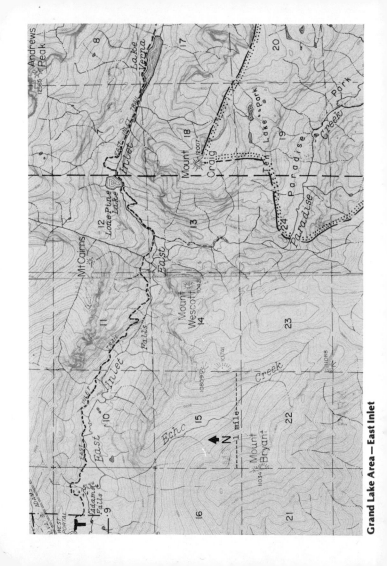

Grand Lake Area — East Inlet

Spirit Lake is located more than a mile from the west (outlet) end of Lake Verna. Three-quarters of the sometimes-soggy trail follows Verna's shore. Past Spirit, the trail takes on an unimproved character for the three-quarters mile to *Fourth Lake*. Past Fourth, the track becomes very sketchy up to *Fifth Lake*, about 9.5 miles from the trailhead.

From Fourth Lake, it is possible to climb steeply to Boulder-Grand Pass for an outstanding view of Fourth, Spirit, and Verna lakes strung out along East Inlet (see "Wild Basin," Ouzel Falls Trail System). The East Inlet chain is an excellent example of paternoster lakes. "Pater noster" is Latin for "Our Father," the first words of The Lord's Prayer; the rosary, a string of beads used as an aid while repeating the prayer, came to be known as a paternoster. When seen from above, a series of lakes in a glaciated valley resemble a string of beads and thus are called paternoster lakes. They might be located either in glacially scoured basins in bedrock or behind rock "dams" — terminal moraines — laid down by a glacier as it melted.

Back at 4.4 miles from the trailhead, the *Paradise Park Trail* branches south from the East Inlet Trail along an easy grade. The way steepens in one stretch before fading to unmaintained status about a mile from the East Inlet Trail. A beaten track continues on into Paradise Park, a research natural area given special protection so that its ecosystem will be preserved as a yardstick for scientific research. As part of that protection, camping and horse riding are prohibited within Paradise Park or *Ten Lakes Park*, a hanging valley that overlooks it. Paradise Park can be reached also via an unimproved trail coming over the ridge from Hell Canyon (see "Indian Peaks, West of the Divide," Roaring Fork Trail System). Folks walking through Paradise Park should exercise even more than their usual care to leave no trace of their passing.

Shadow Mountain and East Shore Trails

Shadow Mountain is not notably high or impressive looking. But an old fire lookout near the summit has a romantic fortresslike quality and has been nominated for addition to the Register of National Historic Places. If it is placed on the register, extensive restoration probably will take place. Perhaps the most significant for hikers will be that the steps on the outside of the tower will be rebuilt, giving hikers access to a view above the trees. You get to the Shadow Mountain Trail via the East Shore Trail.

To reach the East Shore Trailhead drive along the main street of the town of Grand Lake to the corner of Vine Street (a sign there indicates the way to Daven Haven Lodge). Turn south on Vine Street and keep winding in a southerly direction to the bridge crossing the canal connecting Grand and Shadow Mountain lakes. After crossing the bridge, keep heading south for several hundred yards until you run out of paved road. There are a couple of places where you can park along the shoulder; more parking space can be found off the road to the left a few yards farther on. The East Shore Trail begins on the right and probably will be marked with a sign.

Follow it along the shore of Shadow Mountain Lake for .7 mile to the park boundary and then to the Shadow Mountain Trail junction, 1.5 miles from your starting point. The first section of the trail is flat and easy to walk. Most of the way it passes through lodgepole pines, although there are a few sunny stretches where brush predominates.

The East Shore Trail continues to the right along the lake (see below). To climb Shadow Mountain, take the trail to the left, which soon begins to climb at a steady grade up the side of a lateral moraine amid lodgepoles that predominate through most of the hike. Approximately one-half mile from the junction, the Shadow Mountain Trail switchbacks, and you climb a bit more steeply in the opposite direction along the narrow ridgeline of the moraine.

After nearly a mile, the moraine merges with the bulk of Shadow Mountain, and the path bends to the right around the end of the gully between ridge and mountain. Circling a lower summit on Shadow Mountain, the path enters a level area above another gully, then bends to the right along the mountain's flank below the fire lookout. A moderate climb takes you to Ranger Creek, where a narrow wooden trough concentrates water in a tempting trickle. DO NOT DRINK IT. You should carry your own water on this and all other hikes. Untreated water should not be assumed safe. The trough was part of the tower's water system several decades ago.

Leaving Ranger Creek, the trail switchbacks steeply uphill for about one-half mile to a saddle east of the lookout. A right turn away from the trail then leads to the true summit of Shadow Mountain, another half-mile away and 10,155 feet above sea level. The summit is surrounded by trees, which block the view from there.

On the other hand, following the trail to the left from the saddle leads you quickly to the lookout tower. Built in 1932, it stands on a 9923-foot promontory directly above Grand Lake. You may wish to check with the National Park Service before beginning your hike to learn if the steps around the outside of the tower have been rebuilt. If so, you can climb three stories, above the surrounding pine and fir, to an excellent view. Grand Lake lies to the west, and the valley of East Inlet leads away to the east, with Mount Craig on its south wall and the higher tundra-covered slopes of Ptarmigan Mountain and Andrews Peak on the north.

To the southwest, below the even ranks of lodgepole pine tops, Shadow Mountain Lake dominates the scene. Large islands at the southern end are high points on a terminal moraine marking the end of a glacier that once extended 20 miles from cirques easily visible in the Never Summer Range, to the north. South of Shadow Mountain Lake, huge Lake Granby defines the route of the _East Shore Trail_.

Past the point where the Shadow Mountain Trail leaves the shore of Shadow Mountain Lake, the way splits again almost at once. Both branches end up at the same place. The wide path to the left normally is used by horses, the path to the right by hikers. The right-hand path continues along the lakeshore, a bit wetly in places, for 1.3 miles to Shadow Mountain Dam.

You can begin hiking the East Shore Trail at the dam by walking over a dike at the southern end of Shadow Mountain Lake from the National Park Service's Green Ridge Campground. To drive to this campground, turn east from U.S. Highway 34 at the southern end of Shadow Mountain Lake.

From the dam, the East Shore Trail cuts inland up a draw and across a bog to join its other branch, the horse trail. The inland horse trail and the shoreline foot trail both measure about 2.4 miles, junction to junction.

From the convergence of the trails, you walk south along the Colorado River to Columbine Bay, an arm of Lake Granby. After 1.4 miles the _Columbine Creek Trail_ begins on the left and runs to the east up Columbine Creek. The trail was built in the 1930s to provide access for forest fire control. It was unneeded then and is little used today because it has no particular destination.

After a short level stretch, the Columbine Creek Trail climbs steeply above the sometimes marshy valley floor of Columbine Creek. After several stream crossings, it levels and recrosses the main creek. Soon thereafter the track fades away, 2.8 miles from Columbine Bay.

Past Columbine Creek, the East Shore Trail continues for 1.5 miles to cross the boundary between Rocky Mountain National Park and Shadow Mountain National Recreation Area. Both areas are administered by the National Park Service, and the difference between them is of little significance to hikers. Similarly, there is no particular difference to be noted in crossing into Arapaho National Forest (U.S. Department of Agriculture land) when the path heads inland after crossing Twin Creek. You may notice boundary markers about a half-mile later when you reenter the recreation area, and when you leave it again and enter it once more.

Near the end of the trail, the path drops down from Knight Ridge to meet the eastern shore of Lake Granby at Arapaho Bay. The southern trailhead of the East Shore Trail is located at Roaring Fork Ranger Station, 12.7 miles from the northern trailhead at Grand Lake. An easier long trail is difficult to imagine. Mile after mile of lodgepoles and lakeshore, however, might get a bit monotonous after a while.

The ideal way to walk the trail is from one end to the other, having arranged for a car to be left at the end where the hike will conclude. For driving instructions to Roaring Fork Ranger Station, see "Indian Peaks, West of the Divide."

Sagebrush and Indian paintbrush

Destination Tables

You will find the following abbreviations appearing among more common ones in the destination tables on the next eighteen pages:

C.G. = Campground   R. = Ranger

Ck. = Creek   Res. = Reservoir

Fk. = Fork   Rg. = Ridge

L. = Lake   Sta. = Station

Md. = Meadow   T.H. Trailhead

Destination	Starting Point	Distance from Start. Pt. (in miles)	Elevation Gain (in feet) from T.H. to High Point	Altitude (in feet)	Alt. Rank National Park Only	Alt. Rank Including Indian Peaks	Size of Lake (in acres)	Depth of Lake (in feet)	Fish in Lake
Achonee, Mt.	Monarch Lake	6	4,303	12,649		52			
Acoma, Mt.	Shadow Mtn.	4	2,118	10,508	98	131			
Adams, Mt.	East Inlet	5	3,730	12,121	66	93			
Adams Falls	East Inlet	0.3	79	8,470					
Adams Lake	East Inlet	9	2,819	11,210	40	45	4.6		barren
Alberta Falls	Glacier Gorge Jct.	.6	160	9,400					
Albion, Mt.	No Access — Boulder Watershed			12,609		55			
Alice, Mt.	Wild Basin R. Sta.	9	4,810	13,310	12	16			
Andrews Glacier	Glacier Gorge Jct.	5	2,460	11,700					
Andrews Pass	Glacier Gorge Jct.	5.25	2,740	11,980					
Andrews Peak	East Inlet T.H.	7.5	4,174	12,565	39	58			
Andrews Tarn	Glacier Gorge Jct.	4.7	2,150	11,390	27	30			barren
Apache Peak	Long Lake T.H.	6.5	2,861	13,441		9			
Arapaho Glacier Overlook	Rainbow L's. C.G.	6	2,740	12,700					
	Buckingham C.G.	3.5	2,579						
Arapaho Pass	Buckingham C.G.	3	1,785	11,906		6			
	Junco Pond	4.5	1,866						
Arapaho Peak, North	Rainbow L's. C.G.	7	3,542	13,502		6			
	Buckingham C.G.	4.5	3,381	13,502		6			
Arapaho Peak, South	Rainbow L's. C.G.	6.5	3,437	13,397		13			
	Buckingham C.G.	4	3,276	13,397		13			
Arch Rocks	Fern Lake T.H.	1.5	45	8,200					
Arikaree Peak	No Access — Boulder Watershed			13,150		24			

Lake	Access	Dist.	Elev. Δ	Elevation					Fish
Arrowhead	Glacier Gorge Jct.	5.5	3,147	12,387	50	72			barren
Arrowhead Lake	Gore R. Overlook	6	−890	11,130	46	55	34.9		barren
Audubon, Mt.	Mitchell Ck. T.H.	3.75	2,743	13,223		19			
Azure Lake	Gore R. Overlook	7.25	−890	11,900	3	4	13.8		barren
Baker, Mt.	Trail Rg. Rd.	5.5	3,533	12,397	49	69			
Baker Pass	Trail Rg. Rd.	5.75	2,389	11,253					
Battle Mtn.	Boulder Brook T.H.	5	3,194	12,044	68	95			
Bear Lake	On road			9,475	110	144	11.2	33	Greenback cutthroat
Beaver Mtn.	U. Beaver Mds.	2	1,971	10,491	99	132			
Bench Lake	North Inlet T.H.	7.5	1,610	10,150	94	126	6.4	6	barren
Bierstadt Lake	Bierst. L. T.H.	1.4	566	9,416	111	145	7.4		barren
	Bear Lake	1.6	255	9,416	111	145	7.4		barren
Bighorn Lake	Milner Pass	.5	180	10,930	56	72	0.9	6	barren
Bighorn Mtn.	Lawn L. T.H.	4	2,923	11,463	83	115			
Big Meadows	Green Mtn. T.H.	1.8	606	9,400					Brook
Black Lake	Glacier Gorge Jct.	4.7	1,380	10,620	70	94	9.2		Brook
Blue Lake (Indian Peaks)	Mitchell Ck. T.H.	2.5	840	11,320		37	25.7	100	Cutthroat, Rainbow
Blue Lake (RMNP)	Glacier Gorge Jct.	5.5	1,900	11,140	44	53	2.8		barren
Blue Lake, Little	Mitchell Ck. T.H.	3.5	1,353	11,833		7			
Bluebird Lake	Wild Basin R. Sta.	6	2,478	10,978	55	69	22		barren
Boulder Field	Longs Peak R. Sta.	5.9	3,360	12,760					
Boulder-Grand Pass	Wild Basin R. Sta.	8	3,561	12,061					
Box Lake	Wild Basin R. Sta.	6.5	2,240	10,740	66	87	6.4		B Brook
Brainard Lake	On road			10,360		109	15.6	9	Rainbow, Brook, Brown, Suckers

Destination	Starting Point	Distance from Start. Pt. (in miles)	Elevation Gain (in feet) from T.H. to High Point	Altitude (in feet)	Alt. Rank National Park Only	Alt. Rank Including Indian Peaks	Size of Lake (in acres)	Depth of Lake (in feet)	Fish in Lake
Bridal Veil Falls	McGraw Ranch	3	1,060	8,900					
Bryant, Mt.	East Shore T.H.	6.5	2,644	11,034	90	123			
Buchanan Pass	Beaver Reservoir	6	2,676	11,837					
	Monarch Lake	9.75	3,491						
Cairns, Mt.	East Inlet T.H.	4.5	2,489	10,880	92	125			
Calypso Cascades	Wild Basin R. Sta.	1.8	700	9,200					
Caribou	Rainbow L's. C.G.	3.5	2,350	12,310		80			
	Buckingham C.G.	5.5	2,189	12,310		80			
Caribou Lake	Buckingham C.G.	3.75	1,785	11,147	52	52	7	8	Cutthroat
	Junco Pond	5.75	1,866	11,147	52	52	7	8	Cutthroat
	Monarch Lake	9.5	2,801	11,147	52	52	7	8	Cutthroat
Caribou Pass	Buckingham C.G.	4	1,940	11,851					
	Junco Pond	3.5	1,811	11,851					
Cascade Falls	North Inlet T.H.	3.5	300	8,840					
Castle Lake	Wild Basin R. Sta.	6.75	2,650	11,150	43	51	1.8	15	barren
Chapin, Mt.	Chapin Cr. T.H.	1.5	1,814	12,454	47	67			
Chasm Lake	Longs P. R. Sta.	4.2	2,360	11,760	7	9	19.3	100	Cutthroat
Chickadee Pond	Wild Basin R. Sta.	4.75	1,510	10,010	97	130	4.6	4	barren
Chickaree Lake	Onahu Crk. T.H.	1.75	525	9,290	112	146	4.6	4	barren
Chiefs Head Peak	Copeland Lake	7	5,267	13,579	3	3			
Chipmunk Lake	Lawn Lake T.H.	4.1	2,180	10,660	69	92	0.1		barren
Chiquita Lake	Lawn Lake T.H.	5.5	2,810	11,350	30	34	3.7	35	Cutthroat
Chiquita Mtn.	Chapin Ck. T.H.	2.5	2,429	13,069	19	28			
Cirque Lake	Pingree Park	5.25	1,970	11,000	68		2.8	13	barren

Name	Access								Fish
Cirrus, Mt.	Red Mtn. T.H.	5.75	3,757	12,797	26	42			
Clouds, Lake of the	Red Mtn. T.H.	6.25	2,390	11,430	23	25	11.2		Cutthroat
Columbine Falls	Longs P.R. Sta.	4	2,160	11,440					
Columbine Lake	Junco Pond	3	1,000	11,040		64			
Comanche Peak	Corral Ck. T.H.	6.75	2,702	12,702		50			
Coney Lake	Beaver Res.	5	1,439	10,600		95	9	21	Cutthroat
Coney Lake, Upper	Beaver Res.	6	1,779	10,940		71	16	31	Cutthroat
Cony Lake	Finch L. T.H.	9	3,042	11,512	19	21	16.5		barren
Cony Pass	W. Basin R. Sta.	7.25	3,860	12,360					
Cooper Peak	Roaring Fork T.H.	7.75	4,015	12,296		82			
Copeland Falls	W. Basin R. Sta.	0.3	15	8,515					
Copeland Lake	On road		15	8,312		153			
Copeland Mtn.	W. Basin R. Sta.	6.75	4,676	13,176	16	22			
Cracktop	Milner Pass	5.5	2,010	12,760	27	43			
Craig, Mt.	East Inlet T.H.	7.5	3,616	12,007	71	99			
Crater, The	Milner Pass	1	730	11,480					
Crater Lake	Monarch Lake	8.25	1,934	10,280		117	20	78	Brook, Cutthroat
Crawford Lake	Roaring Fk. T.H.	7.25	1,789	10,070		128	2	3	Cutthroat, Rainbow
Crystal Lake	Lawn L. T.H.	7.7	2,980	11,520	18	20	24.8	125	Cutthroat
Crystal Lake, Little	Lawn L. T.H.	7.5	2,972	11,512	19	21	3.7	20	Cutthroat
Cub Lake	Cub L. T.H.	2.3	540	8,620	115	149	10.1	3	barren
Cumulus, Mt.	Red Mtn. T.H.	5	3,685	12,725	28	44			
Dark Mtn.	McGraw Ranch	4	3,019	10,859	93	126			
Deer Mtn.	Deer Rg. Jct.	3	1,083	10,013	105	138			
Deserted Village	North Fork T.H.	3	200	8,160					
Desolation Peaks	Chapin Ck. T.H.	5.5	2,309	12,949	20	32			

Destination	Starting Point	Distance from Start. Pt. (in miles)	Elevation Gain (in feet) from T.H. to High Point	Altitude (in feet)	Alt. Rank National Park Only	Alt. Rank Including Indian Peaks	Size of Lake (in acres)	Depth of Lake (in feet)	Fish in Lake
Dickinson, Mt.	North Fork T.H.	14	3,871	11,831	74	105			
Dorothy, Lake	Buckingham C.G.	3.5	1,940	12,061		3	16	100	Cutthroat
	Junco Pond	3.5	2,021	12,061		3	16	100	Cutthroat
Doughnut Lake	Core R. Overlook	6.75	−890	11,250	36	41	7.4		barren
Dream Lake	Bear Lake	1.1	425	9,900	102	136	5.5	14	Cutthroat
Dunraven, Lake	North Fk. T.H.	10.75	2,280	10,240	88	118	11.2		barren
Dunraven, Mt.	North Fk. T.H.	11.75	4,611	12,571	38	57			
Eagle Cliff	Moraine Park	0.5	786	8,906	109	145			
Eagle Lake	W. Basin R. Sta.	6.75	2,310	10,810	61	80	11.9		Cutthroat
Eagles Beak	W. Basin R. Sta.	7.25	3,700	12,200	63	89			
Elk Tooth	Middle St. Vrain	9	4,210	12,848		39			
Embryo Lake	Glacier Gorge Jct.	3.5	1,120	10,360	81	109	0.5	3	barren
Emerald Lake	Bear Lake	1.8	605	10,080	95	127	6.4		barren
Emerald Mtn.	Glacier Basin C.G.	0.5	637	9,237	108	143			
Emmaline Lake	Pingree Park	5.5	1,930	10,960	95	70	5.7	23	Cutthroat
Enentah, Mt.	East Inlet T.H.	3	2,390	10,781	95	128			
Envy, Lake	Middle St. Vrain	8	2,382	11,020		66	2	18	Cutthroat
Estes Cone	Storm Pass T.H.	2	1,896	11,006	91	124			
	Longs Peak R. Sta.	3.3	1,606	11,006	91	124			
Eugenia Mine	Longs Peak R. Sta.	1.4	508	9,908					
Fairchild Mtn.	Lawn L. T.H.	8.75	4,962	13,502	6	6			
Fair Glacier	Monarch Lake	9.75	3,814	12,160					
Falcon Lake	W. Basin R. Sta.	7.5	2,560	11,060	52	62	7.6		
Fall Mtn.	Corral Ck T.H.	7.5	2,258	12,258	59	85			barren

Fay Lakes	Lawn L. T.H.	6	2,210-2,660	10,750-11,200	41	46	4.6 (Middle)	26	Greenback Cutthroat
Fern Falls	Fern L. T.H.	2.7	645	8,800					
Fern Lake	Fern L. T.H.	3.8	1,375	9,530	109	143	9.2	31	Brook
	Bear Lake	4.7	1,215	9,530	109	143	9.2	31	Brook
Fifth Lake	East Inlet T.H.	9.25	2,459	10,850	59	77	7.4	31	Cutthroat
Finch Lake	Finch L. T.H.	4.5	1,442	9,912	101	135	7.4	15	Brook, Rainbow
	W. Basin R. Sta.	5.3	1,412	9,912	101	135	7.4	15	Brook, Rainbow
Flatiron Mtn.	Corral Creek T.H.	5	2,335	12,335	53	76			
Flattop Mtn.	Bear Lake	4.4	2,849	12,324	55	78			
Forest Canyon Pass	Gore R. Overlook	1.5	-740	11,280					
Forest Lake	Rock Cut	2	-2258	10,298	85	114	7.4	8	barren
Fourth Lake	East Inlet T.H.	8.25	1,989	10,380	80	106	7.4	20	Brook
Fox Creek Falls	McGraw R.	3	660	8,400					
Frigid Lake	W. Basin R. Sta.	7.75	3,315	11,815	6	8	11.9		barren
Frozen Lake	Glacier Gorge Jct.	5.75	2,340	11,580	14	16	7.4		barren
Gabletop Mtn.	Bear Lake	7	2,849	11,939	72	101			
Gem Lake	Twin Owls	1.8	910	8,830	113	147	0.2	5	barren
	Gem L. T.H.	2	1,090	8,830	113	147	0.2	5	barren
George, Mt.	Monarch Lake	10.25	4,530	12,876		38			
Gianttrack	Marys Lake	1.25	1,045	9,091		144			
Gibraltar L., Little	Middle St. Vrain	7.75	2,562	11,200	46	46	5.7	44	Cutthroat
Gibraltar L., Little	Mid. St. Vrain	8	2,562	11,200	46	46	2.0	18	barren
Glacier Knobs	Glacier George Jct	1.75	985	10,225					
Glass, Lake of	Glacier George Jct	4.2	1,580	10,820	60	79	4.6		Cutthroat
Gourd Lake	Monarch Lake	8	2,454	10,800		81	2.0	50	Cutthroat
Grace Falls	Bear Lake	3.25	1,215	10,280					

Destination	Starting Point	Distance from Start. Pt. (in miles)	Elevation Gain (in feet) from T.H. to High Point	Altitude (in feet)	Alt. Rank National Park Only	Alt. Rank Including Indian Peaks	Size of Lake (in acres)	Depth of Lake (in feet)	Fish in Lake
Granby, Lake	On road			8,280		154			Rainbow, Brown Kokanee
Grand Lake	On road			8,367		150			Rainbow, Brown Kokanee
Granite Falls	Green Mtn. T.H.	5.2	1,046	9,840					
Granite Pass	Longs P. R. Sta.	4.2	2,680	12,080					
	Glacier Gorge Jct.	6.8	2,840	12,080					
Green Knoll	Holzwarth Homest	5	3,396	12,280	57	83			
Green Lake	Glacier Gorge Jct.	5.75	2,310	11,550	15	17	3.7		barren
Green Mtn.	Green Mtn. T.H.	2	1,519	10,313	103	136			
Hagues Peak	Lawn Lake T.H.	9	5,020	13,560	4	4			
	North Fk. T.H.	13	5,600	13,560	4	4			
Haiyaha, Lake	Bear Lake	2.1	745	10,220	89	119	15.6	29	Cutthroat
	Glacier Gorge Jct.	3	980	10,220	89	119	15.6	29	Cutthroat
Half Mountain	Glacier Gorge Jct	2.5	2,242	11,482	82	114			
Hallett Peak	Bear Lake	5	3,238	12,713	31	47			
Hayden Lake	Bear Lake	10	2,849	11,140	44	53	7.4		barren
Hayden Spire	Bear Lake	9.75	3,005	12,480	45	65			
Haynach Lakes	Green Mtn. T.H.	8.25	2,286	11,080	49	59	6.4		Cutthroat
Hazeline Lake	Corral Ck. T.H.	4.5	1,110	11,110	47	57	7.4	3	barren
Helene, Lake	Bear Lake	2.9	1,215	10,580	75	100	2.8	3	barren
Hiamovi Mtn.	Roaring Fk. T.H.	6.5	4,114	12,395		70			
Highest Lake	Core R. Overlook	7.75	1,295	12,425	2	2	7.4		barren
Horsetooth Peak	Meeker Park	2	1,572	10,344	102	135			
Hourglass Lake	Fern L. T.H.	6.5	3,065	11,220	37	42	9.2		barren

Howard Mtn.	Red Mtn. T.H.	5.25	3,770	12,810	25	41			
Husted, Lake	North Fk. T.H.	10.25	3,120	11,080	49	59	10.1	21	Brook
Hutcheson Lakes	Finch L. T.H.	8.5	2,382	10,852	58	76	7.4		Cutthroat
Icefield Pass	North Fk. T.H.	11.75	3,880	11,840					
Ida, Mt.	Milner Pass	4.5	2,130	12,880	24	37			
	Timber Lake	6	3,880	12,880	24	37			
Inkwell Lake	Gore R. Overlook	7	–890	11,460	21	23	30.3		Cutthroat
Irene, Lake	Milner Pass	0.5	–150	10,598	72	97	0.7	12	barren
Irene, Lake	Fern L. T.H.	7.25	3,705	11,860	4	5	1.8		barren
Irving Hale, Mt.	Roaring Fk. T.H.	5.75	3,473	11,754		106			
Isabelle Glacier	Long Lake T.H.	3.75	1,440	11,920					
Isabelle, Lake	Long Lake T.H.	2	388	10,868		75	30	37	Rainbow
Island Lake	Monarch Lake	9	3,054	11,400		28	19	39	Cutthroat
Isolation Peak	W. Basin R. Sta.	8	4,618	13,118	18	26			
Italy Lake	Glacier Gorge Jct	6	2,380	11,620	12	14			
Jackstraw Mtn.	Timber L. T.H.	4.5	2,704	11,704	77	109			
Jade, Pool of	Bear Lake	2.75	1,885	11,360	28	31			barren
Jewell Lake	Glacier Gorge Jct.	3	710	9,950	99	132	4.6		Brook, Cutthroat
Jims Grove	Longs Pk. R. Sta.	2.9	1,600	11,000					
Joe Mills Mtn.	Bear Lake	3.5	1,603	11,078	89	122			
Julian, Mt.	Milner Pass	6	2,178	12,928	22	35			
Julian Lake	Timber L. T.H.	5.75	2,800	11,100	48	58	5.5	30	Cutthroat
Junco Lake	W. Basin R. Sta.	6.75	3,130	11,630	11	13	9.2	45	barren
Keplinger Lake	Copeland Lake	6.25	3,374	11,686	10	12	9.2		barren
Keyhole, The	Longs Pk. R. Sta.	6.25	3,750	13,150					
Kiowa Peak	No Access – Boulder Watershed			13,276	18				
Knobtop Mtn.	Bear Lake	6	2,856	12,331	54	77			

Destination	Starting Point	Distance from Start. Pt. (in miles)	Elevation Gain (in feet) from T.H. to High Point	Altitude (in feet)	Alt. Rank National Park Only	Alt. Rank Including Indian Peaks	Size of Lake (in acres)	Depth of Lake (in feet)	Fish in Lake
Lady Washington, Mt.	Longs Pk. R. Sta.	5.5	3,881	13,281	13	17			
La Poudre Pass	Phantom Valley	6.8	1,115	10,175					
Lark Pond	Wild Basin R. Sta.	6.5	2,840	11,340	32	36	4.6		barren
Lawn Lake	Lawn L. T.H.	6.2	2,249	10,789	62	83	48	35	Brook
Lead Mtn.	Red Mtn. T.H.	6.75	3,497	12,537	41	60			
Lily Mtn.	Lily Mtn. T.H.	1.5	1,006	9,786		139			
Lion Lake No. 1	Wild Basin R. Sta.	7	2,565	11,065	51	61	7.4		barren
Lion Lake No. 2	Wild Basin R. Sta.	7.5	2,900	11,400	26	28	3.7		barren
Loch, The	Glacier Gorge Jct.	2.7	940	10,180	93	124	14.7		Brook, Rainbow Cutthroat
Lone Eagle Peak	Monarch Lake	9.5	3,574	11,920		103			
Lone Pine Lake	East Inlet T.H.	5.5	1,494	9,885	103	137	12.9		Brook
Lonesome Lake	Bear Lake	9.5	3,085	11,700	9	11	7.4		barren
Long Lake	Long Lake T.H.	0.5	41	10,521		104	39.5	18	Rainbow, Brook
Long Lake	Roaring Fk. T.H.	7.75	1,639	9,920		134	5	8	Cutthroat, Rainbow
Longs Peak	Longs Pk. R. Sta.	8	4,855	14,255	1	1			
	Glacier Gorge Jct.	10.6	5,015	14,255	1	1			
Lookout Mtn.	Meeker Park	2.5	1,943	10,715	97	130			
Loomis Lake	Fern L. T.H.	5.2	2,065	10,220	89	119	2.8	15	Brook
Lost Falls	North Fk. T.H.	7.4	1,840	9,800					
Lost Lake	North Fk. T.H.	9.7	2,750	10,710	68	91	9.2	21	Brook, Cutthroat
Louise, Lake	North Fk. T.H.	10.75	3,070	11,030	54	65	6.4		barren

Love Lake	Core R. Overlook	5.75	-760	11,260	35	40	1.8	10	barren
Lulu City	Phantom Valley	3.1	300	9,360					
Lulu Mtn.	Phantom Valley	6.75	3,168	12,228					
McGregor Mtn.	Fall R. Ent. Sta.	1.25	2,206	10,486	60	86			
McHenrys Peak	Glacier Gorge Jct.	6.75	4,087	13,327	100	133			
Mahana Peak	Wild B. R. Sta.	7.75	4,132	12,632	10	14			
Many Winds, Lake of	Wild B. R. Sta.	7.75	3,110	11,610	13	15	0.9	6	barren
Marguerite Falls	Fern L. T.H.	3.75	1,285	9,440					
Marigold Lake	Bear Lake	3.5	1,215	10,220	89	119	0.2	2	barren
Marigold Pond	Bear Lake	2.2	1,215	10,580	75	100	0.1	6	barren
Marmot Point	Fall River Pass	0.5	113	11,909	73	104			
Marten Peak	Roaring Fk. T.H.	7.5	3,760	12,041		96			
Matterhorn, Little	Bear Lake	5.5	2,111	11,586	80	112			
Meadow Mtn.	St. Vrain Mtn. T.H.	3	2,832	11,632	78	110			
Meeker, Mt.	Longs Pk. R. Sta.	5.5	4,511	13,911	2	2			
	Copeland Lake	6	5,599	13,911	2	2			
Mertensia Falls	Wild B. R. Sta.	6	1,860	10,360					
Mill Ck. Basin	Hallowell Park	1.6	600	9,000					
Mills Lake	Glacier Gorge Jct.	2.5	700	9,940	100	133	15.6		Rainbow, Cutthroat
Mirror Lake (Indian Peaks)	Monarch Lake	8	2,034	10,380		106			barren
Mirror Lake	Corral Ck. T.H.	6.1	1,020	11,020		66	21	84	Brook
Mitchell Lake	Mitchell Ck. T.H.	1.25	240	10,720		90	13.8	8	Brook, Cutthroat
Monarch Lake	On Road			8,340		152			
Mummy Mtn.	Lawn L. T.H.	8.25	4,885	13,425	8	10			
	North Fk. T.H.	12.5	5,465	13,425	8	10			

Destination	Starting Point	Distance from Start. Pt. (in miles)	Elevation Gain (in feet) from T.H. to High Point	Altitude (in feet)	Alt. Rank National Park Only	Alt. Rank Including Indian Peaks	Size of Lake (in acres)	Depth of Lake (in feet)	Fish in Lake
Mummy Pass	Corral Creek	6.3	1,120	11,120					
	Pingree Park	6.5	2,090	11,120					
Murphy Lake	Green Mtn. T.H.	7.75	2,426	11,220	37	42	7.4		Barren
Nakai Peak	Green Mtn. T.H.	9	3,422	12,216	61	87			
Nanita, Lake	North Inlet T.H.	11	2,240	10,780	63	84	34.4		Cutthroat
Navajo Peak	Long Lake T.H.	6.25	2,929	13,409		11			
Neota, Mt.	Phantom Valley	7.75	2,674	11,734	75	107			
Mt. Neva	Junco Pond	4.25	2,774	12,814		40			
Nimbus, Mt.	Red Mtn. T.H.	5.25	3,666	12,706	33	49			
Nisa, Mt.	Tonahutu Ck. T.H.	3.5	2,233	10,778	94	127			
Niwot Ridge	Long Lake T.H.	4	2,543	13,023		29			
Nokhu Crags	Lake Agnus T.H.	3	2,640	12,485		64			
Nokoni, Lake	North Inlet T.H.	9.9	2,240	10,780	63	84	24.9	50	Cutthroat
North Inlet Falls	North Inlet T.H.	7.6	1000	9,540					
Notchtop Mtn.	Bear Lake	5.75	2,849	12,129	65	92			
Nymph Lake	Bear Lake	0.5	225	9,700	107	141	0.9		barren
Odessa Lake	Bear Lake	4.1	1,215	10,020	96	129	11.2	22	Cutthroat
	Fern L. T.H.	4.4	1,865	10,020	96	129	11.2	22	Cutthroat
Ogallala Peak	Middle St. Vrain	9	4,500	13,138		25			
	Roaring Fk. T.H.	9.5	4,857	13,138		25			
	Wild Basin R. Sta.	9.75	4,638	13,138		25			

Orton, Mt.	Copeland Lake	5.25	3,412	11,724	76	108			
Otis Peak	Bear Lake	6	3,011	12,486	44	63			
Ouzel Falls	Wild Basin R. Sta.	2.7	950	9,450					
Ouzel Lake	Wild Basin R. Sta.	4.9	1,510	10,010	97	130	6.4		Brook
Ouzel Peak	Wild Basin R. Sta.	8.5	4,216	12,716	30	46			
Pagoda Mtn.	Glacier Gorge Jct.	6.5	4,257	13,497	7	8			
Paiute Peak	Mitchell Ck. T.H.	4.5	2,608	13,088		27			
Parika Lake	Trail Rdg. Rd.	5	2,496	11,360		31			
Parika Peak	Trail Rdg. Rd.	6	3,530	12,394		71			
Patterson, Mt.	Green Mtn. T.H.	3.25	2,630	11,424	85	117			
Pawnee Lake	Monarch Lake	8.25	2,494	10,840	78	78	11	22	Cutthroat
	Long Lake T.H.	6	2,061	10,840	78	78	11	22	Cutthroat
Pawnee Pass	Long Lake T.H.	4	2,061	12,541					
	Monarch Lake	7	4,195	12,541					
Pawnee Peak	Long Lake	4.5	2,463	12,943		33			
Peacock Pool	Longs Pk. R. Sta.	4	1,885	11,285	34	39	4.6		Brook
Pear Reservoir	Finch Lake T.H.	6.5	2,112	10,582	74	99	16.5		Cutthroat
Peck Glacier	Monarch Lake	8.75	3,174	11,520					
Pettingell Lake	North Inlet T.H.	10.75	1,970	10,510	79	105			Cutthroat
Pika Lake	Md. St. Vrain	7.5	2,282	10,920	73	73	2.0	10	Cutthroat
Pilot Mountain	Wild Basin R. Sta.	8	3,700	12,200	62	88			
Pinnacle Pool	Red Mtn. T.H.	4.25	2,260	11,300	33	38	3.6		barren
Pipit Lake	Wild Basin R. Sta.	6.75	2,915	11,415	25	27	12.9	50	barren

Destination	Starting Point	Distance from Start. Pt. (in miles)	Elevation Gain (in feet) from T.H. to High Point	Altitude (in feet)	Alt. Rank National Park Only	Alt. Rank Including Indian Peaks	Size of Lake (in acres)	Depth of Lake (in feet)	Fish in Lake
Pool, The	Fern L. T.H.	1.7	245	8,400					
Potts Puddle	Lawn L. T.H.	5.75	2,200	10,740	66	87	3.7	3	barren
Poudre Lake	On road			10,750	65	86			Brook
Powell, Lake	North Inlet T.H.	12.5	3,010	11,550	15	17	12.9		barren
Powell Peak	Glacier Gorge Jct.	7.25	3,968	13,208	14	20			
Ptarmigan Lake	Bear lake	6	2,849	11,460	21	23	21.1		barren
Ptarmigan Mtn.	East Inlet T.H.	9.25	3,933	12,324	55	78			
Ptarmigan Point, Pass	Bear Lake	5	2,888	12,363	51	74			
Rainbow Lake	Fern Lake T.H.	7	3,585	11,740	8	10	12.9		barren
Rainbow Lakes (#3)	Rainbow L's. C.G.	0.5	240	10,200	122	122	4	14	Brook
Ramsey Peak	Pingree Park	7	2,552	11,582	81	113			
Rams Horn Mtn.	Marys Lake	2	1,268	9,314		142			
Red Deer Lake	Middle St. Vrain	7.25	1,734	10,372		108	16	58	Brook; Suckers
Red Mountain	Red Mtn. T.H.	5.5	2,565	11,605	79	111			
Red Rocks Lake	On road			10,160		125	6.5	4.5	Rainbow
Ribbon Falls	Glacier Gorge Jct.	4.5	1,330	10,570					
Richthofen, Mt.	Phantom Valley	6.5	3,880	12,940	21	34			
	Lake Agnes T.H.	2	2,640	12,940	21	34			
Rock Lake	Gore R. Overlook	6.5	−1,700	10,320	82	111	5.5	10	Cutthroat

Rock Lake, Little	Core R. Overlook	6.75	−1,700	10,320	82	111	3.7	20	Cutthroat
Round Lake	Roaring Fk. T.H.	6.25	2,879	11,160		49			
Round Pond	Bear lake	2.5	845	10,320	82	111	0.2	1.5	barren
Rowe Glacier	Lawn L. T.H.	9	4,660	13,200					
Rowe Glacier Lake	Lawn L. T.H.	9	4,560	13,100+	1	1	7.4		barren
	North Fk. T.H.	13	5,140	13,100+	1	1	7.4		barren
Rowe Mtn.	North Fk. T.H.	14	5,224	13,184	15	21			
	Lawn L. T.H.	10	4,644	13,184	15	21			
Rowe Peak	North Fk. T.H.	13.5	5,440	13,400	9	12			
	Lawn L. T.H.	9.5	4,860	13,400	9	12			
Saddle, The	Lawn L. T.H.	8.25	3,858	12,398		90			
St. Vrain Mtn.	St. Vrain Mtn. T.H.	4	3,362	12,162					
St. Vrain Glaciers	Md. St. Vrain	8	2,562	11,200					
Sandbeach Lake	Copeland Lake	4.2	1,971	10,283	87	116	16.5	40	Rainbow
Satanta Peak	Junco Pond	4	1,939	11,979	100	100			
	Buckingham C.C.	4.5	1,858	11,979	100	100			
Sawtooth Mtn.	Beaver Res.	6.5	3,143	12,304	81	81			
Shadow Mtn. Lake	On road			8,367		150			Rainbow, Brown, Kokanee
Shadow Mtn.	East Shore T.H.	5	1,765	10,155	104	137			
Shadow Mtn. Lookout	East Shore T.H.	4.8	1,533	9,923					
Sharkstooth, The	Glacier Gorge Jct.	4.75	3,390	12,630	36	54			
Sheep Mountain	McGraw Ranch	2	1,838	9,678	106	140			

Destination	Starting Point	Distance from Start. Pt. (in miles)	Elevation Gain (in feet) from T.H. to High Point	Altitude (in feet)	Alt. Rank National Park Only	Alt. Rank Including Indian Peaks	Size of Lake (in acres)	Depth of Lake (in feet)	Fish in Lake
Shelf Lake	Glacier Gorge Jct.	4.25	1,980	11,220	37	42	3.7		barren
Shipler Mtn.	Milner Pass	2.2	567	11,317	86	118			
Shipler Park	Phantom Valley	1.7	60	9,120					
Shosoni Peak	Long Lake T.H.	4.25	2,487	12,967		31			
Signal Mtn.	North Fk. T.H.	6	3,302	11,262	87	120			
Signal Mtn, South	North Fk. T.H.	5.5	3,316	11,276		119			
Skull Point	Pingree Park	7.5	2,996	12,026	70	98			
Sky Pond	Glacier Gorge Jct.	4.6	1,660	10,900	57	74	11.2		Brook
Snowbank Lake	Wild Basin R. Sta.	8	3,021	11,521	17	19	7.4		barren
Snowdrift Lake	N. Inlet T.H.	8.75	2,620	11,160	42	49	9.2		barren
Snowdrift Peak	Bear Lake	8	2,799	12,274	58	84			
Solitude Lake	Glacier Gorge Jct.	4.5	2,180	11,420	24	26	7.4		barren
Solitude, Lake	North Inlet T.H.	8.5	1,180	9,720	106	140	2.8	4	Cutthroat
Spearhead, The	Glacier Gorge Jct.	6.25	3,335	12,575	37	56			
Specimen Mtn.	Milner Pass	2.2	1,739	12,489	43	62			
Spectacle Lake, Lower	Lawn L. T.H.	5	2,810	11,350	30	34	7.4	80	barren
Spectacle Lake, Upper	Lawn L. T.H.	5.25	2,820	11,360	28	31	11.2	60	
Spirit Lake	East Inlet T.H.	7.75	1,899	10,290	86	115	8.4	20	barren
Sprague Glacier	Fern L. T.H.	7.75	3,705	11,860					Brook

Feature	From								
Sprague Glacier Lake	Fern L. T.H.	7.75	3,705	11,860	4	5	5.5	9	barren
Sprague Lake	On road			8,710	113	146	12.9	9	Rainbow, Brook
Sprague Mtn.	Bear lake	9	3,238	12,713	31	47			
Spruce Lake	Fern L. T.H.	4.6	1,515	9,670	114	148	3.7	8	Rainbow, Brook
Static Peak	Lake Agnes T.H.	2.5	2,640	12,560	40	59			
Steep Mtn.	Cub Lake T.H.	4.25	1,458	9,538	107	141			
Stone Lake	Roaring Fk. T.H.	6.75	2,879	10,643		93	6.0	8	Rainbow, Cutthroat
Stone Man Pass	Glacier Gorge Jct.	6.25	3,240	12,480	23				
Stones Peak	Bear lake	10	3,447	12,922		36			
Storm Pass	Storm Pass T.H.	1.5	1,140	10,250					
	Boulder Brook T.H.	3.75	1,400	10,250					
Storm Peak	Longs Pk. R. Sta.	6.25	3,926	13,326	11	15			
Stormy Peaks	Pingree Park	5.25	3,118	12,148	64	91			
Stormy Peaks Pass	Pingree Park	5	2,570	11,600					
Stratus, Mt.	Holzwarth Homestd.	5	3,636	12,520	42	61			
Sugarloaf Mtn.	Pingree Park	6.25	3,090	12,120	67	94			
Sundance Mtn.	Trail Ridge Road	0.5	446	12,466	46	66			
Tanima Peak	Wild Basin R. Sta.	8.5	3,920	12,420	48	68			
Taylor Glacier	Glacier Gorge Jct.	5.25	3,913	11,800	17				
Taylor Peak	Glacier Gorge Jct.	6.25	3,678	13,153	23	23			
Teddys Teeth	Marys Lake	2	1,268	9,314					

Destination	Starting Point	Distance from Start. Pt. (in miles)	Elevation Gain (in feet) from T.H. to High Point	Altitude (in feet)	Alt. Rank National Park Only	Alt. Rank Including Indian Peaks	Size of Lake (in acres)	Depth of Lake (in feet)	Fish in Lake
Tepee Mtn.	Lake Agnes T.H.	2.5	2,060	12,360	52	75			
Terra Tomah Mtn.	Milner Pass	6.75	2,010	12,718	29	45			
Thatchtop	Glacier Gorge Jct.	5	3,428	12,668	34	51			
Thunder Falls	W. Basin R. Sta.	7.25	2,420	10,920					
Thunder Lake	W. Basin R. Sta.	6.8	2,074	10,574	77	102	16.5		Cutthroat, Brook
Thunder Mtn.	Phantom Valley	7.25	2,980	12,040	69	97			
Thunder Pass	Phantom Valley	6.3	2,271	11,331					
Thunderbolt Peak	Monarch Lake	6.25	3,592	11,938	88	102			
Tileston, Mt.	Lawn L. T.H.	4.5	2,714	11,254	88	121			
Timber Lake	Timber L. T.H.	4.8	2,060	11,060	52	62	10.1		Cutthroat
Timberline Falls	Glacier Gorge Jct.	4	1,210	10,450					
Timberline Pass	Trail Rdg. Rd.	1.75	566	11,484					
Toll, Mt.	Mitchell Ck. T.H.	5.25	2,499	12,979		30			
Toll Memorial	Rock Cut	0.5	260	12,310					
Tourmaline Lake	Bear Lake	4.5	1,115	10,590	73	98	1.8	12	barren
	Fern L. T.H.	4.8	2,435	10,590	73	98	1.8	12	barren
Traingle Lake	Monarch Lake	9.25	2,774	11,120		56			
Trio Falls	Wild Basin R. Sta.	7.25	2,800	11,300					
Twin Lakes, Lower (Radcliff Pond)	Wild Basin R. Sta.	3.5	1,270	9,770	105	139	4.6	15	Cutthroat

Twin Lakes, Upper	Wild Basin R. Sta.	3.5	1,290	9,790	104	138	1.8		barren
Twin Owls	Twin Owls T.H.	0.5	869	8,789		116			
Twin Sisters Peaks	Tw. Sisters T.H.	3.7	2,338	11,428	84	95	4.6	5	barren
Two Rivers Lake	Bear Lake	2.5	1,125	10,600	71				
Tyndall Glacier	Bear Lake	4.75	2,725	12,200					
Upper Lake	Roaring Fk. T.H.	7.25	2,879	10,730		89	7	6	Cutthroat
Verna, Lake	East Inlet T.H.	6.9	1,809	10,200	92	122	33.1		Brook
War Dance Falls	North Inlet T.H.	7	1,260	9,800					
Watanga Lake	Roaring Fk. T.H.	4.25	2,509	10,790		82			
Watanga Mtn.	Roaring Fk. T.H.	5.5	4,094	12,375		73			
Wescott, Mt.	East Inlet T.H.	5.5	2,030	10,421	101	134			
West Creek Falls	McGraw Ranch	2	600	8,160					
Windy Gulch Cascades	Upper Beaver Meadows	2	680	9,200					
Wuh, Mt.	Bear Lake	2.5	1,286	10,761	96	129			
Yellowstone Canyon, Little	Phantom Valley	4	940	10,000					
Ypsilon Lake	Lawn L. T.H.	4.5	2,180	10,540	78	103	7.4	55	Cutthroat
Ypsilon Mtn.	Chapin Ck. T.H.	3.5	2,874	13,514	5	5			

Suggested Readings

Backpacking: One Step at a Time, Harvey Manning, Random House, New York, 1973.

Pleasure Packing: How to Backpack in Comfort, Robert S. Wood, Condor Books, San Francisco, 1972.

Mountaineering: The Freedom of the Hills (third edition), Peggy Ferber, editor, The Mountaineers, Seattle, 1974.

Backpacking with Small Children, James and Ann Stout, Thomas Y. Crowell Company, 1975.

Backpacking Equipment: A Buyer's Guide, William Kemsley and the Editors of *Backpacker* Magazine, Macmillan Publishing Co., New York, 1977.

Simple Foods for the Pack, Vikki Kinmont and Claudia Axcell, Sierra Club Books, 1976.

The Well-Fed Backpacker, June Fleming, Victoria House, 1976.

The Outdoorsman's Medical Guide, Alan E. Nourse, M.D., Harper & Row, 1974.

Mountaineering First Aid: A Guide to Accident Response and First Aid Care, Dick Mitchell, The Mountaineers, Seattle, 1974.

A Field Guide to Western Birds, Roger Tory Peterson, Houghton Mifflin Company, Boston, 1969.

Wildlife Country: How to Enjoy It, edited by Alma Deane MacConomy, National Wildlife Federation, 1977.

High Country Names, Louisa Ward Arps and Elinor Eppich Kingery, Rocky Mountain Nature Association, 1972. (history)

Raising the Roof of the Rockies, Gerald M. Richmond, Rocky Mountain Nature Association, 1974. (geology)

Rocky Mountain Mammals, David M. Armstrong, Rocky Mountain Nature Association, 1975.

Plants of Rocky Mountain National Park, Ruth Ashton Nelson, Rocky Mountain Nature Association, 1976.

Alpine Wildflowers, Beatrice Willard and Chester O. Harris, Rocky Mountain Nature Association, 1975.

Index

286